Unquiet Days ═══

Unquiet Days

At Home in Poland

Thomas Swick

Ticknor & Fields · NEW YORK · 1991

For information about permission to reproduce selections
from this book, write to Permissions, Ticknor & Fields,
Houghton Mifflin Company, 2 Park Street,
Boston, Massachusetts 02108.

Library of Congress Cataloging-in-Publication Data

Swick, Thomas.
Unquiet days : at home in Poland / by Thomas Swick.
p.   cm.
ISBN 0-395-58563-5
1. Poland — Description and travel — 1981–
2. Poland — Social life and customs — 1945–
3. Swick, Thomas.   I. Title.
DK4081.S95   1991   91-12103
943.805 — dc20   CIP

Printed in the United States of America

Book design by Lisa Diercks

BP 10 9 8 7 6 5 4 3 2 1

Sections of "Warszawa" appeared in *The American Scholar, The
North American Review,* and *Catholic Twin Circle.*

"Great Night" was published in a slightly different version in
Commonweal.

"War Months" was published in part in *Ploughshares.*

A section of "The August Pilgrimage" appeared in *Catholic
Twin Circle.*

The author gratefully acknowledges permission
to quote from the following works:

Pan Tadeusz by Adam Mickiewicz, translated by Kenneth Mackenzie,
1964, Polish Cultural Foundation, London.

Marian Zalecki, "Theology of a Marian Shrine —
Our Lady of Czestochowa." (Marian Library Studies, No. 8).
University of Dayton, Dayton, Ohio, 1976.

For
my mother and father

He came to believe that the machinations
of power, how it was organized and wielded,
who governed whom and by what means, all
this was less important than a nation's soul;
its character; its religion; its humor and
art and music and literature.

Ian Hunter, from
Malcolm Muggeridge: A Life

Contents

PROLOGUE   1

I. WARSZAWA
   AUTUMN   13
   WINTER   28
   SPRING-SUMMER   70

II. THE ENGLISH
   LANGUAGE COLLEGE
   81

III. WAR MONTHS   131

IV. GREAT NIGHT   169

V. THE AUGUST
   PILGRIMAGE   179

VI. WAITING FOR THE
   STEFAN BATORY   259

EPILOGUE   267

Prologue ══════

Prologue

THE GENESIS of this book can be easily traced back to a small bed and breakfast hotel in Paddington where I spent a week in the fall of 1976. I had come to London after a year in France (winter study in Provence, summer farm work in Alsace) to catch my ship, the *Mikhail Lermontov*, back to America. Coming out of Paddington Station, I soon found myself on a street lined with hotels and, after examining the lobbies of a handful, I chose one not in any way distinguished from its neighbors, called the Mitre.

My first afternoon in the city I spent hunting for books. One that attracted me (my resources were low, so my taste discriminating) was *Foreign Faces* by V. S. Pritchett, the account of a trip he had taken in the early 1960s to the countries of Eastern Europe. I retired with it to the Serpentine and read in the waning afternoon sunlight. Returning to the hotel, I stopped into the bar before going up to my room and ordered a beer from an attractive barmaid. I remember taking a seat by the far wall and pretending to watch a BBC documentary on chimpanzees. The barmaid was a study in brown — short brown hair, lively brown eyes, tight brown sweater. I assumed she was Irish. Finishing the beer, I returned for another and lingered awkwardly for a while, until the young woman asked my country of origin. I told her and asked her the same. She answered, quite unexpectedly, Poland. With a motion almost of legerdemain, I produced my book and, after pointing out the chapter on her homeland, insisted that she borrow it — not so much so she would read it, but so she would have to see me again to return it. As I left she was gamely asking a customer how to make a Bloody Mary, a drink that he still insisted on receiving even after hearing her frank denunciation of the ruination of vodka by tomato juice.

Hania, a nickname for Hanna, was a breakfast waitress and chambermaid at the Mitre Hotel, and only that one evening a substitute barmaid, as most nights she was to be found working at a conveyor belt in a shandy factory, her second job. All this I discovered on our first date, a rather soggy trek around the West End on one of her rare days off. She was also, I learned, an econometrics major at the University of Warsaw. She had been coming to London most of her student summers to make money and to improve her English, which was already fluent, clipped, and hurriedly produced. (When she said "I beg your pardon," the phrase came out as a single word.) She had an aunt in Kensington with whom she had stayed until the woman took to keeping a chicken in the bathtub. I shared a red telephone booth with her one day while she conversed with this relative — my first introduction to spoken Polish — and still recall being impressed by the immense obscurity of sound and the machine-gun rattlings of the rapidly repeated "yes": *Tak tak tak tak tak.*

We returned to our respective countries and conducted an epistolary courtship, which resulted in Hania's coming, after a year, to the United States. She stayed for nine months, auditing courses at Princeton while I wrote for the *Trenton Times*. Four months after her departure,

I went to Poland, presumably for a year. On the way I stayed for a few weeks with my farm family in Alsace and experienced another serendipitous turn of fate.

One day while I was picking cherries in a distant orchard, some relatives of the family arrived from Strasbourg. They mentioned that a young Polish woman named Jolanta was visiting with them on a Methodist Church exchange program and asked if I would be interested in meeting her. I said I would be and a few days later was driven down to Strasbourg after supper.

Jolanta did not know French and welcomed the chance to speak English, which she did exceedingly well. She showed a certain amount of bemusement at my desire to live in Poland, and then tenderly described her hometown of Warsaw, which had already taken on for me the tantalizing, slightly ominous allure of a foreign city one is going to live in never having seen. In the center of this city, she told me, was a renowned English school. Her father was the director.

Two weeks after this meeting I boarded a train in Strasbourg and made a late-night, last-minute change in Cologne. In the morning I saw the Berlin Wall from my compartment window, and later gazed out at the lackluster landscape of western Poland, before being finally reunited with Hania at the dusty, provincial Gdansk Station in Warsaw.

I promptly went to see Jolanta's father, Mr. Kuczma, who lived in a large apartment above his famous English Language College on Plac Zbawiciela, Savior Square. Apart from being the school's director, Mr. Kuczma was also a Methodist minister, and successfully combined, at first glance, the gravity of both. We chatted in a room of very heavy furniture under a portrait of John Wesley;

Mr. Kuczma listened patiently to my story and kindly offered me a job. My career as a teacher, together with my life as a Polish breadwinner, began.

Though my contract was for the full school year, my visa would expire after the first semester in February. So in January Hania and I began the unpleasant process of obtaining an extension. The visa office was located then (this was 1979) on the first floor of a solemn building on Warsaw's well-named Raven Street. Visits there made me queasy. The waiting area, dimly lit and windowless, was surrounded by numbered offices out of which clerks in sweaters would regularly emerge, lock the doors behind them, and then bustle down the corridor carrying forms or decks of shuffled passports. The few chairs were usually all taken by Arab men, stymied by questionnaires (the model forms in English and French were most of the time in use) and assisted by gum-cracking blondes. On the walls hung not picturesque travel posters nor even more understandable socialist slogans, but blanched advertisements for "Western" goods sold in Warsaw's dollar shops. Cinzano and Sony. The wait could take hours; the interview fruitless minutes. ("You don't have the 2-S form. You have to get it from the Ministry of Education. We don't do anything for you until you have that form.")

On our third visit, Hania, who usually came along to translate, was asked to wait while I was taken upstairs to a previously unseen realm. As I was led along the corridor I noticed that some of the doors we passed were padded. My escort opened a door, asked me to take a seat inside, and handed my file to a full-bellied man sitting behind a perfectly empty desktop.

In poor English the man recounted aloud my recent

past and noted my desire for a longer visa. I nodded. "Well," he said, "if you help us, we can help you."

I asked him to elucidate. He said that as a foreigner (pronounced to rhyme with porringer) working at the English school I was in the unique position of meeting both Poles and other "foreingers." He suggested that it would be helpful to him and his office if I could take notes on what they were saying and come to him with these comments every week. The work, he said, would be not unlike the journalism I had practiced in the United States.

I refused, repeatedly, as he continued to advertise the work. Sensing futility, he at last relented: "Well, if that's your answer, then there is not anything we can do for you."

Hania was surprised, though not awestruck. (Polish friends had had similar interviews when requesting passports.) She teased me for not asking at least about the salary. Mr. Kuczma commented philosophically: "It all adds up to your experience." He said that, should I ever return, I would always have a job at his school. Three days later I was on a train to Athens. The rest of that winter and all of that spring I spent in the northwestern town of Arta, where I had found a job teaching English.

It was in Greece that my love of Poland truly blossomed. I had gone there inspired by the writings of Fermor and Durrell and a little frayed by the unrelenting cold, hardship, and tawdriness of Warsaw. Yet everything in Arta — the mischievous students, the incompetent director (who, despite the prominently displayed Cambridge Certificate of English in his office, barely spoke the language), the childish men, the subjugated women, the purdah of the cafés, the disdain for learning, the highly romanticized though professionally infuriating sloth — made me pine for Poland. Returning for the Pope's first historic visit that June (despite my dubious history, I received a two-week tourist visa without difficulty), I could not have seen Poland at a better time. My Mediterranean interlude impressed on me the special character of people who live under harsher climates and regimes, and encouraged me to adopt the Poles as other writers had the Greeks.

At the end of that summer I returned to the States, as Hania did to the University of Warsaw. My obsession became clear one day while meeting in New York with a magazine editor, who, after hearing my numerous ideas for stories on Poland, said in frustration, "We need something that will be good graphically," to which I replied, "Polish posters!"

One day in May 1980, I sat down at a scarified desk by the Slavic literature stacks in Princeton's Firestone Library and wrote a long letter to Hania. I cited the advantages of my returning to Warsaw, marrying her, regaining my job at the school, and remaining a full two years. This, one of the most important letters I have ever written, never arrived — though I did, on September 10, ten days after the signing of the Gdansk shipyard strike agreements and the founding of Solidarity. A week later I was teaching again.

A month later Hania and I were married, at the Palace of Weddings in Warsaw's Old Town. I stayed for two extraordinary years (September 1980 to September 1982) as planned — teaching, traveling, writing articles (until the imposition of martial law), and keeping an extensive journal that, at the end of my stay, was graciously sent home to me by a Dutch friend in her embassy's diplomatic pouch.

At home, my interest in Poland did not wane. In Philadelphia, where we moved after Hania's acceptance to the University of Pennsylvania, I continued teaching English to recent Polish immigrants. I enjoyed the weekly escape, after my dull editing job in the city, to the old Polish working-class neighborhood of Richmond. Here the life I had so recently lived renewed itself.

As soon as we had saved enough money, Hania and I returned to visit. Our first trip back together in the fall of 1985 was perhaps the most moving, watching from the plane as the first heartrendingly grim and homey apartment blocks slid into view. We returned again in the fall of 1988. Each trip produced a lengthy article, which, after the usual round of polite rejections, found a home. I went anxiously back in 1990, to see the new Republic, to close a decade of attachment to Poland, and to close this book.

A few years ago I wrote to V. S. Pritchett to tell him of the momentous role one of his works had played in my life. He replied on a handwritten postcard: "So happy to hear a book of mine has been enjoyed by you and with such delightful after-effects."

What follows is, I hope, one of them.

— Thomas Swick
Fort Lauderdale, Florida
1990

I
Warszawa

Autumn ══════

I FIRST WENT to Warsaw in the fall, that season of sullen skies and sorrowful anniversaries that the Poles call "golden." My apartment was on the top floor of a modern building in the northern neighborhood of Żoliborz, and each morning I dressed in darkness, looking out onto the soaked walls of the identical gray block across the way and the rows of yellow headlights creeping through the drizzle on Słowacki Street. It seemed the wettest place I had ever known. As testament to this, on weekends at the train station I saw families coming home with high-handled wicker baskets filled with mushrooms. In contrast to southern cities, where life moves outdoors, here the weather came inside: buses bore a scent of pressed, sodden material, and their windows steamed at varying degrees for weeks at a time. Shops, restaurants, cafés, and offices all presented murky pools inside their doors and the soggy black outlines of galosh prints up and down their halls. Waitresses with naturally red cheeks (and as bitter as the Baltic winds) wore tight wool sweaters, while the sedentary cashiers and postal clerks, constantly besieged by drafts, bundled in gray thermal vests. I developed a liking for tea, served steaming in glasses, which warmed the hands and possessed a rich, mahogany hue. And as much as I cursed the rain, I admired the Polish word for it: *deszcz*, so similar to the shivers — *dreszcze* — it often gave.

Not every summer, I was told, ended with a seven-month cloud cover. "In 1939 we had the most beautiful autumn imaginable," my wife's aunt always marveled. "It was as if *le Bon Dieu* freely opened up the heavens over Warsaw for the German bombs." There is much in the municipal poetry of precipitation. I own an anthology of four centuries of verse about Warsaw which contains numerous references — as much for the realistic depiction, I am sure, as for the romantic imagery — to fog and rain. Jarosław Iwaszkiewicz, in his "Autumn in Warsaw," speaks of "misty boulevards and soft furs," and Antoni Słonimski writes in his poem "In Warsaw":

> *A dark, closed-up café*
> *An empty street without day*
> *Between the wet leaves of the lantern*
> *Fog*

One of my favorite Polish cartoons, by the illustrator Andrzej Mleczko, depicts a man in the rain, stepping headlong into a puddle on an unpaved road. Apartment blocks crumble and electrical wires topple behind him, as he intones: "I belong to the realm of European culture. I belong to the realm of European culture. I belong to the realm of European culture."

I took a bus downtown in the morning to prepare for my day's lessons. Seats were rare, as was, at certain hours, space. Stout bodies, further padded by topcoats, bunched together in one tight mass, while the doors took minutes to close due to the protuberance of extraneous riders, usually young men. (The same situation reigned on trams, where an alarming bell accompanied each attempt.) I most profoundly experienced this enforced closeness in the morning, when passengers, wrenched from the solace of their beds, coughed, wheezed, and dredged up sputum in the best traditions of a nation addicted to nicotine. Exiting then required feats of strength: I would often be knocked off balance by round, muscular matrons, my book bag, ungiving, caught behind me. On the sidewalks I frequently found those who had just gotten off a bus or tram taking a second or two to straighten their coats, adjust their hats, and generally regroup. It was not uncommon to find a button or two missing.

Always on the buses I would try to work my way to a window. Looking out at the city I would see long rows of featureless shops, with small windows and heavy metal doors, out of which often coiled the landmark queues, or "tails," as the Poles themselves, with a descriptive eye, called them. In the display windows of the state clothing stores mannequins stood unconvincingly, frozen in time as well as expression. Their straw-colored tufts of hair seemed never to be combed. The downplaying of privatization made for a simplicity of shop names. I read in close succession, SHOES, CLOTHES, VEGETABLES, BOOKS — signs that gave a street the somewhat nostalgic flavor of a storybook town in a grammar school reader. At night, some came aglow in a lovely, unmodern neon script.

Shopping also took a novel form, something that, as a first-time foreigner I realized when, finding myself on a downtown street, especially waiting to cross, I was approached and politely asked where I had bought my shoes. There were few things more terrifying in daily life to the beginning learner of Polish than the interior of a Warsaw shop. Taking my place solemnly in a queue, I would gape at the potent, listless insolence of the bluefrocked shopgirls, wondering what incomprehensible contumely they would unleash when my turn came. Though, as often as not, the most butcher-faced softened on hearing my speech (my first glimpse of the favors awaiting a foreigner in a country that routinely discriminates against its own kind).

Even in our neighborhood shops, I noticed that the residents had established little or no rapport with the clerks who served them regularly and unwillingly. I hardly blamed the girls, spending their days in the state's damp, dimly lit stores with the cheerless produce. (The sight of potatoes spilling from a trap door and then being shoveled off a soiled floor was new to me, though I liked the bulbous pickles and cold crisp strips of uncooked sauerkraut retrieved from barrels.) Once, near the end of my stay, in a state craft shop on Puławska Street, I watched an idle, elderly customer bantering casually with a young assistant and was jarred by the realization that it was the first time I had witnessed such an exchange in Poland.

To avoid having to speak, I went to the local self-service market. Here, on dark evenings, I would stand in a line, often stretched outside, of housewives waiting for the metal baskets needed for entry as they were relinquished by those coming out. Inside were shelves of plainly wrapped bags of sugar and flour, crookedly labeled bottles of vinegar, lusterless boxes of *herbatniki* (cookies) with the consistency of sawdust, half loaves of two-day-old bread pointed upright like portly missiles and with a torn, brown piece of paper nearby for use in testing their degree of petrifaction. Near the cashiers would usually stand the plastic crates of milk sold in sacks, also plastic and often punctured, which caused an expanding white film to cover the concrete floor. I can remember one evening following down numerous aisles the trail of milk left by a woman who, unwisely, had placed that item at the top of her list.

Shopping was not done for pleasure, but for survival; the faces in the shops and on the streets were those of weary scavengers. It was impossible to imagine a Varsovian going out to walk the boulevards and, like Charles Lamb in London, drawing sustenance from the crowds. Except during demonstrations.

Hania and I took our midday meals at the private home of a woman who lived on Adam Mickiewicz Street, an unfortunate address, I thought, for the poet loved good food and wrote of it eloquently. A long table, or rather series of tables, was set up in her living room, occupying it entirely. From one to three in the afternoon, the hardened regulars wandered in, wished those who had already started *smacznego* (*bon appétit*), and found themselves places at the feast. Pani Basia, a thickly set, mustachioed woman, would wamble out of her tiny pre-war kitchen (of which we could glimpse only the grease-streaked stove) with watery soup. Minutes later (Poles eat with remarkable speed, and fortitude), she'd reappear with the day's ration of unidentifiable meat, lumpy potatoes, and runny side of grated, boiled beets. A tricolor plate of brown, white, and purple. We never received dessert, though one day for dinner Pani Basia served macaroni topped, for some reason, with a whiskery mush of stewed raspberries. There was little in the way of dinner conversation. Upon finishing, each diner would rise and, head politely bowed, utter "thank you," to which everyone seated would reply the same.

I taught English three days a week, and on my days

off explored the city, often with dissatisfaction. The combination of a socialist system and a northern climate made Warsaw unattractive to visitors drawn to the life of the street. There were no ethnic neighborhoods lively with immigrants, as Westerners are used to finding in their capitals, and even if there had been, life would have been contained indoors. If one did not like Poles, it was an intolerable place to be. As befits a city built on a plain and then destroyed, there were (outside of the Old Town) no hidden alleyways or steep back streets. Everything was open, spacious, relentlessly planned. The closest the quotidian city came to the picturesque was, I suppose, in its old housing courtyards: green oases of quiet, occasionally with a statue of Mary as a centerpiece, behind grim portals.

The city possessed a shabbiness that seemed to me heightened by its overcast sky, which not only echoed the dominant shade, but precluded any possibility of release from it. Worn wooden doors led into unlit corridors; in the more modern apartment complexes, missing ceiling tiles exposed the as yet intact plumbing systems. Unlatched doors opened and closed with the wind. Secretaries tapped on heavy, curvaceous typewriters, and in the cafés leaden cakes sat in vintage cooling cases. Milk bars looked too grimy to serve anything as pure as that white liquid. Everywhere paint was chipping and the ironwork on balconies rusted. There was no such thing as an attractive lawn.

After some weeks I found that the two places in which I felt at home in Warsaw — places that seemed to transport me to a more familiar world of affluence and upkeep — were the churches and the hotels. The churches — both the Gothic and Baroque monuments in the Old Town,

and the modern chapels in the more run-down neighborhoods — exuded an air of workmanlike completion
that was paralleled only in the new hotels (foreign-built)
like the Victoria and the Forum. The capital, it appeared,
served two masters: God and the Westerner. And I wondered: Was it treating the Westerner as God, or, perhaps, vice versa? Like many Poles, I began to use both
the churches and the hotels as retreats — soothed by the
wax tapers on the altars, the chocolates in the dollar
shops — from the grotesqueries outside.

The longer I lived in Warsaw, which I came to love, the
more I saw, though never loved, in fall. As with more
northern cities, Warsaw's pace quickened in autumn, as
its citizens returned from their month (or more) at the
lakes, at the seashore, in the mountains, or in the West.
On the major shopping streets, Marszałkowska and Nowy
Świat, it once again became difficult to pass through
a shop door unaccompanied. Though many people —
with that broad Polish view of holidays — took off again
for the mountains in September.

On the streets young people walked with large, cut
sunflowers, picking out the seeds and lending a strange,
primeval tone to their otherwise contemporary aspect.
Before the school year, they lined up overnight on Savior Square to enroll in classes at the English Language
College where I taught. The flower peddlers, ageless,
tatterdemalion women who had not been away anywhere, squatted on stools in downtown streets behind
buckets of gladiolas and asters. The *woda sodowa* (soda
water) vendors sat impassively by their parasoled carts,
the days of their five-glass service numbered. Theater
posters proclaiming the fall season colored the wooden

fencing around never ending construction sites (grand productions in themselves, with their own thick plots of intrigue and tragedy), artistically drawn and with a continuing theme of heads opening up. At Przy Teatrze, the tiny restaurant next to the Syrena Theater, the sour white soup *żurek* replaced the cool pink *chłodnik* on the menu. Grocery stores filled with their last bounty before the winter, and one could find any number of small, generously bruised apples. At the Różycki Bazaar across the Vistula River in Praga, middle-aged harridans stood in clusters with Western-made sweaters held to their chests; farther along salmon was laid out on white-papered tables, and salami, rosy pink in its chalk white casing. On Embassy Row the Bulgarians posted color photographs of yet another successful harvest, while next door the Americans ran a particularly needling report on the attributes of solar heat. For the military anniversary in October, a headquarters building on Victory Square ran its red-bannered slogan, "The Polish People's Army: The Faithful Guardian of Socialism and Independence," a message I read for the first time in 1980 from the backseat of a Fiat on my way to the Palace of Weddings to be married.

In autumn, schoolchildren tramped to Łazienki Park to gather fallen chestnuts, chancing upon those rare cloudless days when the sunlight suffused the yellow leaves in a riotous affirmation of the title "Polish Golden Autumn" (*Złota Polska Jesień*). On fair Sundays, pianists played Chopin in an open-air concert, and older couples shuffled down the leaf-strewn lanes in reveries of nostalgia and melancholy. It was not only the season but the city. For this generation, Warsaw is, more than anything else, a city of the departed. There are those departed in the war — friends, siblings, classmates — and remembered on a depressingly high number of neighborhood streets with a tablet ("On this spot on 20 June 1944 Nazi soldiers murdered seven civilians"), fresh flowers, and a votive candle. There are the family members departed, dead from various cancers, diseases of the heart, liver, kidneys, and lungs, also, no doubt, prematurely, in this country lacking in technology, pharmaceuticals, and a sense of preventive medicine. They, too, are remembered at their gravesides on All Souls' Day. Lastly there are all the sons and daughters, nephews and nieces, godchildren, departed, emigrated to new futures in the West. Łazienki in autumn is filled with people whose lives have been slowly, inexorably, emptied of loved ones.

Warszawa. The feminine name comes, according to legend, from a fisherman couple, Wars and Sawa, who once gamboled on the banks of the now polluted Vistula River. The city's symbol is a mermaid, unique among her kind, raising sword and bearing shield. Her unknown soldier fell in the Polish-Soviet War of 1919 to 1920, a fact that causes pleasure whenever one of the Soviet Union's representatives, on official visit, lays a wreath at his tomb. She has borne numerous foreign influences and occupations — August von Platen called her "the Thermopylae of Poland" — and the names they have sometimes given to her evoke images of drastically different cities.

Varsovie is the city seen in eighteenth-century prints, in which elegant coaches driven by liveried coachmen rumble through the Old Town. The Warsaw Uprising, in the last days of the occupation, was enacted here, resulting in an almost total devastation of the site. After the war, the red-roofed clutter of Gothic, Renaissance, and neoclassic structures was painstakingly rebuilt to look its former self, often, when photographs were unavailable, from the rich detail in Bellotto's paintings. A Polish child born abroad and raised in a house decorated with old Warsaw prints can, in an unthinkable passage through time, go to the capital today and on these streets find an identical urban landscape, "the most beautiful," wrote Kazimierz Brandys in *A Warsaw Diary* of Krakowskie Przedmieście, "in Europe." Of the accompanying world of Francophone nobility — nannies imported from Paris and menus in French at the Bristol Hotel — there is little trace, though I used French, before I learned the much more beautiful Polish language, to communicate with my wife's collection of elderly aunts. One of them, born in St. Petersburg, told of going with her mother to the English Shop on Nevski Avenue, the same one the Nabokov family patronized for Pears soap.

ווארשה was a city of shopkeepers, tradesmen, and Talmudic scholars. Here Yiddish newspapers were published and Hassid banquets held; Zionist societies conducted meetings and boys in gabardine attended *cheder.* Today Jewish Warsaw is a theater with headphones for simultaneous translation, and a cemetery. It has become, worldwide, an unending polemic.

Warschau I see written on a train leaving Berlin. It is a name barked harshly by the stationmaster, like "Achtung!" with none of the soft syllabic sliding of Varsovie. The train's destination is a city in which all the civic statues have been toppled, with the exception of that of Copernicus, whose profession has neatly been changed to "German astronomer." The diurnal metropolitan routine is one of roundups, ration cards, partisans, death,

and — eventually — detailed, systematic demolition. "In
1939," Czesław Miłosz has written, "the old Warsaw vanished spiritually; it vanished physically when the Nazis
destroyed it at the end of the war." A good number of
older Poles still speak German.

Варшава was the postwar city. Its two most physically
prominent legacies, Constitution Square and the Palace
of Culture, are buildings whose designs miraculously
exceed their names in portentousness. The square is a
great, arcaded area of flat pillars, state shops, and purposeful housing, its walls decorated with muscular la-
borers and one formidable mother with child in socialist
realism relief. The palace, larger and even less loved
than the square, is a soaring, crenulated tower — a gift
from the Soviets — sprawled at the city's epicenter and
dominating its horizon. The Poles' favorite comment on
it, best heard while walking the five minutes past it, is:
"It's small, but in good taste." Inside the bureaucratic
city, with its locked office doors and halls papered with
slogans ("We can succeed only along the true path of socialism"), its beefy men in ministries sitting behind desks
with nothing atop them but a telephone, the mark of
Варшава was everywhere. The language, though, and
its new social terms of address, like "Comrade" — even
among party members — never caught on.

Warsaw, that prosaic name tied to a pact, fits the contemporary city. As in many of the world's capitals, English has become the language of the young: they study
it and dance to it and wear it on T-shirts and pins. Students frequently came to my classes with buttonry proclaiming such thoughts as "TV Lies," "Anti-Socialistic
Element," and "I'm a Sexual Genius." One of my favorites was, "I would rather have a bottle in front of me

than a frontal lobotomy." For years, news, especially local, came from the BBC and Voice of America. And for all Warsaw's plainness, its name reveals, with a reversal of its parts, an irreversible truth: Warsaw. Saw war.

Less than one hundred years after replacing Krakow as the capital of Poland in 1596, Warsaw suffered at the hands of an invading army. In the middle of the seventeenth century, Swedish forces overran Poland, wreaking some of their greatest destruction in the capital. After their retreat, much of the city, including the Royal Castle, had to be rebuilt, not for the last time.

In 1794, the Kościuszko Uprising against Russia was declared in the capital, as in other parts of the country, and saw the massacre of thousands of Varsovians. With the surrender of the city, the Republic of Poland ceased to exist, and its parts were carved up like meat for lions: the east for the Russians, the south for the Austrians, and Warsaw for the Prussians.

The city, like the country, did not acquiesce. The 1830 November Uprising against the Russians, who had since assumed administrative power over Warsaw, cost more lives. It too was unsuccessful, and its repercussions were appalling — while, at the same time, harbingers of things to come. Estates were confiscated, leaders were condemned to death, and thousands of officers were transported to Siberian labor camps. Out of this failed insurrection came, as well, the great "emigration of talents," that included Fryderyk Chopin and Adam Mickiewicz.

World War I, which saw the rebirth of Poland, also saw the death of 450,000 Polish soldiers. And yet the loss seems almost insignificant in light of what was to follow.

The German occupation of Poland, following the invasion of September 1, 1939, changed forever the face of the capital, and of the country as well. One of the first things a foreign visitor is taken to see in Warsaw is the film in the Old Town museum of the destruction of the city. It is as if to say: nothing about the country can be understood without first comprehending the incalculable devastation of the Second World War. The documentary begins with peaceful scenes of Varsovians strolling in the summer of 1939, played to the background music of Smetana's *The Moldau.* These are followed by pictures of the first bombardments and, later, actual footage taken by the Germans as they carried out their house-by-house destruction.

Just as the Second World War overshadows the First, so tends the German occupation of western Poland to overshadow the Soviet occupation of the east. Yet between 1939 and 1941, the Soviet Union deported over half a million Polish civilians. Crushed into boxcars like cattle, in the most grisly extremes of temperature and privation, many never survived the journey. At the same time the Soviets established a policy of spoliation — of land, property, cities, lives — so complete that it caused many people to assume the foreign presence was only temporary. For if the Soviets really meant to stay, the Poles reasoned, why would they be destroying everything?

In a nation of suffering, Warsaw suffered terribly. From 1939 to 1945, six million Poles — nearly one in five — died; about half of these were Polish Jews; 700,000 were Varsovians. Survivors who returned to the city after the war found it unrecognizably in ruin. Now famous are the photographs of vast acres of unrelieved rubble, half skeletons of buildings, and the occasional cross protruding unscathed out of the wasteland.

●   ●   ●

All Souls' Day, known as "Day of the Dead" in Poland, is celebrated on November 1 and is as much a part of fall as Christmas is of winter, and Easter of spring. In Warsaw all offices are closed, and residents go to the cemeteries, particularly Powązki, the city's largest.

The first year I was surprised to see the crowds, the lopsided provincial buses lined up outside the gates as if for a football match. The flower peddlers did a good business in memorial wreaths, chrysanthemums (because they support the cold) and candles.

The weather was always raw and wet. Hania led me, turning deftly down avenues of tombs, to her parents' graves far in the back. Even after numerous visits I could never find them on my own. We passed porous sepulchers, old family plots, their corners overgrown with vegetation, and marble plaques garbed in moss. Weatherbeaten busts topped Gothic pedestals, and crosses, more numerous than trees, traced a low, Calvary-inspired horizon. As we walked I would read under my breath the names on the tombs — Szewczykowski, Chołoniewski, Znamierowski, Koisiewicz, Pniewski, Pruszkowski. At many of the plots, mothers had rolled up sleeves, children had been sent with buckets for water, and together they cleared the autumnal debris of leaves and twigs. At others, flowers had been carefully arranged in jars of water and candles had been left to burn. It was a tenebrous, cozy, classical place whose appeal, other than for remembrance, was evident.

At dusk we would head to the nearby military cemetery, walking, like Young Goodman Brown, with "a grave and dark-clad company." Here in the darkness and mist the world became one of outlines and forms. Rows of cupped candles stretched far into the distance. Masses

of overcoats brushed beside us in the Alley of the Meri-
torious. The drizzle fell on flames that smoldered, sending up an agreeable scent of smoke and wet bark. More
dark forms passed, alternately blocking and releasing
the candlelight. We found the makeshift monument to
Katyń (the site of a massacre of Polish officers by the
Russians during World War II), its white and blood red
banner tied between trees and bathed, one year, in the
unnatural white light of an ABC camera crew's equipment. We found, in their special sections, the graves of
the insurgents of the 1863 Uprising, the soldiers and
POWs of World War I, the defenders of Warsaw in 1939,
and the soldiers of the Home Army. Here, at the last,
stood tall ordered rows of simple crosses made, fittingly,
from the felled trunks of young birch trees. Before the
graves gathered a silent, meditative populace, the faces,
some tearful, illuminated by the candle glow. As a foreigner I too found the sight moving, not the least because
the names and ages on the plaques — Zbigniew 17, Jerzy
20, Urszula 18, Krzysztof 16 — were the same as those of
my students.

Winter ═══════════

"I DON'T MEAN to sound *tribal*," Stefan said, "but how are you getting your food?"

We were sitting at a glass-topped table on the second floor of a café on Marszałkowska Street, just around the corner from our school. Some dim fluorescent lights made partially visible a low-ceilinged room containing about forty such tables with chairs, all of them empty. The only other customer, a drunk, was at the bar eulogizing horses. A young, sullen waitress brought us two bottles of Krakus beer, both losing their labels, and two moderately clean glasses.

"We've been thinking of hiring a cook," I said.

"Now that winter's coming," offered Stefan helpfully, "you may want to consider suicide."

Stefan was a sandy-haired, slightly rubicund young man with a mischievous gaze. We always sat next to each other in the teachers' room, a depot of eccentricity, and made the most of the ten-minute class breaks (twenty minutes at six o'clock for tea) with countless, to-be-continued conversations. Born in Poland, Stefan had grown up in Australia, a fact which accounted for his native fluency in English. When I asked him once what he had done in Australia for so many years he answered characteristically, "Went to the beach." Another time he admitted to having been an early reader of *Mad* magazine. He returned to Poland as a teenager and went, well prepared, into the *Anglistyka* Department at the University of Warsaw.

If he had taught the two obligatory years in a state school, I never knew where. Already, he seemed a fixture at the English Language College. At the first fall faculty meeting, he had attracted notice by suggesting that English be the required usage at all times within the school, even among the Polish teachers, who predominated, and even at tea. It was one of his few suggestions that the director found acceptable. Lately Stefan had become interested in the Grotowski method of acting and its application to language teaching. He had also instituted a suggestion box.

He never talked of Australia and appeared more than at home in Warsaw. He was one of those people who carry their own private world within themselves, and so are generally oblivious to surroundings and amenable anywhere. He showed a bemused interest in the United States, picking up tidbits of trends from newsmagazines and asking me for clarification. He saw America, not unlike Poland, as a country with tremendous potential for mirth.

Our beers consumed, we got up and walked through the broken lines of vacant tables. The drunk had now transferred his adulation to bison. The two waitresses, with equally bored expressions, sat scraping their cigarette ends across the bottoms of their ashtrays, gazing out at the blackened windows and waiting to go home.

Out in the cold night air, Stefan noted, "A small taste of Warsaw café society," then added, with a look of incomprehension, "and people in Kracow claim that theirs is superior."

The street was empty and still. The concrete pillars of

the Marszałkowska Street arcade stretched in darkness toward Constitution Square where a small yellow light glowed; first steady, now wobbly with the approach of an old tram.

Warsaw once possessed a fabled café life. In the period between the two world wars, cafés and cabarets thrived in the unfamiliar, tantalizing spirit of national independence. Literary coteries gathered around their favorite estaminets (the *Skamander* group of Słonimski and Tuwim frequented Ziemiańska), and figures from the arts spent their youthful nights in club rounds. Mieczysław Fogg sang his impossibly romantic tangos, and Pola Negri could be seen escorted through the smoke-filled interiors.

Even before this time, cafés and their clientele enjoyed notoriety. In the book *Sketches and Pictures from Warsaw Life*, approved by the "elder censor" in 1857, an entire chapter is devoted to "Wags of the Salon," among which — indeed, deemed "the most worthy of the title 'wag'" — is the café wit. According to a census of the period, there were exactly 4,008 wags in Warsaw in that year. It is worth looking at the census for other populations.

In Warsaw, a city of nearly 180,000 people, there are

Geniuses of the first rank	165
Geniuses of the second rank, i.e., great talents	523
People of scientific training, in a word, brilliant folks	3,002
Amateurs of literature and science, and patrons of the arts	2,873
Wags	4,008
Social reformers	386

Progressives	half the population of Warsaw
People who make an impression	5,738
People who could be great, if not for this or that	2,642
Phenomenally beautiful women	indefinable number
Pretty women	all who are not ugly
Ugly women	none
People who are known to be simpletons	a very considerable number, with the exception of those who are pronounced to be
People who themselves admit to being simpletons	0,0

In the early 1980s, Varsovians still met at cafés during the day, work hours being a popular time. But the place for evening entertainment was the family apartment. The variety of menu and refinement of company were invariably greater at home, and one could usually count on it to be free of insolent personnel. Home was private. It was also clean. If, as was once said in France, the Frenchman invites you to his café because he is embarrassed by his home, the Pole invites you to his home because he is embarrassed by his café. And home, for a Varsovian, is an apartment.

Warsaw is a city of apartments. Apartment blocks line every street and rise up out of lots in clusters, creating a topography that is clean, scattered, redundant, and thickset: a riparian plain strewn with rectangular boxes. There is no area of the city without these blocks, no residentless financial sections or uninhabitable warehouse districts. If an apartment has a view, it is of other apartments. The unvaried, humdrum sight used to depress me on the Grójecka Street tram, looking up as I would at block after block of stunted, symmetrical balconies. On this thoroughfare, with its stark, contemporary housing, I saw something in Hania's lament (which she had once shared as we walked along the Seine) that Paris had been saved in the war, and Warsaw ravaged.

Every city of course is a city of apartments, but not as absolutely as Warsaw. It took me months before I saw a house, in a secluded neighborhood of houses, and this was home to an American embassy family. The word for apartment, *mieszkanie*, is derived from the word *mieszkać*, "to reside, to live."

There are the elegant apartments in the Old Town, reserved, one was always told, for artists and writers. There are apartments, like the "Gomułkas," whose minute dimensions reflect the austere measures of the leader in whose time they were built. There are apartments off of Łazienki Park, once designated for retired party hands. There are horrid, award-winning apartment complexes of the 1960s, built to house thousands and referred to derisively by Poles as "anthills." There are prewar apartment houses heated by coal and cleaned by chimney sweeps who carry large, leather, bristle-topped satchels swung across their black, Victorian, double-breasted shirtfronts. (It is this collection of buttons, I suppose, which mandates that, upon seeing a chimney sweep, you clutch at yours, and not let go of them until — and here the custom loses me — a woman wearing spectacles passes by.) There are desirable apartments on the placid, tree-lined streets off Filtrowa, and mean, decrepit ones across the Vistula in the working-class district of Praga. There are apartments high above

Jerozolimskie Avenue, where one can hear the trams as they come ringingly on and off the Poniatowski Bridge. There are apartments with addresses as sublime as Joke Street, Incomplete Street, Wild Boar Street, and Winnie-the-Pooh Street. In Muranów, the former Jewish quarter, apartments stand slightly elevated, John Gunther tells us, because of the rubble and corpses underneath. There are apartment buildings whose walls still bear the scars of machine-gun fire. Ringing the city are the newest complexes, rising tall, sleek, and miserly out of erstwhile potato fields. (Here, as in other parts of the city, a horse-drawn peasant wagon will sometimes appear: a wrenching scene in winter as the horse breathes vaporous clouds and the peasant drives with enormous gloves while hunched inside his heavy coat.) Plain and monotonous in daylight, these dwellings become futuristic cities at night, ribboning the darkened land with unfathomable, seemingly endless walls of light.

The winter sun in Warsaw sets, often unseen, in midafternoon. Then the windows of all these apartments come aglow, recalling, especially in the Old Town, a scene from a childhood Advent calendar.

If there is one thing Warsaw is more than a city of apartments, it is a city lacking apartments. Varsovians spend the majority of their lives in apartments, much of the time talking about apartments, which compete with politics as a primary topic of conversation. Discussions are precise ("He got a forty-three-square-meter apartment in Żoliborz"), and the numbers, so intimate to Poles, conjure up immediate images.

The wait for apartments in years is somewhere in double figures, with the usual, well-connected exceptions. Parents put their newborn babies on waiting lists.

A studio apartment (called a *kawalerka*, after *kawaler*, or bachelor) often houses a family. Lovers borrow friends' apartments for afternoon trysts. In the larger, one-bedroom apartments, three generations sometimes live together in varying degrees of harmony. A common choice for newlyweds is not so much where to live, but with whose in-laws. One of Hania's university friends married a classmate and moved in with his family, sharing his room. After seven years the couple decided on a separation. With no place to go, she took to sleeping with her head at the foot of the bed.

Poles still leave the village and the countryside to come to Warsaw. Despite the overcrowding, there are no street people. Thousands await apartments, but almost everyone has a home. "What are the three prerequisites for happiness in Poland?" went a joke popular at the beginning of martial law. "To have your own job, your own apartment, and your own opinion." Were Bolesław Prus alive and writing today his great novel of the city (a book without which, Antoni Słonimski once conjectured, Warsaw would never have been rebuilt), he would title it not *The Doll*, but *The Apartment*.

Hania and I frequently went on afternoon visits to her aunts' apartments, setting out in the cold winter twilight as the city's workers headed home. The idea of having all of one's family and lifelong friends a tram ride away was novel for me. We would jump off in some nondescript neighborhood and locate the local flower peddler, Hania in her Western clothes miraculously communicating with a threadbare ancient. The buildings were unanimously humble in design and old enough not to have elevators. The stairs were illuminated by a timed hall light that always extinguished itself before our ascent. Bare, chipped

plaster walls; cold, unwashed concrete landings; a uniformity of faceless doors. Feeling the wall, we found the
bell, which emitted a harsh, high-pitched gravelly ring
that sometimes set off a domestic bark, then the approaching pat of slippered feet across a parquet floor.
Inside, in the warm luminosity, one found an elegant
apartment. Never have I seen doors so solidly divide
such disparate worlds.

Though consisting of only one room, Aunt Masia's
apartment was the most striking. An elaborate folding
of curtains permanently concealed the windows and
gave the room, along with its occupant, the period air of
a theater set. The room itself was high-ceilinged and
furnished in a jumble of fine oak chairs, writing tables,
divans, and cabinets. Near the dining table sat an ornate
silver tray displaying countless small *objets* of gold and
silver. In one corner, near a window, stood a bookshelf,
and in front of it two chairs turned slightly toward each
other as if for conversation. Aunt Masia still made some
money tutoring English: once we had come and found a
student, Jerzy Maksymiuk, director of the Chamber Orchestra of the Warsaw Philharmonic, grinning wordlessly in farewell as he walked sideways out of the room,
dragging in self-conscious fashion a large sack across
the floor. On one wall hung a great portrait of Masia's
second husband, a dark, handsome man dressed in riding breeches and holding a crop. Like many pictures
hanging in old Warsaw apartments, this one possessed a
small tear in the canvas: the unmistakable mark of a dis-
rupted life.

Masia would greet us with some objurgation toward
the regime, which seemed to me, and perhaps to her,
ages removed from that interior. She was an unconven-

tional woman, tall and brittle, of a type not found in the frumpy meat queues outside. She wore slacks, smoked cigarettes — which she would pluck out of a gold, mono-grammed case — and enjoyed spirits, especially Scotch, which she always took the opportunity, in honor of our visit, to consume. She held strong, if only slightly out-dated opinions, and appreciated the company of young people. A devoted grandson dropped by regularly to read aloud to her because of her failing eyesight (a cur-rent selection was *Bitter Glory*, a history of Poland be-tween the wars, written by an American), and his sister, a French major, would stay for hours, contradicting everything her grandmother said.

The Petersburg aunt, Kira, though also in her seven-ties, was more animated. She had an impressive reper-toire of Revolutionary tales (she had fled Russia in a freight train, sharing a car with the Japanese ambas-sador) and romantic histories, both of which she nar-rated in a bemused, breathless voice that frequently de-veloped into an uncontrollable chortle. Aunt Kira, my wife once informed me, had had at least two husbands and numerous dalliances and had imparted to Hania her cheerful philosophy that "Men are like buses: if you miss one, another will be along shortly."

One aunt, Basia, was infirm, looked after by an obedi-ent male cousin who would lead us into the main room and station us at either side of her so that we could both speak directly into her feeble, though tremendous ears. She was always dressed in the same monotone layers of timeworn cardigans and skirts, her speckled hand ca-ressing the curve of her wooden cane. The setting al-ways had the character of an audience. Basia would ex-pound on various topics, a popular one being the beauty of my wife, whom she called, as did some of the other aunts in my presence, "*la petite.*" Hania blushed appreciatively and after our visit would talk of the atrophy of her aunt's mind. Basia worshiped as history's three greatest men Napoleon, Piłsudski, and De Gaulle, and saw as the embodiment of evil on earth whoever was the current first secretary. Like many of an older generation, she was critical of youth. "I don't understand these young people today," she would explain angrily. "Why don't they go to Jaruzelski's house and slit his throat? Why don't they simply string him up and hang him from the highest lamppost? Why they don't do that, I can't for the life of me understand. If I were even twenty years younger," she would proclaim, pounding her cane on the floor, "I would be the first one at him."

Aunt Janusia, who lived with her second husband off Puławska Street, was my favorite. A tiny, energetic woman, she dressed always in black and resembled the widows one sees ducking into churches on weekday mornings in small towns in France. She taught French and looked French, with a wizened face and a small, hooked nose, though her eyes were blue and benevolent.

Her absentmindedness was legendary. Arriving for five o'clock tea, we would find her at the door, her stockinged feet in dilapidated slippers. After a moment's thought she would exclaim, "Haneczka, how nice of you to drop by unexpectedly. Just passing through the neighborhood? Bolek! Hania and *le monsieur* are here!" One wondered by what unimaginable methods she contrived to keep her pupils. She was known to invite half a dozen people to dinner and then kiss her husband good-bye as she went off to see a movie. It was told that one day shortly after the war she had asked a man passing by to mind her goat, which she kept in the yard for milk, while she went down the street to buy some bread. Instantly forgetting the deal, she took off on a jaunt. Returning that night she was surprised to find an unfamiliar, irritated man sitting with her pet. Her present boarder, a middle-aged priest, often retrieved — in the most inappropriate company — her newly washed nylons from his freshly pressed coat pockets.

Once settled we were served tea in cups and on rare occasions the exquisite holeless Polish doughnuts, *pączki*, made at home or, just as triumphantly, purchased at the Blikle Shop on Nowy Świat Street. Everything about Janusia was quickened: her movements, her speech, obviously her memory. Nibbling her doughnut, she carried on an accelerated conversation with Hania while Bolek, sitting mute in his armchair, kept an untrusting eye on the door. Janusia was seventy-two and showed no signs of slowing down. Hania sometimes accompanied her to the cemetery to lay flowers on the family plots and came back exhausted from feeble attempts to keep pace. One could see her whisking by the shoppers on Puławska Street, but it was impossible to imagine her standing stationary in a queue.

The shelves in Janusia's apartment were lined with classics, bad novels, mysteries, and detective stories from the Livre de Poche series, none of which could be taken out without displacing a member of the family, honorably framed. Aunt Janusia had come from a large family in eastern Poland and, with her first husband, had created another; photographs filled every bit of shelf space and available desktop. There were sepia prints of Georgian manor houses, sylvan parks, high-collared men with luxuriant mustaches (one in a coat of vague military appearance, wearing a sash and an astrakhan hat), long-skirted ladies leaning on swings, and cherubic, flaxen-haired children sitting atop ponies. In one, three peasant women offered a large round loaf to Hania's great-grandmother in an annual harvest enactment. Interspersed with these were modern color photographs of grandchildren in jeans hamming it up on a wooden pier in the Mazurian lakes, and the ever popular postcards of the Pope. From the support bars of the shelves were tied long strands of colored ribbons, blue, red, yellow, green, which made any time in Aunt Janusia's apartment feel like the day after a holiday.

Hania and her aunts never seemed to tire of talking; I mostly listened, astounded by the constant banter and shared jokes. Farewells, when they came, were prolonged by still more news, gossip, well-wishing, inquiry, as we stood minutes in the antechamber, suited for the cold. "The English," Hania taught me early, "leave and don't say good-bye. The Poles say good-bye and don't leave."

What always struck me on such visits was the natural cheerfulness of these women. They had begun lives more privileged, and continued lives more depleted (materially) than anyone I had ever known, yet they accepted their fates with equanimity. They complained no more than anyone else in Poland, a good deal less in fact, and almost never of personal misfortune or physical ailments. Age, so often the thief of humor and serenity, seemed of little consequence to them. A religious faith, at least for Aunt Janusia, was partly responsible. No doubt too, the early lessons of irretrievable loss of property and wealth had seasoned them somewhat for the later, incontestable ravages on mind and body.

Most of our younger friends who had apartments lived in the more recently built ones. They were usually far from the city center and usually at primary points on the compass, most frequently south. These "modern" buildings, owing to a lack of maintenance, deteriorated quickly, and their overall appearance was saved only by the fact that vandalism had not yet taken a hold on Polish urban life. Their bare lobbies were gained through clanging doors linked by muddy paths. Yet their most depressing features by far were their corridors — narrow, poorly lit, unfinished runways that stretched institutionally past thirty or more portals.

Here, as well, I was pleasantly startled to find the comfortable home behind the penitentiary door. Though consisting of the same number of identically sized rooms, the apartments each took on the unique character of their inhabitants. Furnishings were usually few and simple — tables, chairs, and beds made of light pine in a contemporary Scandinavian design. But added to these were appurtenances — wood paneling in the foyers, country-style cupboards in the kitchen, handsome coatracks, bookshelves, and nightstands installed and hand-carved by the man of the house. It was rare to meet a Polish male who could not make a piece of furniture. One of our friends, after whittling and sawing into existence most of his family's possessions, set to work on a peasant figure, in the naive tradition, which eventually stood five feet tall in the vestibule. Coming out of the long corridor into his apartment was like putting down *Brave New World* for *Uncle Vanya*. Of course much of this artisanship was called into being simply by the unavailability of things to purchase. But it was also, more importantly, a way to make an intimate refuge, a mortal pronouncement, in state housing.

Stefan's apartment was the exception. In the same complex as that of the woodsman, it had been little altered by personal design. I saw it for the first time on a dull, damp Saturday afternoon on which I had been invited for tea. Stefan greeted me at the door ("Let me take your coat. Still have it, I see. Must not have come by bus") and led me into the living room. It was small enough that the dining table, placed against one wall, nearly bridged the other two. A large television set monopolized an opposite corner. The soft colorful debris of children's toys littered the shag carpet. On the wall was hung, or rather, was taped, a cutout photograph of the Pope.

"I'm going to take the girls for a walk," their mother announced, suddenly appearing in the doorway.

"Poor Zosia, she's been run around all day," Stefan explained.

"I've been run around for the last eleven years," riposted Zosia, before firmly closing the door behind her.

"The vaunted Polish feminine charm," said Stefan. "But then, people in the States don't know much about Poland, do they?" I told him they didn't. "The same in England. They don't know anything about Poland. In France as well. In Germany, well, in Germany they do" — his voice dipping to a hush, the corners of his mouth turning up — "because we took some land from them.

"Let me show you something while the women are gone." He led me into the girls' bedroom. The door opened only partly because of the table behind it. Around the room, desks abutted beds that squeezed between dressers, leaving little in the way of floor space. Books and papers and stacks of magazines sat atop the tallest pieces and teetered precariously. Opening a top desk drawer, Stefan pulled out a sheaf of typewritten papers that bore the unpolished look of *samizdat*.

"This," he began, lifting the first few pages, "is a piece

entitled 'Notes to the Nation on Proper Etiquette During the World Cup Matches.' There's something of a soccer hysteria in this country, and I have drawn up some helpful behavior tips, so we do not embarrass ourselves. Just a little thing I did in my free time."

Another piece was titled "Scenes from Warsaw Life" and consisted of short, descriptive notes:

- "Honey from the Bee Shop" on Puławska Street. In the window, below the store sign, an attractive, wooden sign proclaiming "The Elegant Honey Drink." Underneath it a crude, handwritten cardboard sign reading: "Out of honey."

- Mannequins in shop window in Constitution Square modeling new suit jackets but shirtless due to shortages.

- In milk bar on Marszałkowska Street a man sitting with his head in his soup.

There is a Polish expression, *pisać do szuflady*, "to write for the drawer," used for those people whose writings (primarily political) were not suitable for the official press and were relegated to the safe shelter of apartment dressers. Engagement in this form of writing demanded a rare, inscrutable feeling for the saving grace of words and thought. For it was not just the random, recording job of journal entries, but a formal process of creation which Stefan practiced. And one had to remember that there were not only no papers in which to print his work, but no cafés in which he could spend long afternoons entertaining his confreres, tossing down vodka and sharpening his wit. Here, in this furniture-

filled room of a meager apartment, was his literary do-
main. It was in the spring of 1979, a little more than a
year before the emergence of Solidarity, when I asked
him if he found it disturbing to think that there was no
chance of official publication.

"Well, I'm used to it," he said. "When I think about it, it
does bother me. But I try not to think about it. You know
I spent some time in Australia and I know something
about the West. In fact, I feel myself to be part Western.
In Poland, we have an advantage because we have more
freedom than any other Eastern European people. And
at the school, as well, we're in a better position than teachers at other schools to try new things. That's why I put
up that suggestion box. You see, people in Poland are
blocked. I want to do something that will push them a bit,
that will," he added, pausing, "unblock them."

Varsovians live in well-toasted apartments, and the sensation on coming out into the sparkling night air, after
hours in a cramped, low-ceilinged, smoke-filled room,
was liberating. No matter how much I had drunk or
eaten, the frigid temperatures instantly cleared my head,
while numbing my fingers and toes. I studied the shivering taxi queue, and the dragon-breathed bus stop pa-
trons, and then chose my torture.

I suffered in these winters more than I had in any
others, not simply because they were colder, which they
were, but because I spent more time exposed to the cold.
On the bitterest of winter afternoons, I would stand outside in a food line for an hour and then wait another forty
minutes for a tram. The cars were unheated, and I stood
holding, with gloved hands, the icy metal of the seats.
Then I would make the long walk home from the tram

stop in darkness, passing the somber forms of a heart-wrenching queue, planted there since morning, rigid with cold and waiting for meat.

The word for cold, *zimno*, sounded cold to me, especially when the first syllable (begun as the French *g* in *Gigi*) stuttered through chattering teeth. It derives from the word for winter, *zima*. For the long season, Warsaw's streets came alive with furs and pelts and dead animal skins interspersed among drab woolen coats. Young men sometimes wore ankle-length sheepskin coats from the Tatras, some double-breasted and with mats of a discolored shag in Rastafarian points at the collar and cuffs. When sporting the high astrakhan hats, they possessed a roguish, hetman allure. Young women, likewise, were often extravagantly wrapped, with soft scarves drawn tightly across their mouths and hats pulled down low over their brows, giving them the mystery of the Muslim chador. Passing them on the street, I frequently saw only eyes, cerulean and watery, peeking out. Many wore limp foxes around their necks, the still sharp eyeteeth calmly clamped around the feathery tails. The most popular were silver, but there were also white foxes and red. In class, female students placed them on the windowsills in what I first interpreted, with professorial concern, to be unnecessarily predatory poses. Yet their comfortingly slack countenances came to represent for me the wild — which seemed intoxicatingly near — and a time (here, at least, not yet passed) when man by necessity clothed himself with its skins.

A hat was an essential item in Warsaw winters, and to go about without one was to risk any number of strong rebukes from middle-aged Cassandras (with which Warsaw was filled). These stout ladies favored for themselves dumpy wool caps, set back slightly on their heads and knit in sedate shades of brown or blue, yet occasionally I'd spot a lurid lime or tangerine. Along the same lines were slightly more aesthetic, pancake-shaped caps. Also popular were globular hats, white or brown, resembling whiskered soccer balls, and their hybrid, with fuzzy sides all the way around a smooth cloth top. Men wore heavy fur hats made from the coats of nutrias, the earflaps tied at the top to make a four-walled fortress for the head; also gray astrakhans with flaps running across the backs and with protective visors; also in this style, sleek muskrat and fine dark fox. There were Greek fisherman caps, Basque berets, an occasional fez, and the odd British bowler. The rare elderly gentleman could be seen with young lamb pelts dyed and fit onto his lapels to match his hat. Equally fetching for ladies were exquisite mink pillbox hats. I once saw one of these set far down upon the brow of a stunningly beautiful woman on a bus, her dark hair pulled thickly into a braid and the attached tail of a raccoon falling in back of her red-rimmed ear.

Winter seemed already mature by Christmas, which came with little outward display. Some state shops on Nowy Świat and Marszałkowska streets pasted crude paper decorations onto their windows, few of which held for longer than a week. A handful of plywood shacks went up just before the holiday to sell tawdry ornaments. There were no city light displays or main square Christmas trees. The most visible sign of the holiday's approach was in the growth of the queues, sometimes as long as a block. The longest formed outside fish shops, where Poles waited with dedicated patience for the traditional carp. This bony fish was purchased live and, for un-

beatable freshness, allowed in some households to oc-
cupy the family bathtub before its ultimate journey to
the kitchen.

There was always a heroic aspect of the hunt involved
in Warsaw shopping, which was intensified, of course, at
Christmas. My first year I took great pride in waiting
three hours in line for a bunch of bananas, a feat that at
one point was recorded on film by an NBC camera crew.
I divided my shopping between the real world of Polish
shops and the dream world of Pewex stores, which accepted dollars (from Poles as well as foreigners) and sold
a perennial holiday assortment of chocolates, cookies,
nuts, liquors, cigarettes, teas, and coffees all year. It was
always fascinating to see the intense pleasure brought to
a Polish household by a tin of English breakfast tea or
Danish butter cookies. I recall after one Christmas meal
sitting around the table, when all the presents lay scattered and ignored, and watching Hania's cousin study
with unqualified admiration the velvety green box of
After Eights, with its plush interior of individually filed
mints.

Shopping was always more of an adventure than a
duty for me. Hania, in the midst of the food crisis, told
me: "I see no need for you to stand in queues. It's not
your fault our country is in a mess." "But it's not your
fault either," I insisted. "Oh, in a way it is," she answered.
"In a way it's the fault of all of us."

After her mother's death, my wife, an only child,
whose father had also died, moved from Żoliborz to a
larger, two-bedroom apartment in the western district
of Ochota. The apartment occupied the top corner of a
simple four-story building recently constructed amidst
older tenements in a cul-de-sac. The cracked plaster

wall of one of these houses greeted us in all weathers and seasons from our place at the kitchen table, the most popular spot in the apartment. Even bathed in sunlight, the place filled me with an ineffable sadness. To one side of our building was a taxi depot, and in the front, across a street, was a field where displaced peasants planted crops.

We lived in Ochota with Hania's "aunt," Jadwiga (Jadzia for short), who was not a blood relative but a close friend of Hania's mother from Szymanów, the Catholic boarding school they had all attended as girls. She had moved from Lodz with her daughter, Małgorzata (nicknamed Gosia), a shy, forty-year-old anesthesiologist who worked at a nearby hospital. These friends of the family — Hania always spoke of them as aunt and cousin — were more like mother and sister to her. It was Aunt Jadzia who, on our return from the Palace of Weddings, greeted us at the apartment door with a shaker of salt ceremoniously balanced atop a loaf of bread.

Jadzia was a solid, portly woman, a very recognizable type in her bulging housedress and kitchen slippers. She spent almost all of her waking hours in the kitchen, cooking countless soups and then sitting down for restorative teas. The kitchen was also a recognizable, socialist type, with its double-paned windows (a gauzy bundle of farmer's cheese often dangling from the handle), its snug refrigerator, its unsound linoleum table set against one wall and surrounded by child-sized stools, the only furniture that would fit. The two-year-old walls were hopelessly charred. I had no idea of the universality of our little *kuchnia* until I saw a picture in the book *A Day in the Life of the Soviet Union* which showed it nearly identically reproduced in a housing complex in Leningrad.

Jadzia always occupied with authority the stool closest
to the wall, packed in tightly between the table and the
refrigerator. When our dog, Jap, a hybrid boxer, settled
down next to her she could be pinned inside for hours.
Then Hania or Gosia would reset the kettle. Jadzia's
preferred posture was slightly forward with both elbows
on the table, her weary chin resting in an upraised palm.
She had a white mane of hair, somewhat unruly in the
morning, large brown eyes, and a pouchy face that occasionally bore an expression reminiscent of neurasthenia.
She was an excellent mimic, and interspersed her regular lamentations on the bitterness of war, the tragedy
of Poland, with comical imitations. These relieved her
mournful air. Though a gentle woman, she grew equally
animated in anger, which was all too easily induced (and
all too frequently for her fragile heart) by the evening
news. Sitting at the kitchen table day after day, her listless resignation alternating with her role as raconteur,
she seemed a Slavic version of the bounteous black nannies of early Hollywood movies.

Apart from her children she was sustained by two
events in recent times: the election of the Polish pope
and the founding of Solidarity. She took the movement
immediately to heart, endeared to it as a nationalist and
as a Catholic. (One of the union's original demands, and
one of the first the government implemented, was the
weekly radio broadcast of the Sunday Mass from Warsaw.) Whenever Lech Wałęsa appeared on television,
speaking in his jarringly direct and incautious fashion,
Jadzia sat in her armchair as if listening to music.

She spoke fluent French, the result of having been
sent as a child, before Szymanów, to a boarding school
in Belgium. As a young girl she had been chosen to

present a bouquet of roses to Clemenceau on his state visit to Poland, an event which was frequently replayed in our kitchen.

I called her "aunt," *ciocia* (pronounced "cho-cha"), and addressed her respectfully, if a bit awkwardly for me, in the third person. "Would aunt like some tea? I didn't know that aunt was running late." I habitually overpraised her cooking for the pleasure such compliments gave her. Actually, for what she had to work with, she was not untalented; in fact, she was a vast improvement over the professional woman on Adam Mickiewicz Street. Though every day seemed to produce a familiarly brothy soup, a thin, breaded cutlet, and a side of boiled potatoes generously ladled with cooking grease. Less formal meals consisted of stale bread or matzo crackers spread with whatever was available: cheese sometimes, jam and butter usually, horseradish always. I remember during one difficult month spreading undue amounts of horseradish on a matzo cracker so to feel especially full. If I rushed out in the morning without my breakfast, Jadzia would scold me with maternal hurt, to which I could have easily replied: "But I did have breakfast — at last night's supper!" What I would have given during those years for a single grapefruit.

In my first months I attended morning Polish classes, though I could have gotten, and eventually did get, better instruction sitting with Jadzia in the kitchen. She spoke with a slight Lvov accent, according to Hania, and took enormous satisfaction — as only certain people in certain languages do — in the *sound* of her words. As a child she had wanted to be an actress (not an acceptable profession in those days for proper ladies), and it showed in her Polish. She delivered the thickly knotted consonants and susurrous constructions with flourish. She had a few favorite litanies that she would deliver powerfully, her eyes wide and her brows arched high, often on a popular theme of Soviet hegemony.

Jadzia kept company at tea with Hania, Gosia, or Bocia, Hania's authentic aunt. Bocia was physically and temperamentally Jadzia's opposite: petite, prickly, and illnourished. She was thoughtful without being warm, and when I confessed that I found her difficult I was somewhat relieved to find that everyone else did too, even Jadzia, who would spend hour upon hour with her in the kitchen, inhaling the smoke from her Sport cigarettes.

Bocia visited us, several days a week, but would not permit anyone to come to her apartment in the center of Warsaw (a rule that had held since her husband's death twenty years earlier). She often brought fresh fish, which required an entire morning to purchase, for our cat, Osmond. She had her own stool, at the head of the table, and her own dented cup for tea: she was particular about such things. Between sips she would nervously work a stub into her yellowed, plastic cigarette holder, looking down at the procedure through the thick lenses of her spectacles. She was a decorous alcoholic, and her small hands and head shook in a way that made them seem to be on strings controlled by a slightly inexperienced marionettist. Similarly, a lifetime of nicotine had introduced a deposit of phlegm in her throat that, in all the years I heard her cough at it, she never expelled.

At Christmastime the activity in the kitchen intensified. The apartment would be enveloped in the viscid aroma of *bigos*, an elaborate sauerkraut stew that Jadzia would cook for days and we would eat for weeks. It gets better the longer it sits, I was always told. She also baked, filling trays blackened by age with numerous cookies and velvety cakes, the latter getting the best of her ration cards for sugar.

On Christmas Eve, Leszek, Gosia's longtime fiancé, who lived with his wife and two teenage children, brought a small tree. Leszek was about fifty, an engineer with peasant looks (blond hair, sloping nose, ruddy complexion) and a courtly manner. Despite his unorthodox personal life, he shared many traits with Jadzia: he was strongly nationalistic and, in theory if not practice, Catholic. Yet his unclear intentions toward Gosia made his relations with her mother something of a series of polite misgivings. Indeed, he would always return home for the Wigilia meal, kissing Jadzia's hand as he went.

Polish Christmas officially begins on December 24, when the first star is spotted in the evening sky. The name for Poland, *Polska*, is derived from the word *pole*, meaning "field," and many of the holiday's traditions (as in other Christian lands) are still those of the countryside. Our Wigilia (literally, vigil) would usually begin much later, and with much less extravagance than is called for. Traditionally this dinner, as a sort of supreme example of the paradox in Polish life, is both a fast and a twelve-course meal. It is technically a fast in the sense that it is meatless — the only one of the two traditions, in those days of economic decrepitude, that was consistently honored.

The table was set, not, as is customary, with a bedding of straw beneath the cloth, but always, no matter how tight the seating, with one extra place. ("For the Russian soldier," was the joke in the Christmas of Solidarity, made almost prescient the following year.) At each person's place was the *opłatek*, a long, consecrated wafer, often embossed with a biblical scene. Before sitting down to eat we would each take this bread about the room, offering a piece to everyone else with wishes for the coming year, and then receiving the same, in a ritual dance of snapped wafers, kissed cheeks, and gladsome recitation.

This done, the fast began with the serving of soup: spicy cream of mushroom or *barszcz*, its bright, decoratively red broth washing over "little ears," as the delicate, submerged *pierogi* filled with ground mushroom are called. Following the soup came herring or carp, with more *pierogi* — this time filled with sauerkraut — and boiled potatoes. We drank wine, and sometimes vodka. "Fish," pronounced Bocia, "have to swim."

It was always astonishing to see, despite the paucity of the marketplace, how many of the obligatory foods did appear at this meal, and the importance everyone attached to their appearance. It seemed of little consequence to me whether we would have carp this Christmas, but to Jadzia and the others it was a matter of the utmost seriousness. Over time I grew to appreciate this businesslike attention to small details amidst seasonal shortages, for it had in it something of the symbolic resistance of a coerced people. As long as they had carp on their Wigilia table, all had not yet been taken from them.

Dessert consisted of Jadzia's cakes, many of them containing poppy seeds, so that the lucky diner who had survived to this point without choking on a fish bone now faced the inevitability of several little black seeds lodged between the teeth. Afterward we would exchange presents and head out to Mass.

Normally, we went to the local church, but my first

year we went to St. John's Cathedral in the Old Town. We walked, at that usually lifeless hour of the night, with packs of worshipers over the glistening cobblestones. Crowds of figures hurried to the entrance; some young men let out piercing, drunken shouts; a few policemen sheltered in doorways. At the cathedral the parishioners backed out into the street, overflowing the vestibule. We pushed our way through (how often we pushed our way in Warsaw!) and gained entrance. I had never before seen a church so filled. The side aisles, as well as the nave aisle, were impassable with standing celebrants, as was the space before the altar rail, so that anyone sitting in the first pews saw only the backs of those standing in front.

The cathedral was built in place of its predecessor after the destruction of the Second World War, in a style known as Mazovian Gothic, in some places plain, in others ornate. It possesses a high altar, this night bordered by seven stately pines. The service was officiated by one bishop and four priests; to the side stood choirboys dressed in their black-and-white cassocks. The carols, though not familiar to me, were intensely moving. There is a strong tradition of Polish carols, their beauty never marred by play in department stores or supermarket aisles. The nineteenth-century poet Mickiewicz (often called the Polish Byron), while lecturing in Paris on Slavic literature, discussed the carols, calling them "the nucleus of the national poetry." Musically they are impressive, with influences as diverse as folk songs and baroque chorales. There is a haunting, almost elegiac lullaby, "Sleep, Little Jesus," and a stirring, sonorous hymn, "God Is Born," taken, tradition has it, from a polonaise played at a coronation of Polish kings. The still-bundled participants sang these familiar songs with a heavy, purposeful air that resounded powerfully in that vaulted nave. Their faces, hardened by labor, were thoughtful and somber. The spirit of Christmas, which works a kind of facile, outward cheer in Americans, here seemed to have the opposite effect of quiet introspection. After the benediction the great gathering headed slowly out into the cold and darkness of Świętojańska Street and then dispersed in a thousand pensive directions home.

On Christmas Day, Andrzej, Jadzia's son, would arrive from Lodz with his thirteen-year-old daughter, Urszula. Andrzej was a true communist, not only an atheist but an employee of the party — a career choice that had tested a mother's love as few such choices do. In his early forties, he had boyish features almost constantly clouded with unease. When we had finished our *bigos* and were lingering around the table with our tea and After Eights, Andrzej would talk gravely about the mood in his office, which was always dour. Like his mother, he possessed a good sense of humor and his laughter at family get-togethers grew sometimes into cachinnations that seemed designed to eliminate momentarily the troubles of his working world. It was from him that I first remember hearing the Polish words for: "In my humble opinion . . ." When Leszek entered into this gathering the possibility of discord became so great that Polish punctiliousness was stretched to new and taxing heights.

Upon Leszek's return, Gosia and Hania and I would go with him for an afternoon walk in the Old Town, he and I leading, the women following behind. Gosia, like many chronically shy people, was an unstoppable talker when paired with someone close, and she and Hania could walk arm in arm for hours. I learned not to mind.

Leszek was from the beginning an interesting companion. He impressed me as an authentic Warsaw character. He had grown up in Żoliborz, and as a child saw partisans battling Nazis in his neighborhood. In 1946, when the city lay in ruins, his parents sent him to stay with relatives in Zakopane, a resort town in the mountains. The theory was that even if food was as scarce, the air would be salubrious. Leszek once told of going to the Zakopane post office and picking up a package from his parents which contained a single loaf of bread. He was so hungry that he stood in the street and devoured the entire gift at once. Rather than construct a morality tale about how he should have made it last the week, Leszek claimed that no meal subsequent had ever surpassed that stale bread.

Indeed, he took no pleasure in food: he ate every meal with supreme indifference, proceeding through it with a workmanlike demeanor until he had methodically extinguished every bit of grizzle and grease. He never left a drop of soup, a scrap of meat, a sip of compote; in this, as well as in other ways, he highlighted for me the deficiencies in my own, cosseted character. Instead of enthusiasm for food, he expressed gratitude for it, which he and many others of his generation simply regarded as necessary to exist.

Leszek had finished the polytechnic with a degree in engineering, that exalted profession in the new socialist experiment. (Doctrinal songs of the period bore titles such as "We Are Building a New House.") He worked for a state firm, constructing roads and highway bridges, but was never tempted by the idea of party membership. He was a virulent anticommunist.

His professional career was enhanced by two healthy

children and a coterie of boyhood friends. (I knew nothing of his failed marriage, as he never spoke of his wife except to call her, when the occasion demanded it, "the mother of my children." I learned that she was emotionally unstable, a fact that Leszek used to explain his need to stay home until the children could look after themselves.) He practiced gymnastics once a week with a crowd from his school days, and had gone every summer for the last twenty-five years with the same group of friends and their children on a two-week canoe trip in the Mazurian lakes. Except for one or two excursions to Lake Balaton in Hungary, he never traveled abroad.

As we walked along Krakowskie Przedmieście Street, Leszek showed himself to be a man of infinite curiosity, knowledgeable on a plenitude of subjects. His specialty was Polish history, and he retained facts with a keenness not unlike the insistence on carp at Christmas. For both the carp and Leszek's version of history were under threat from higher powers.

From the beginning he conversed with me in Polish, speaking slowly and listening patiently. It was a dual lesson in language and history. At every block something inspired him to tell its past: the Copernicus monument, the Prus statue, the university gates, the Bristol Hotel, where I had the rare opportunity of enlightening him with the rumor, picked up from a Fulbright scholar, that Mary McCarthy had written her novel *The Group* while a guest. (Stefan, thinking of the hotel's famously bad service when I gave him this same literary nugget, replied, "Yeah, while waiting for her coffee.")

We would then walk through the Old Town, stopping at the churches bunched along its cobbled streets to visit the crèches. It was a popular Warsaw activity at Christmas, similar (to use a profane comparison) to window-shopping in New York City.

I can't recall ever being ill at Christmas, though every winter brought me novel ailments. Coming home from school or shopping I would be weak from the force of the cold, my skull pounding as if packed with ice. Hot baths, which I slipped into blissfully, left me limp. The unrelenting cold and my long, daily exposure to it were compounded by a deficient diet and lack of sunlight. We kept vitamins in iodine-colored vials on the kitchen table, along with a vast array of suspicious medications that Gosia had collected from her hospital, and Hania's family constantly forced these down my throat whenever I ate. I could not be counted on to take them myself, owing to a certain distrust of Polish pharmacology. (I had seen the cafés, I could just imagine the laboratories.)

Hania and Gosia frequently checked my eyes for jaundice; Jadzia regularly complained that I looked pallid (*blady*, with a soft *a* as in *blah*, one of those Polish words whose sound perfectly conveys its meaning). She would pull her hand down over her face, which, newly unveiled, mimicked my supposed atrophy. I discovered boils on the backs of my hands and experienced the thrill of bronchitis for the first time in my life. I developed an asthmatic cough from the cat, though, because I was so fond of him, I attributed it to the carpet. Gosia periodically arranged tests and x-rays for me without the wait, and I would count the cigarette butts on the cement steps as I walked from floor to floor. In the lobby, grim, tubercular men stood smoking in ancient bathrobes, and down the corridors rakish doctors made their rounds in clogs.

I came down with *zaziębienia* (colds), *grypy* (flus), un-nameable viruses, each one knocking me out for a few days, a fate I accepted with only a little reluctance. There can be few recuperative experiences more pleasurable than that of convalescing in a household of Polish women. This sentiment was, however, called into question one winter when I developed an extraordinarily high fever and, after consultation in the kitchen, a nurse was summoned to give me "cups."

The woman arrived and, after taking off her coat in the antechamber, was led into our bedroom. She carried a round tray filled with twenty-six identical bulbous glasses, a box of matches, a stick with a cotton wad at the end, and a bowl of rubbing alcohol. She dipped the cotton stick into the alcohol, set it aflame, swirled it quickly round the rim of a glass, which she then deftly deposited onto my bare back. She did likewise with the other twenty-five. Then she covered me and told me to lie still on my stomach for the next fifteen minutes. I did as I was told, feeling halfway between a freak show artist and a theater marquee advertising my act. The only sensation I felt other than extreme humiliation was an occasional pinching. When my fever eventually subsided, the cups were given due credit. And even if they hadn't helped, rationalized Hania, as she did with every home-made cure, from bitter herbal teas to garlic sandwiches to steaming glasses of boiled raspberries, they had done no harm.

As in most cities, social life picked up around the holidays, and to foreigners Warsaw became an unexpectedly attractive capital. It offered a native population with a tradition of hospitality and cultivation of outsiders, and a diplomatic community that was small enough to be familiar and accessible. In these two aspects it seemed to be the exact opposite of Paris, with its disingenuous natives and its multifarious and diffuse foreign contingents. In fact I often wondered why Warsaw, with its perennially strong dollar, had not yet replaced that city as the preferred refuge of American writers.

Attending parties of the *corps diplomatique*, even the informal gatherings of office staff, held for me an almost forbidden fascination. A dimly lit bus carried us through deserted streets, their shops not only shuttered but, we knew, depressingly empty behind the shutters. Brought to our stop, we walked to the special residences, sometimes with a secret policeman as the doorman, of Western embassy personnel. Once inside our host's apartment, I would feel like an Englishman who has just walked onto Gibraltar from Spain. I found in all of these homes an unmistakably familiar climate, not of affluence, but rather of simple and inalienable comfort — a common material vernacular — that was all the more powerful for seeming so illusory. No matter how many visits I made, I could never quite get over these little dreamy pockets of the West with their snack foods, their Cuisinarts, their glossy magazines spread out on their glass coffee tables — in barren Warsaw.

In December 1978, I experienced what Poles for years after referred to as the "winter of the century," *zima stulecia*. On the night of the twenty-ninth the temperature dropped to minus twenty degrees Celsius. The mercury in a thermometer that my mother had thoughtfully sent, which showed the temperature in both Celsius and Fahrenheit, disappeared at the bottom. The next morning the cold was accompanied by snow and wind that by noon increased to a tremendous pitch. Sitting in our neighbor's apartment, on the top floor of our building, we watched in the west hoary gusts flailing unobstructed across the open spaces. On the radio we heard that electricity was failing in some sections of the city and that the rapid accumulations were causing trams to stop in their tracks.

I put on wool trousers over long underwear, two pairs of socks, two heavy sweaters, coat, gloves, scarf, hat, and boots and left for my afternoon English classes. On the street, buses were stalled and huge crowds, moving and jumping to stave off frostbite, were gathered at the stops. When a bus finally arrived, everyone fought toward it, not caring so much where it was going, but hoping only for some relief from the blizzardy pelt. When I eventually made my way on, I found that the floor was a sheet of ice. Sandwiched as we were, though, there was no chance of falling. The windows were completely etched by frost of the most beautiful, crystalline delicacy, so I had to guess at my stop, and start fighting toward the exit, at the one before.

To my astonishment, all of my classes were well attended, and students who came in late did so with apologies. When I told one young man that he looked like he had just got back from Siberia, he rejoined, "Better to be coming back than to be going to." In the teachers' room, Stefan invited me to join him the next morning for tennis.

It snowed all night in varying degrees. When I stepped out at five-thirty, a fine mist was coming down. Physically, it was still night, and not a vehicle moved along the dark streets. I walked through high banks to the tram stop and waited, racquet in gloved hand. I was the only person or thing about. After fifteen minutes of painful cold, I glimpsed a single light in the distance and watched with cautious belief the slow arrival of an empty tram. I gave the driver an icy wave with my Slazenger and felt pride in believing that, to all he had seen in a lifetime of civic transport, I had added something new.

I changed at the Rondo downtown, and with Stefan nowhere in sight, made walking rounds in the underground passage. After about fifteen minutes he appeared, shivering in a short wool coat and a tight beanie. His Roman nose had a purplish hue and his eyes were rheumy. "We have only two problems in Poland," he informed me cheerfully as we walked upstairs. "The weather and our neighbors."

The gym, in a student residence on Narutowicz Square, was unheated, and the floor was marked with the boundary lines of every indoor sport known to man. We played for an hour and a half.

That evening, New Year's Eve, the temperature dropped to minus twenty-seven, and a new storm blanketed the city with additional layers. We went out to go to a nearby party, and found a stinging, horizontal snow and a deep, hyperborean calm. My eyes no sooner filled with tears than the tears froze. We hailed a bus that was full of flushed, half-faced creatures buried in fur. The frosted windows gave the interior the unnatural brightness of a theater set, and I got a feeling of having intruded upon a private party.

The apartment to which we were invited was without heat, and the host welcomed the few of us who'd made it in the hope that we could add some. The burners on the kitchen stove were on high flame, and the living room was strewn with pots and pans of boiling water, regularly refilled. Strands of foam rubber had been glued along the sides of windows, and blankets had been rolled and placed at their bottom crevices. Our host distributed vodka, as well as the weather report from Moscow. "It's minus thirty there now."

"Serves them right."

"It's awful for the children," said a mother, ignoring these remarks. Her children slept in the next room, bundled in quilts.

"It's healthy to sleep in cold conditions."

"But it's not the weather, you know. It's the politics. We had enough coal. We had more than enough coal. But we exported it. It's absurd that we should be without it now. There's no reason why we shouldn't have heat."

"All right," offered her husband. "A toast." He poured out the vodka evenly. "If it goes to minus thirty, we change the government. If it goes to minus forty, we change the system."

On the first day of the new year a natural disaster was declared. Schools were closed, and many office workers were told not to report the following morning. All holiday resorts had closed down, as had the Warsaw airport. The newscasts never gave measurements of snow accumulations, though we were told that the sun, which we hadn't seen in a week, would set at 3:24 P.M. Several temporary blackouts occurred, the finest in the middle of a news report on the subject. Our hot tap water came and went.

The following day those who did report to work were given shovels (flat wooden boards tied to sticks) and asked to excavate in drifts taller than themselves. There were few maintenance crews to clear the thoroughfares; instead citizens — foundrymen, engineers, lawyers, professors, scientists, prisoners — amassed the stuff, sometimes filling trucks and vans with it as if for export. Senior citizens and children were exhorted not to go outside, and men were requested to surmount their vanities and not refrain from face creams, earmuffs, and other protective, nonalcoholic measures. On the radio a man sang that people are morally improved when they are cold. A meteorologist urged all apartment dwellers to put blankets and other insulations against their windows, which was a bit like being told at sea to close your porthole shutter. Christmas was over, and winter was just beginning.

Toward the beginning of February, it is the custom of Varsovians to head south, not to escape the winter but to delight in it. Their destination is the Tatra Mountains, a range of the Carpathians which rises up starkly between Poland and Czechoslovakia and dangles their common border like a treacherous high wire from peak to peak.

The Tatras were for a long time the favored resort of the Polish intelligentsia. Any literary biography with pictures is sure to feature its subject with his circle in Zakopane. The mountains provided Polish artists with not only rest but inspiration; there is in the national literature a vast amount of Tatras poetry, penned by everyone from Warsaw aesthetes like Iwaszkiewicz to native-son bards like Tetmajer. Figures as diverse as Karol Wojtyła (before he became pope) and Arthur Rubinstein took their holidays in the Tatras. Lenin hid from the secret police in nearby Poronin before going on to Switzerland.

In recent times the Tatras have become more prosaic, filling up with students on winter break. While there has been great interest in skiing, the mountains also fulfill that almost physical need that many Poles have for nature. Leszek was one of them, not only with his canoe trips away from civilization, but with his Sunday passion for walks in the woods. Though I did not share this feeling — I would always motion for a stroll in the Old Town instead — I understood it. More than a way of simply testing oneself in a primitive environment, which is for many people a sort of cleansing, the Polish immersion in nature was a conscious retreat from the degradations of an alien system, and as such provided a purification that Sierra Club members could never dream of. The Poles who flocked to the Tatra Mountains and the Mazurian lakes gave a whole new meaning to the phrase "getting away from it all."

One winter during my February break, Hania and I went to the mountain village of Kościelisko with Leszek and Gosia. They were both meticulous travelers and packed a month's supplies, including food provisions, in Leszek's venerable Syrena. The theory was that one queued in Warsaw's empty shops before going anywhere because the shops elsewhere were even emptier. To their unlabeled tins, which looked as if they dated from the occupation, I added a can of Krakus ham which my parents had recently mailed us. Leszek and Gosia regarded its arrival with tempered amusement, while Hania headlined the event "the repatriation of the Polish pig."

Squeezed in among our supplies, we headed south from Warsaw, passing from the last towering apartment block immediately into the low, featureless plain. The city transformed itself into country with alarming ease.

As with all previous rides into the environs of Warsaw, I found this one hopelessly depressing. The villages that sprang up so haphazardly seemed nothing more than clusters of square, flat-roofed houses unsystematically placed, constructed of the cheapest brick and concrete, and connected by lanes of horse-trod mud. The walls of some houses were begun in one material, continued in another, sometimes reverting to the first, leaving an unsightly mosaic to the financial vicissitudes of the owner-builder. I could look upon the flat tableland, stretching undiminished on either side, and entertain thoughts of the charges and forays, the sudden troop offensives and fatal tank aggressions, indeed the whole long and varied panorama of foreign incursion that had thrived on that ground.

It was not until we were on the other side of Krakow — one of the sootiest cities of architectural value in all of Europe — that we could begin to make out the glad changes, in man and nature, that convince the traveler that he has journeyed. The earth rose from its sleep, from flat to mountainous, from brown to white. Farther along the air changed from damp to dry, the forests from deciduous to conifer. As we puttered upward in Leszek's Syrena the horse-drawn wagons became horse-drawn sleighs, the three-room apartments of the city became three-story houses, and the brittle hodgepodge of the peasant hovel gave way to the Arcadian wood of the mountaineer hut. There is a saying, which every Polish schoolchild learns, about the last of Poland's Piast rulers, Kazimierz the Great, that he "found Poland built in wood and left it built in stone." Since then it has been rebuilt of brick and cement and cinder block, and it is, for anyone coming into the Tatras, a joy to find wood again. Even the bus stops here are neat, timbered A-frames. When, after driving for over eight hours, we arrived in darkness in Kościelisko, a fine snow was falling, lights were dim in response to a weakened power supply, and we were warned of the approaching mountaineers' sleighs by the crystal tinkling of small silver bells tied about the horses' necks.

The first morning we walked to Zakopane, the cultural capital of the Tatras. Most of the houses we passed were built of wood, the newer ones glazed and golden, the older ones more darkly grained. The authentic mountain houses have a layer of tightly braided straw between each log. Sitting next to some of the houses was a miniature model, also arched and wooden, to house the *owczarek podhalański*, the fluffy snow-white dog of the the Tatras, similar to the Samoyed in its benign expression. Leszek led us onto the street where the great families of Zakopane have always lived and then down into the center, where an old wooden church, characteristic of the region, stood beside a connecting cemetery. Most of the memorials were wooden, too, simple crosses with etched floral designs. One grave displayed an unusual representation of Christ which I had seen at a small chapel along the side of the road the day before. The primitively carved figure was wearily seated with his head tilted heavily into his hand, his face bearing an expression of vast woe. It reminded me of Jadzia at our kitchen table. Leszek explained that it was a popular pose in Polish religious sculpture and was called "Christ Worrying."

Each day after that we headed in another direction, entering at some new point the range that loomed in front of us. We hiked in the Chochołów Valley and also, after a winding bus ride, to Lake Morskie Oko, the "Eye of the Sea," 4,570 feet above sea level. The eye was frozen, or closed, at the base of rocky precipices, and we could see a thin, diminishing file of hikers walking across it. This land of an eerie, Ice Age discontinuousness, so close to Czechoslovakia, has long been a point of contention between the two countries. The man credited with gaining it for Poland is Count Zamoyski, who owned a great deal of the surrounding property. An eccentric aristocrat, he is said to have slept on his desk using the *Oxford English Dictionary* as a pillow. On our way down the mountain we were awarded with a clean, sunlit view into Slovakia (as everyone here called it): snowy pine forests and an impalpable quiet, pierced only by the faraway voice of a tiny figure on the other side of the border below, calling after his horse and sleigh.

We ate at restaurants or shelters high in the folds. The fare was edifyingly good: bowls of *żurek* (described on translated menus as a "sour Polish peasant soup") with bits of kielbasa and half of a hard-boiled egg — one's own Morskie Oko. Also plates of hot *bigos*, with its own, often unidentifiable bits, and crumbly brown bread, hot cups of wine, or glasses of hot beer with a lone clove gaining the surface. There was also a drink known as "mountaineer's tea," which Gosia joked was probably half tea and half vodka before learning that it was.

On Sunday, Leszek drove us to Mass at the village church of Chochołów. We took seats in the back, breaking the segregation of sexes in the pews. The men on our side had all set their rounded felt hats upright on the pew in front of them. Soon after we were seated, the congregation began singing a hymn without organ accompaniment, unfortunately the only such, and the most beautiful. The mountaineers have an idiosyncratic singing style best accompanied by fiddle or violin, or left alone. It is characterized by a certain anarchy of pitch, various voices at seemingly random moments breaking out above the others in what black gospel singers might call "soul" or "inspiration" but what at times seems reminiscent of the piercing glossolalia of Arab song. At the end of the service we learned our first news since leaving Warsaw — that a special service was to be held on Tuesday evening in Zakopane for the state of Poland.

When we arrived most of the town and tourists were already gathered, so that the crowds of faithful filled the vestibule and blocked the entrance before spilling out the doors. Minutes before the service was to begin a troop of mountaineers, elegant in fancy dress, came out of the shadows behind the church like some recreated ancient guard. All carried carved walking sticks, and some, shoulder bags, a sign that they were traveling overnight from distant villages. They wore clinging white wool trousers with ankle pompoms of red and black and a wide black stripe running up the sides to a colorful spurt of embroidery on either thigh. (Generally similar, the intricacies of this design vary according to family, like the kilt plaids of Scottish clans.) On their feet were black boots or more traditional, canoe-shaped loafers of soft leather with laces tied halfway up the calf. On their heads were the domed black hats with their enigmatic band of white seashell and proudly mounted eagle feather. Some of the men wore white capes, wildly embroidered about the shoulders, over billowy white blouses; others, sleeveless brown sheepskin vests. The whole array was untouched by modern times save for the scattered shoulder bags and the pins of Solidarity. After all the concern of the preceding months, we felt a great relief in watching this pageantry, which had not changed over so many years and so many occupations.

On our last day, we took a stroll through the village and found a wedding party outside the church, waiting to depart. Four sleighs were lined against the churchyard gate; the bridal sleigh was tied to two handsome white mares, each with a pine branch tied above her mane like an evergreen plume. The drivers loitered about in white trousers and leather coats, sharing rounded, unlabeled vodka bottles with the village ruffians. When the newlyweds were seated in their sleigh, the two groomsmen, dressed in flowing brown coats with a tricolor ribbon drawn across the front, mounted their steeds. Thus stationed in the middle of the street they sang on horseback, in loud and quavering voices, a prothalamion to the young couple. After several more unintelligible verses they began a slow trot, followed in turn by the sleighs, the whole procession moving quietly across the snow to its three-day fête.

I was reminded of Hilaire Belloc, who wrote, after recounting a traditional English Christmas,

> This, which I have just described, is not in a novel or a play. It is real, and goes on as the ordinary habit of living men and women. I fear that set down thus in our terribly changing time it must sound very strange and, perhaps in places, grotesque, but to those who practice it, it is not only sacred, but normal, having in the whole of the complicated affair a sacramental quality and an effect of benediction; not to be despised.
>
> Indeed, modern men, who lack such things, lack sustenance, and our fathers who founded all these rituals were very wise.

The following day we drove back to Warsaw, returning to a city and a government with a new prime minister since we had been there the week before.

Spring-Summer ═══

ONE FINE EVENING in May, with chalk dust still fresh on my hands, I was picked up outside school by our English friend Andy and his Mexican friend Roberto for an initiatory tour of Warsaw by night.

The only taste I had had of this world was an evening at the Palace of Culture, which, oddly enough, contained a nightclub. That night the stripper, a stout woman, had circled the stage several times in a long cape before peremptorily dropping it to the ground. She had successfully brought socialist realism to the art of striptease. But I was to see none of that tonight, Roberto assured me. A tall, goateed, rather distinguished looking student of economics, he had in common with Andy a playboy streak and a Mexican wife.

Our first stop was at Kamieniołomy, a nightclub in the old Europejski Hotel named after the quarry where prisoners are sent to hammer rocks. We parked and turned down a dark side street whose single sign, vertically set in white neon letters, read DANCING. The only other distinguishing mark of a club was the group of Libyans gathered at the door. The bouncer came with the news that there were no more tables; Andy invoked the name of the Mexican embassy; the doors were opened and the Libyans followed us in. Roberto said, "They're not in our party," and we gave our coats to the cloakroom attendant, who was typical of his profession, with a reptilian face, emaciated features, and platinum teeth. He puffed on a cigarette while struggling with our trench coats (God knows how he managed in the wintertime) and paid absolutely no attention to the mild scuffle now going on behind us.

We descended some stairs and entered a cozy, medium-sized room lit by red bulbs set atop bogus brick walls. It was almost completely empty. We were led across the raised dance floor to a table. A waiter in a dull red jacket handed us menus. There were two choices, chicken or duck. We ordered one of each and they arrived on plates unadorned by any other animal or vegetable. Our request for Chianti was refused, and a few minutes later we were brought two outrageously expensive French wines, which we declined. For dessert there was only brandy and peanuts, presented to us wrapped in a thick red napkin on a silver dish and accompanied by an elegant serving spoon. The room continued to fill with people who were urged to get up from their tables (as if the food didn't provide enough encouragement) and dance.

At about eleven an unshaven man appeared and sang enthusiastically. He was followed by eight women in provocative outfits whose performance combined the worst aspects of ballet, gymnastics, and exotic dancing. A not untalented woman then sang "I'll Never Fall in Love Again" and "I'm Just a Woman in Love." A magician and a stripper both rather unimaginatively made things disappear. About this time we decided that the entertainment in Warsaw nightclubs was not to be found in the entertainment, and left.

We walked in the cool night air across Victory (formerly Piłsudski) Square to the Victoria Hotel. The hotel,

part of the Inter-Continental chain, was the most lux-
urious in Warsaw, centrally located with a view of the
square and the Grand Theater. The mahogany and
marble lobby, with its hanging plants, was bedizened
with prostitutes who stood in a row, one every few feet,
resembling a loosely formed receiving line. They were
uniformly attractive, gracious, and elegantly, if a bit
overly, dressed. Three came forth and took our arms as
we headed past. Here the nightclub, Czarny Kot (Black
Cat), was full, and our new friends suggested we all go
someplace else together. We declined, and they returned
to their places.

If one never went to hotels in Warsaw one rarely saw,
or at least recognized, a prostitute. There was no red-
light district; how could there be in a socialist country
"free" of Western decadence? And since the business
was primarily international, serving the Victoria, the
Forum, the Grand, the Europejski, the Metropol, and
the Polonia, the ladies had no need to walk the streets.
They were the reverse of the Pewex shops in that they
offered native goods to a predominantly foreign population. But like the Pewexes they also balked at złotys.

Warsaw hotels, especially the third-class ones like the
Grand and the Metropol, were also surprisingly marked
by the presence of Arabs, who spent hours upon hours
in the lobbies and cafés. It was, in fact, in the bar of the
Victoria Hotel that Mohammed Daoud Oudeh, a ring-
leader of the Munich Olympic siege, was gunned down
in 1981. Disciples of Khaddafi would appear from time
to time on Nowy Świat Street, passing out English translations of the Green Book. One always found them at
the visa office. Though some actually stayed in the hotels,
many rented apartments for a month or longer. They
were almost all men, predominantly young. A Libyan ac-

companied one of my female students to class one night, and after the lesson I asked him to explain Warsaw's attraction to his people. He told me simply that it was more affordable than Paris or Berlin (he was taking a month-long vacation after finishing medical school) and offered the two things he could not get in his own country: women and alcohol. Poles were generally not well disposed toward their Arab visitors, and I came to think of it as poetic justice that a people who had for so long grumbled about Jews were now vexed by Arabs.

The Czarny Kot was a dark, low-ceilinged room with secluded black booths and a sunken bar bathed in a velvety green light. It was lined with prostitutes. Some sat with their backs to the bar, chatting amicably with a few male clients and exhibiting generous lengths of leg. Others were turned the opposite way, nursing beers or glasses of mineral water. We moved to the center of the bar to make our orders, and a young man rose and asked us in English if we'd like his seat.

"No thanks," I said. "Are you here for the city planners' conference?"

"No, I'm a journalist for UPI. A photographer. From Los Angeles. In fact, I just got in today." He had a boyish face and a clean, frank expression. "You know, I'll be honest with you. I can't believe my eyes. I've just been here one day and God, this is too much to believe. I never expected this. You know, I used to live in Las Vegas, and that place is hooker city. But these girls make the girls there look like dogs. There are so many and they are so beautiful and so well dressed and they all seem to speak English. I feel like a kid in a candy store. But listen," he said, a bit more confidentially, "tell me, are they pretty clean?"

"That's hardly for me to say."

"Because, you know, I had one already. And I wouldn't want to spoil my wife who's clean — I wouldn't want to mess up her body fluids. But I was really impressed with that girl I had. You know, I don't like the 'slam-bam-thank-ya-ma'am' thing. But it wasn't like that at all. She was really nice. I don't know if she was acting, but she really seemed to enjoy it. Anyway, it was great for my ego. And then she didn't just get up and leave. We talked a lot, you know, about all kinds of things — the government and stuff. So a great day for me, really — my first day in Poland and I got a picture out and I got laid. What more could you ask for? You know," he said confidently, "I think I could live here."

"They close at three."

"No, I mean in Poland."

"But you have no idea what it's like. You spend your time in the Victoria bar. Besides, you're here in a good season. It's spring. In winter it's completely different."

"But you know that just makes it more interesting. The harsh climate, the greater sense of turmoil and difficulty. The feeling of being followed. Jesus, I was thinking about that today. You know I'm probably being followed, and what do they see? The American journalist comes to Poland and the first thing he does, he gets laid."

Those first warm weeks of May always transformed the city, the blossoming linden and chestnut trees sprinkling the gray with buds of green. Young men bought bunches of violets or lilies of the valley for their girlfriends and kissed their hands. Windows all over the city opened wide, letting out the winter air, and walking past them I could sometimes hear in unison from radios a few brief cords of Chopin's Polonaise in A Major.

The downtown streets filled with people, and I took time in the balmy afternoons to watch them pass: teenage girls hurrying along arm in arm with their mothers; young men in blue jeans and U.S. Army–style jackets; young mothers leaving their babies in carriages while they went inside shops; the occasional military bureaucrat in his olive green uniform; idle Arab men, frequently with a blond escort; middle-aged functionaries carrying worn briefcases; peasants in for a day's shopping; stout matrons walking their dachshunds; and stylish, beautiful young women who, faced with all the inconveniences of shortages and uniformity, still dazzled with the tying of a scarf, the cut of a skirt, the braiding of hair, or even the way they balanced their small leather bags low on their hips. Warsaw was, in fact, the only city I knew where the women were more fashionable than the mannequins.

On warm days the crowds went about in short-sleeved dresses and shirts, and occasionally my eye gazed down to find the concentration camp number on my neighbor's arm.

The traditional spring queues formed for ice cream and visas. The most visible creamery was the state-run Hortex, though there were private ones with loyal clienteles, more felicitous names — Green Hut, Palermo — and daily flavors of lemon, vanilla, chocolate, and strawberry. Connoisseurs of chancelleries discussed their individual merits: "the West Germans are the easiest — same day service"; "the Austrians are tough." Walking by the U.S. embassy on Piękna Street one found whole families gathered in the courtyard, sitting on the grass on flatly spread pages of the party daily, *Trybuna Ludu*.

Small private shops sold the season's first tomatoes at unaffordable prices, while the cheaper dill was sold in bulk. Its scent infiltrated kitchens all over the city, just as its taste would sabotage every soup and sauce till autumn. At home Jadzia put thinly sliced cucumbers into sour cream for a refreshing salad with the most unbecoming springtime name of *mizeria*. She also made *chłodnik*, a cold Lithuanian soup as worthy as gazpacho or vichysoisse, containing chiefly red beets, curdled milk, cucumbers, and pickles. It appropriates the other half of the hard-boiled egg from winter's *żurek*, setting it down in a dill-and-parsley-dotted pool of flamingo pink. Mickiewicz, in his epic poem *Pan Tadeusz*, extolls its goodness:

Mężczyznom dano wodkę; wtenczas wszyscy siedli,
I chołodziec litewski milcząc zwawo jedli.

The men were given vodka; then everybody sat,
And in silence Lithuanian chłodnik briskly ate.

The May that Cardinal Stefan Wyszyński died, Warsaw underwent another transformation. Few modern cities, including Rome, have witnessed a religious pageant as magnificent.

The funeral was set for Sunday, and on Saturday I went to view the coffin in the Seminary Church on Krakowskie Przedmieście Street. Far from the church I found the end of the queue that had been stretching since morning. It snaked its way back and forth along the main thoroughfare, which, closed to traffic, had become the weekend promenade. Warsaw had a pleasantly odd feeling of detachment and suspended time: the city seemed to have no other business than remembering its cardinal, and the presence of the state, always constant, seemed magically to have vanished. In a rare moment, Varsovians appeared to possess their city.

The next day was fair and warm. At Victory Square, I found a tall wooden cross looming over a mass of people, and took my place in a line about three-deep along Królewska Street. The entire route was strewn, from church to square to cathedral, with the accumulated flowers of four days' homage. There were few police visible; instead groups of Solidarity members with armbands restrained the crowds. The procession arrived, shortly after four, led in an emphatically slow step by a crucifer, his right hand clasped at his heart; a chalice bearer; a thurifer; two candle bearers; and one young man carrying a walkie-talkie.

They were followed by various lay groups, walking in a dirgeful tread and carrying enormous wreaths proclaiming their affiliation: Polish Drivers Association, Warsaw Steel Mill, Poznan Solidarity Chapter. There were academic participants in black robes, and, in three distinguished cases, resembling the Dutch masters in their roll collars. There were the regional groups in native costume: the proud mountaineers in white capes; Krakovians in their puffed pantaloons of candy cane stripes; Silesian miners marching solemnly in large numbers and wearing their black, brass-buttoned jackets topped by circular casquettes of tall purple plumes; and steelworkers in white cowboy hats. Coming behind was a great mass of churchmen and women: long defiles of priests, many young, so that one could see how Poland has become a world exporter of clergy. Rows of older priests, each bearing a chalice, preceded these. The nuns, I think, were the most remarkable, a hooded gray wave of them; more than I had ever seen before, more perhaps than I had seen throughout my life.

Then came the higher orders of the Church: bishops who filled the street with their tall miters; Orthodox priests in salt-and-pepper beards, who had traveled far to be here; cardinals in luminous robes of heliotrope. When the coffin arrived it was not pulled by a carriage but borne by volunteers. Behind it marched the leaders of Solidarity — Lech Wałęsa prominent among them — government officials in their dark suits, and countless diplomats, emissaries, and dignitaries from abroad. The Mass was said in Polish by an Italian cardinal.

Finally, there was the procession to the cathedral and the final resting place. Moving with it, I climbed the base of a column by St. Anne's Church to get a better view. Heads hung out of the wide open windows across the street, while Castle Square filled with bodies tightly packed. When the coffin emerged, it became all I could distinguish, bobbing downward atop a sea of heads in its slow, choppy passage to the cathedral, as its bells, as well as those of all the Old Town's churches, tolled in requiem.

The summer months in Warsaw possessed an air of genteel languor that was intensified by the dusty streets and unmowed parks. Those without passports were often at the lakes or in the mountains, and the trams rumbled along half full. Rarely did it get hot, and when it did the queuers looked more miserable than if they had been in a midnight frost. (I remember Leszek once complaining, when the temperature had reached a pleasant eighty-five, that it was "so intolerable it sapped one's strength.") Swimming pools accommodated with feebly chlorinated water and women wore high heels with their bikinis to enhance their legs. After a strenuous set of tennis on parched clay courts there was lukewarm soda from a coolerless canteen or — the Poles' favorite refresher in any season — a steaming hot glass of tea. Downtown afterward my thirst would be so great that I would take a communal glass from a *woda sodowa* vendor, forgetting for the moment that the street slang for this drink could be roughly translated as "tuberculosis cola."

Frequently the summers were cold and wet. "We're having a mild winter this summer" is a not wholly inaccurate Polish expression. It was usually so when we were camping, which I tried at all costs to avoid. It was not just that I hated camping but that I felt at home in Warsaw.

I enjoyed going out in the morning with my book bag swung across my shoulder, buying the morning's copy of *Życie Warszawy* at the kiosk and then traveling and transferring with a native's knowledge on the buses and trams. The closeness and familiarity of the city made it quite common to run into a friend, or, failing that, to have my ear bent by a stranger. I would drop into the British Institute to take out a novel, or the American embassy library for a week's worth of *International Herald Tribunes*. I might go for lunch to the little restaurant next to the Syrena Theater on Litewska Street, which featured a cartoon of Mr. Stroganoff astride his *boeuf*.

Though the contemporary bookstores were for the most part worthless, there were wonderful secondhand bookshops, *antykwariaty*, where I would rummage amidst the dust, pulling out prewar magazines, prints, and literary classics. I loved going to the reading rooms, especially the one at the corner of Nowy Świat and Jerozolimskie — the crossroads of Warsaw — inhabited by combatants of the *ancien régime*, sitting erect in their bemedaled suit coats and threadbare ties, discussing Poland. Here, in these smoky depositories of an international press, one could read on sticks the daily papers from Warsaw (including the bright red headlines of Polish sports), Sofia, Moscow, and Prague. When I could no longer stand the smoke I would jump on a bus to Ujazdowski Park or the nearby, secluded Dolina Szwajcarska (Swiss Valley) and appropriate a bench for reading. I have never spent as much time sitting in parks as I did in Warsaw.

On one of the last days of August the famous overnight line formed in Savior Square, composed of students eager for a place in the English Language College, and once again a queue brought the summer to a close.

II
The English Language College

THE ENGLISH LANGUAGE COLLEGE occupied the lower half of an imposing, angular, prewar building in Savior Square in downtown Warsaw. Its sooty stucco walls rose up with a few architectural flourishes — two French windows leading out onto a stone balcony on the third floor, a vertical row of suspended bay windows at the corner. From the outside it was impossible to tell where the classrooms ended and the apartments began. With its nine stories and slightly top-heavy perch, the building loomed over the square, which was really a circle, circumnavigated by cars and bisected by trams. The square also contained a church, a bookstore, a café, the central fish market, a grocery store, and a women's clothing shop. Upon the school's front wall, two passages of scripture were engraved in Polish. The first was from John: "And ye shall know the truth and the truth shall make you free." The second, Matthew: "Come unto me, all ye who travail and are heavy laden, and I will refresh you."

Though officially called Ośrodek Języka Angielskiego, the school was known familiarly as Szkoła Metodystów, for it was owned and governed by the Methodist Church of Poland and Mr. Kuczma, its director, was a Methodist minister. The school itself had been founded by a small group of American Methodists in 1921, along with similar schools in Lvov (then part of Poland), Poznan, and

Katowice; of these, only the Warsaw school had survived. Except for closure during the German occupation, it had been in continuous operation since its
founding. Virtually any enterprise in Warsaw connected
with learning English is popular; the specific combination of tradition, private ownership, and church affiliation was especially attractive to generations taught by
the state, and had made the Methodist School a city institution. Thousands of Varsovians had attended, if only
for a semester.

Despite the religious connection, the curriculum
was wholly secular. The Methodist School functioned
uniquely as a private evening school for English, and accepted at a very reasonable fee anyone over fifteen
years of age. During my time more than four thousand
Poles were enrolled. Most of them were in high school
or college, where, very often, they were already taking
courses in English that they deemed, for a variety of
reasons, to be insufficient. Lessons were fifty minutes
long, three times a week, on alternate days. The program
consisted of eight semesters over four years. It was not
unheard of for students to finish and then enroll again,
not because they had learned nothing, but because it had
been time pleasantly spent. Attending evening classes
here had become for the younger generation the thing to
do in Warsaw. It was one of the consequences of the city's
deficiency in providing legitimate entertainment.

The institution, for all its size, was run along the lines
of a mom-and-pop store. Mr. Kuczma usually came by
at three to see that all the teachers had arrived, and then
appeared again for tea at six. He was rarely present
when the night's classes ended at nine. He was a short,
thickset, robust man with a head of steel gray hair thrust
back from an impressive widow's peak. He always wore

a coat and tie. He had a superintendent's passion for order, yet when it deteriorated he usually exhibited (like many Poles of his generation, who bring to every crisis the experience of greater, unimaginable ones) a calmly philosophical bearing.

Downstairs in the school office his wife worked, handling the mammoth queues in the long days of registration and dealing with transfers, dropouts, and complaints the rest of the time. Jolanta, the eldest daughter, did turns teaching, substituting, and registering when she was not in America studying linguistics. The son, Krzysztof, a theology student, also substituted, and the youngest child, Anna, performed clerical tasks until she was old enough for classroom duty. The entire family had learned English from the father, who had taught it to himself after the war and spoke fluently, but now with an accent heavier than his children's.

From the start, the school enchanted me with its old-fashioned atmosphere and that queer, flattering camaraderie one often feels from foreigners engaged in work with one's own tongue. The teachers' room, located behind the French windows on the third floor, filled between classes with people who seemed to be of unclassifiable nationality: in their clothes and physical appearance they were unmistakably Polish, yet as soon as they spoke, the words, and often the accents, were English. There were, of course, varying degrees. One young woman, Maria, had an English father and had grown up in England, which made her sound impeccably British. There was a middle-aged floozy who wore tight slacks and piled her dyed red hair high atop her head; she spoke with a riveting, flawless New Jersey accent. (When I asked Stefan about her odd behavior, he explained to me quietly: "She went to America once and has never quite gotten over it.") A few of the men also favored American speech, though the general preference — especially among the recent, predominantly female graduates of the *Anglistyka* Department at the university — was for British English. Stefan's was the lone voice in support of Australian.

The teachers' room was divided by a tall partition into a smokers' section and a nonsmokers' section. Each half was identical: high-ceilinged, narrow, and spare, with a long table stretched from one end to the other and surrounded by about a dozen armless dark wooden chairs. A tall wardrobe stood in the front. By the windows in each section sat a small table, atop which were placed a tray with glasses and a green or brown bottle of Mazowszanka mineral water. Coming in before three I would pour myself a glass, upending the colorfully skirted peasant girl on the label. In this room for the nonsmokers hung a large world map.

My first day Stefan had found a seat for me at his end of the table near the window. I don't remember our first exchanges, though I know that I found him instantly likable. The other teachers were just as accommodating and showed none of the resentment I half expected from people who had studied years for a position I had suddenly gained simply by virtue of my birth. There was a very tall, thin, serious young man named Janusz who wore unfashionable black-frame glasses that gave great intensity to his slightly oily face. To his left sat Krystyna, a pretty young blonde; she rarely spoke but would lean her head interestedly on her hand while listening to our conversation. The half-Anglo Maria sat on my right, a pert, fussy woman, and next to her sat Piotr, a curious, if not suspicious character. He wore his black hair in a bristly crew cut and favored a heavy green Mao jacket, which, no matter what the temperature, he never seemed to remove. His thick glasses constantly slid down his nose and he would repeatedly, and emphatically, re-set them with a militarily precise movement of his middle finger. While across the table Janusz read a much-thumbed copy of *The Russians* by Hedrick Smith, Piotr would sit with a contraband issue of *Playboy* underneath his attendance folder. Beside Piotr sat Grzegorz, a husky, rubicund man in his forties who wore plaid flannel shirts and often began conversations with me by saying, "I heard on Voice of America today . . ."

Far away at the other end of the table gathered the older teachers, joined by Mr. Kuczma at six o'clock for tea. Ludmiła, though only in her thirties, was already the archetypal schoolmistress and in that role would share small talk with the director, while next to her Mr. Romanowicz would delicately work at the wrappings of his sandwich. He had boyish features, a sturdy nose and longish gray hair that dropped down slightly in the back over his turtleneck. He was a dedicated bachelor and, as much as one could be in Warsaw, an epicure; his talk often centered on culinary delicacies, showing, if noth-ing else, an excellent memory. "Before the war we chil-dren used to receive the most exquisite marzipan," he would remark wistfully, before biting into his stale cheese sandwich. Miss Wiaderny joined this group, though she was oblivious to food, taking her nourishment instead from the timeless rules of English grammar. A captious septuagenarian whose taut face bore the lines of years of careful enunciation, Miss Wiaderny had spent most of her life at the Methodist School. She came in no matter what the weather, to substitute, or simply to lend her voice, usually unsolicited, to the ongoing linguistic de-bate. Her faculty for finding fault had sharpened over the years and had combined with the natural intrusiveness of the lonely aged. She was an undying Anglophile, the only teacher at the school who gave me the impression that, as an American, I was unfit to teach English.

Occasionally our sedate conversations would be drowned out by bursts of hearty laughter from the smokers' room, which was occupied exclusively by women — some veterans and recent graduates, but mostly young mothers who appreciated the hours (when husbands were home to watch the children) and alternate days off. Once I asked one of the women what they talked about so fluently, and she replied, in an accent verging on cockney, "Oh, you know, Tom, the Polish woman's classic lament: kitchen, cooking, queueing."

My students were mostly in high school or college, with the occasional middle-aged engineer hoping for an assignment in the West. I had one class of beginners; they filled a long, narrow room on the second floor with their expectant, clear-complexioned, inarticulate faces, experiencing for the first time in their lives a teacher with whom they could not communicate, by whom they could rarely expect to hear their names pronounced correctly. A typical attendance sheet began:

> Waldzińska Jadwiga
> Sieregiejczyk Urszula
> Matejczuk Iwona
> Kurszyński Wojciech
> Tchor Aneta
> Szewczyk Andrzej
> Chmielewska Katarzyna
> Szczypior Zdzisław

The student body, like the faculty, found women in the majority, a disproportionate number of them extremely fetching. Many appeared, in fact, to dress up for class, their hair washed, their outfits matching, their faces radiant. Squeezing my way down the circular staircase between classes I would wonder if I had ever seen so many beautiful girls in one place: luxuriant dark hair brushed against coat collars and blond wisps were drawn back to reveal porcelain cheeks. There were a few sirens but more of a characteristic wholesomeness that made me think of that school, indeed, of that stairwell, as the *ne plus ultra* of feminine charm in Eastern Europe.

Returning to the teachers' room was always a bit like coming back to your corner after a round in the ring. Stefan would be sitting perfectly still at the far end with his textbooks closed in front of him, concentrating on the application of body language to English instruction. "Sometimes I go into the classroom and just sit," he said to me once. "That gets their attention. Then I begin to talk and they lose interest. Can it be," he asked, beginning to smile, "that we've been going about it the wrong way all these years?"

As the semester continued, Janusz finished *The Russians* and passed it on to Ludmiła. Maria complained about the plainness of the room. "Why don't we put up some nice posters instead of that boring map?" "I like maps," I said, and got a second from Janusz. "Just look at the Soviet Union," he would say. "Such an enormous country with so much fertile land and so many natural resources. Why, they should be the richest, most productive country on earth. And what are they? They're a backward, inefficient, incompetent fiefdom that has to import grain from the United States."

"You heard about what would happen if the Soviet Union took over the Sahara?" asked Grzegorz. "There would be a shortage of sand." Miss Wiaderny would importune me across the table: "Mr. Swick, do you use the pluperfect tense in America?" while Mr. Romanowicz reminisced about a special poppy seed roll his mother used to bake for holidays.

As the days grew shorter — by December it was nearly dark when we arrived at three — Piotr began bringing a thermos of tea spiked with rum. He expounded on the medicinal qualities of this drink and offered us each a shot into our tea at six. (The school, with its high, antiquated ceilings, was difficult to heat, and teachers and students dressed in sweaters most of the year.) Teatime lasted twenty minutes. The glasses were always too hot for me to pick up, especially when the charwoman, a leathery, good-hearted widow, filled them to the brim, which she often did for me out of what Krystyna said was "deference to America. See Tom, our glasses are not so full." I would hurriedly gulp down the contents a minute before the bell.

Over the course of the semester my teaching abilities improved, and I received armfuls of flowers on Teachers' Day and my Name Day. At Christmas I was immeasurably touched by gifts that I knew had not come easily.

I grew to like the students and began lingering after the bell instead of retreating to the teachers' room. Initially taken by their charm and politeness, I became impressed by their intelligence, maturity, and sense of humor. ("Mariusz, give me a sentence using the word *conscience*." "I looked in the dictionary for a definition of *conscience*.") Their courtly manners were shown when an exercise demanded a conclusion to the phrase, "Don't talk to the teacher . . ." "With your hands in your pocket,"

offered one young man who, when asked for an explanation, said that no Pole would ever dream of speaking
to any superior in such a disrespectful fashion.

They were quick to laugh — the other teachers informed me that Polish students are the easiest audiences
in the world — but their laughter seemed precious to
me because of their circumstances. How could I not
have admiration for high school students whose chosen
Friday night activity was attending English lessons, remembering how I had spent my time at that age? I constantly compared them to American students and grew
in awe of how they thrived with so much less. Of course,
what I saw as deprivation was all they had known, at
least the ones who had not yet been abroad, which included most. Yet their effervescence on cold dark evenings in a foreign city not only brought me out of recur-
ring depressions, but made me question what possible
right I could have to such a mood. Indeed, the inscription from Matthew on the wall outside, "*Pójdźcie do mnie
wszyscy którzy . . .*," seemed to apply more to me than to
my students.

In the first week of February I learned that I would
not receive a visa to stay for the following semester. At
school I told Mr. Kuczma that I had something to discuss with him privately. We went into the library, next to
the teachers' room, and I described my interview. He
shook his head, his face bearing a look of understanding
and disdain, and made his helpless comment about the
enrichment of my experience. He assured me that there
would always be a job for me at the Methodist School,
should I ever return to Warsaw. Janusz, when I told the
teachers at tea, said, with his lips tightly pursed: "The
bastards."

At the next day's classes I told my students that I

would no longer be their teacher, explaining only that I had been refused a visa. (I had been cautioned never to discuss anything even remotely controversial in the classroom. "You never know," Piotr had added, "who your students are.") They seemed genuinely annoyed. One young woman, Ilona, asked touchingly if there was anything they, the students, could do. I assured her there wasn't. After my last class with the beginners a tall, lovely girl with the lilting name of Jolanta Jankowska approached and, employing a phrase I had never taught them, said softly, "'Tis a pity. 'Tis a pity."

My next sight of the Methodist School, a year and a half later, came on a warm, pleasant evening in September, just as the last classes were letting out. I had arrived in Warsaw the night before, ten days after the signing of the Gdansk shipyard strike agreements and the founding of Solidarity. The great gray building in Savior Square stood unchanged. The curved, tree-shaded front walk was lively with students gathered in groups and young men waiting to meet their girlfriends after class. Within this crowd I easily spotted Stefan standing under the glistening leaves of a linden tree. Shortening somewhat the magisterial length of his nose was a new, short-haired, light brown mustache.

"You go to these Solidarity meetings and everybody has a Wałęsa mustache," he explained. "I think he ought to go into business. Wałęsa T-shirts, Wałęsa pillows, Wałęsa drinking cups."

His apartment was just as I remembered it, unevenly furnished and in disarray. Beside the taped picture of the Pope on the wall was a new Solidarity banner in the distinctive, jumbled red script. Stefan's wife brought out supper, *kanapki* — delicious, one-sided Polish sandwiches of butter, tomato, salami, shredded cheese, hard-boiled egg, and cayenne pepper — while he apprised me of the current situation. The movement, which from my reading in the States I had thought was centered only in a few factories and shipyards, had spread throughout the country; there were now Solidarity chapters starting up at countless firms and institutions, including the Methodist School. Stefan, in fact, had become its chairman. Some of the teachers, he said, showed apprehension, though most unequivocally embraced the changes. The following week I began teaching again.

The teachers' room hummed during the class breaks with endless discussion, often with several people talking excitedly at the same time. It became ever harder to hear the bell, and harder to pull away when it became evident, often by Mr. Kuczma's timely presence, that it had gone off. Added to the world map, and the bottle of Mazowszanka in the corner, was a bulletin board for the school's new Solidarity union.

In our room Krystyna had departed to teach Polish at the American embassy, but most of the others remained. Janusz was passionately involved in the latest events. Piotr was, if anything, even more inscrutable than before. He still wore his heavy green Mao jacket, but now with a Solidarity pin prominently stuck above the pocket. He had begun making lists and pouring out glasses of mineral water for endless toasts. "To Wałęsa!" "To free trade unions!" "To the revolution!" Maria joined him while Grzegorz watched with a bemused skepticism. Mr. Romanowicz appeared unfazed, as did Miss Wiaderny, whose first words on seeing me back were, "Mr. Swick, do you have any explanation as to why the British say 'He got a rise' while the Americans say 'He got a raise?'"

At the end of the month Stefan organized a Sunday

afternoon meeting at his apartment for those wishing to register officially as members of the school's Solidarity union. About twenty-five teachers attended — more than half the faculty, including all from our end of the table and most of the ladies from the smokers' room. Stefan began by apologizing to me for conducting the meeting in Polish, stating that the subject demanded it. He discussed the present situation, as well as he knew it from the meetings he had been to, and then outlined the objectives of the union at our school. There followed an orderly discussion, Stefan handling the questions deftly and intelligently. At the close, everyone gathered to sign on as members. The calmness of the meeting was so complete that I underestimated the risk these teachers — most of them with families — were taking by putting their names on that list. I thought of Stefan's uncle who had been deported — an incredible historical incident to me, but a fact of life that was never far away for these people. Bottles of beer and glasses of tea were brought out from the kitchen, and the teachers lingered to talk a bit before departing. When everyone had left, Stefan kindly offered to drive me home. Halfway there I remembered that, with Hania and the family away in Lodz for the weekend, I had left the place a mild ruin.

"I have to apologize for the apartment," I said. "It's a mess."

"Don't worry about it," Stefan replied, his face lightening up for the first time in hours, "the whole country is a mess."

The teachers began to speak Polish more often among themselves, even Stefan, the originator of the proposal to ban its use two years earlier. One of the shibboleths that had come out of the negotiations in Gdansk between the

government and the workers had been "to speak like a
Pole to a Pole," something that was hardly possible in
any other language. Using Polish was a way of reassert-
ing national identity — an idea at the core of Solidarity — and it inevitably allowed for a more natural form
of communication. This return to their own language
made the teachers seem more real to me, and I liked the
hard, masculine sounds — "*Cześć, kolego!*" (Cheers, colleague!) — that now echoed down the halls.

After lunch at the American embassy cafeteria, I would
stop at the tiny bakery on Mokotowska Street for two
pączki to have with tea. Three, which I often desired, was
more difficult, if not impossible, to say: *trzy*. When I was
very hungry I would ask for two (*dwa*), and then say
quickly, "*Może jeszcze jeden*" (Maybe one more). I would
stuff the grease-spotted paper wrapping into my book
bag and walk the two long blocks to Savior Square. I was
often the first to arrive and, after hanging up my coat in
the wooden wardrobe, I would go to the Mazowszanka
bottle to quench my thirst, begun by pickle soup.

I had an unprecedented four of my six classes in
Room 26, used for faculty meetings. It was large with a
bay window that gave it additional corners, and because
of its depth the teacher's desk sat regally atop a foot-
high platform in the front. The numerous tall windows
looked out onto Savior Square, and the sun, in those
rare moments when it reminded us of its existence,
came flooding through, warming the wooden chairs and
students' backs. The windows all possessed deep ledges
that were piled high in winter with heavy coats. In the
evening, I could see out of one window the dark steeples
of the Church of the Savior across the way; through another, atop the roof of the apartment opposite, the glass

in a Bulgarian wine advertisement refilled again and again by synchronized neon. I found my two favorite classes in this room — the beginners' class at six o'clock and an intermediate at seven.

At nine the school day ended discordantly as teachers grabbed their coats and rushed down the steps for their buses and trams. At home, anywhere from twenty minutes to one hour later, the dog would greet me at the door, the cat would glance up at me from our bed, and Jadzia would reheat the day's thin soup or start an omelet. Then I would pull a stool up to the kitchen table, where Hania and Gosia and sometimes Leszek would be at their usual places, drinking tea.

I had Tuesdays and Thursdays free. I attended Polish classes for a time, and in the evenings privately tutored an officer of the Ministry of Education who was responsible for my work permit. Hania and I had met him during the first week of my arrival in the cavernous ministry building on the Boulevard of the First Polish Army. Because the meeting was conducted in Polish, only upon leaving did I learn from Hania — who knew better than I the importance of favors in Polish life — that I had agreed to teach him English.

Wojtek, as he requested I call him, lived near us in a building as imposing as his ministry, in an apartment smaller than his office. His English was much worse than I had hoped, and he was at an age and of a density that made it unlikely that it would get much better. He seemed uninterested in drills and handed over a letter, written in English and addressed to the Ministry of Education, that he wanted me to translate for him. It concerned the expulsion from a dormitory of one Nigerian student by another. The student exchange program with Nigeria, I soon learned, was one of Wojtek's specialties at the ministry. Before I left he asked me to appraise his pronunciation of phrases he had worked on in preparation for the next day's visit of the Nigerian ambassador. "It is a pleasure to welcome you." "Good afternoon." "We are going upstairs." "I am walking with you to the door." "I would like to stress, my English is not the best."

In the middle of October a sheet was pinned to the bulletin board in the teachers' room listing sixteen demands of the school's Solidarity union. They included, among other things, a reduction in class length (from fifty to forty-five minutes), the installation of humidifiers in the classrooms and of a telephone in the teachers' room, and the permission to use articles from *Newsweek* and *Time*, as well as from the Polish papers *Polityka* and *Kultura*, as classroom texts. Stefan, with the help of a few other teachers, had drawn them up. "What are the chances they'll be accepted?" I asked him. He smiled. "I'd say they're about as good as those of the Russians invading."

A few days later during tea, Piotr put his radio on the table (he had begun bringing it to school and listening to it during the breaks) and turned up the volume. The announcer gave the news that Solidarity had officially been registered that day in a Warsaw court as a legal union. Piotr, along with Stefan, Maria, Janusz, and Grzegorz, greeted the news with cheers. At the other end of the room, Mr. Kuczma said dryly, "It was to be expected."

The Solidarity bulletin board filled with scraps of information, clipped articles of note, dates of meetings, quotes, and poems. An interesting document appeared,

obtained by Solidarity, which indicated the salaries of secret police for various assignments. One of the most lu-
crative was the nine-day pilgrimage on foot to the shrine
of the Black Madonna in Częstochowa, which I hoped to
take part in before I left Poland. One evening I found a
statement by Wałęsa which someone had pinned up:
"Tanks can guard us but they can't make us work." A
few days later, a Tennyson sonnet:

> *How long, O God, shall men be ridden down,*
> *And trampled under by the last and least*
> *Of men? The heart of Poland hath not ceased*
> *To quiver, tho' her sacred blood doth drown*
> *The fields, and out of every smoldering town*
> *Cries to Thee, lest brute Power be increased,*
> *Till that o'ergrown Barbarian in the East*
> *Transgress his ample bound to some new crown: —*
> *Cries to Thee, "Lord, how long shall these be?*
> *How long this icy-hearted Muscovite*
> *Oppress the region?" Us, O Just and Good,*
> *Forgive, who smiled when she was torn in three;*
> *Us, who stand now, when we should aid the right —*
> *A matter to be wept with tears of blood!*

The government began to acknowledge some of its
mistakes, and disclosures became routine. The public
started to take journalists seriously. But while people
were encouraged by the new style of the press, they were
not always uplifted by the contents of the news. One day
at lunch, Krystyna and I discussed the previous evening's
television report on the destruction of historic buildings
in Kracow by insidious, uncurbed pollution, which the
commentator had said was the worst in Europe. "It was

so disgusting," Krystyna said. "I had no idea things were so bad. For years they told us things were going well, and even though you didn't believe it, you had no idea just how bad everything was. Now all of a sudden you hear of nothing but our deterioration. I can't take it all at once."

In the shops, supplies were dwindling fast, and their absence began to monopolize conversation. At the beginning of December queues for butter stretched longer than they had two years before for meat. "I went from one shop to another," said Hania one evening, "and nothing, nothing, nothing. No sugar, no potatoes, no butter, no rice."

"Everywhere you go there are nothing but cans of green peas," commented Mr. Romanowicz at school. "There must have been a bumper crop of peas this year."

"I heard," said Grzegorz, "that the butter rationing is going to be equal to that which it was during the occupation."

"Which occupation do you mean, Mr. Chodziński?" asked Mr. Romanowicz, grinning.

"The German occupation, of course."

"You know, I will give the Germans this much: they made excellent use of our school during the occupation. According to reports they had in our basement one of the most deliciously lascivious nightclubs east of Berlin."

"During the occupation," said Mr. Kuczma, quickly steering the discussion back to its original theme, "we used to get one egg a month."

"In Warsaw during the occupation," proclaimed Mr. Romanowicz, "you could get anything you wanted. We had champagne and caviar. Yes, caviar. It was smuggled through the front."

"Well, you know what they're saying," said Stefan with his penchant for synthesis. "With Gomułka we had socialism. With Gierek we had materialism. With Kania we will have cannibalism."

Things were not going well with the Nigerians, either. The latest letter had come to Wojtek from the embassy, though it had been written by students at a provincial technical school. It had our minister completely stymied, and I soon saw why. It couched numerous complaints in florid, painstakingly diplomatic language. I told Wojtek as simply as possible that the students were demanding some action on the part of the ministry with regard to their complaints. Wojtek reacted to this skeptically, no doubt seeing the rebellious mood of Solidarity infecting everyone.

First, the Nigerian students expressed a desire for textbooks and notebooks (they had been given none). Second, they asked for lab uniforms (they had not received these either). Last, they urged that something be done about the "equipment" in their dormitory rooms. In closing, the students begged "the honorable minister to save our souls," or else they would assume that "you are playing on the intelligence of the Nigerian nation." Wojtek gathered all this in with a child's sense of discovery, his eyes opening wider, his voice "oooooing" louder, at each translated sentence. I sensed that he regarded these students as belonging to a lower sphere, and I felt great pity for them as the helpless victims of one of those "harmless" communist pledges of "friendship and cooperation with our African brothers."

As the year neared its close, the general fidgetiness grew under the much publicized — at least in the West —

threat of invasion. At school during tea we listened to the BBC or Voice of America on Piotr's radio. Four days before Wigilia, the BBC announced, "Aleksei Kosygin is reported to have died." Grzegorz commented, "Now, that was a nice construction."

The last class day before the holidays, I arrived at school with the verses of carols I planned to copy onto the blackboard. I knew from my first year that teaching religious carols would be permitted (in Polish, all carols are considered to be religious) and that my expectations should not be high: "We Poles are not musically gifted," Elżbieta, one of the teachers, had warned me then. "Except for the mountaineers in the south, we are a nation off-key."

I had prepared some of my favorite carols — "Angels We Have Heard on High," "What Child Is This?" "I Saw Three Ships" — and one that seemed a perfect piece of diction, if not vocabulary, for learners of English, "The Twelve Days of Christmas." I assigned each student a day — because of the size of the classes, we went around several times — and pointed to each as his turn came. It was a great success, with "twelve lords a-leaping" neatly changed in one class to "twelve Poles a-queuing."

Opening the door to my five o'clock class, I found the room dark, save for four white candles burning in a pine wreath atop my desk. The silence was broken by "Do You Hear What I Hear?" played from an unseen recorder. As my eyes adjusted to the darkness, I began to make out the triumphant, impossibly moving faces of my students.

At tea we gathered, teachers and students, for the traditional carol sing in the front hall downstairs. Mr. Kuczma stood on a platform in his black shirt, white tie, and jacket, leading the singing of "Hark! The Herald Angels Sing" and "God Rest Ye Merry Gentlemen" loudly and energetically and giving no cause to refute Elżbieta's theory. One of the ladies from the smokers' room, the matronly Mrs. Iwanowska, played the piano. The students, crowded into the room shoulder to shoulder, gave the carols their all, singing with difficulty the odd-sounding phrases, yet with feeling that showed on their faces. To end the assembly, Mr. Kuczma played a recording of "Silent Night" sung by an American Mennonite woman who had taught at the school a few years earlier. The sight of Catholic students gathered by a Methodist minister to hear a Mennonite soloist in a communist country appealed to me.

In my seven o'clock class, Tadeusz and Maggie stood up to present me with a bottle of champagne each. "Merry Christmas!" "But where did you get this?" I asked, incredulous. "People are queuing for butter." "Welcome to Poland," said Ryszard joyfully. I suggested that we open the bottles, but immediately realized we had nothing to drink the champagne in. "Thinking you will ask," said Wiesław, as he proceeded to dig two dozen glasses out of his bag. One bottle just barely made a round. We drank to Polish-American friendship, then popped the second cork.

On the last school day of the year, Stefan, Piotr, Grzegorz, Janusz, Maria, and I joined the ladies in the smokers' room for a drinkless toast. "To 1981," said Mrs. Iwanowska. "Let's hope it will be better than we expect it to be."

Shortly into the new year Elżbieta approached me at school one evening and asked if I would be interested in taking on another private pupil, her mother's internist, Dr. Urszula Zięba. Reluctantly, I agreed. As usual, the opportunity to see another apartment, another life in this city of lives stacked one upon the other, intrigued me; if only, I mused, I could give a single lesson, like a curative vaccine, and never have to return with weekly doses. Also, I thought, we could use the money. At home everyone had heard of Dr. Zięba; Gosia, though never having worked with her, knew of her forbidding temperament.

I took a tram one Thursday afternoon to the Mokotów district and found the quiet street where she lived. Rows of small, cozy homes were broken, on one side, by a six-story apartment house. I was surprised to find that Dr. Zięba's address corresponded to this building. It was a typical Warsaw tenement, circa 1960. The entrance door hung wide open and the front hallway was bare concrete. The light did not work, and I walked up several flights of stairs in darkness, hearing the echoes of doors opening furtively on other floors and smelling the garbage pails left outside.

Dr. Zięba greeted me at the door, shook my hand firmly while looking down at her shoes, and led me through a narrow hallway to a small, cell-like room containing a couch, a chair, a desk pushed against a window, and a wall lined with books.

"Would you like some tea?" she asked me in Polish, and then went off to make some, returning with two deep mahogany glasses. She was a thickset woman in her sixties with a severe appearance; her deeply furrowed face looked gray and weary. She sat on the couch, I in the chair, and explained her situation. She was more and more frequently called to England and the

United States for medical conferences, and while her English was passable, she found it difficult to hold a serious conversation. If I would be willing to come once a week, for two straight hours of conversation, at a reasonable fee, she would be most indebted to me. All this she said without changing expression. I agreed and, after finishing my tea, shook hands and departed.

With much misgiving, I returned the following week. I had suffered the agonies of hour-long conversations with other students; the thought of two hours, with a grave middle-aged doctor in a specialty known for its arrogance weighed on me as heavily as the low winter clouds. Because the trams ran so irregularly, and I was particular about not being late, I arrived ridiculously early. I wandered around the neighborhood and counted the minutes to the dreaded lesson. As usual, I was cold and hungry. I passed a kiosk, a stark, windowed box that sold nothing edible but which exuded an aroma that I had come to think of as the essence of Warsaw: a hollow and unsatisfying smell of stale tobacco, yellowed paper, and shampoo, which, inhaled deeply on an empty stomach, always filled me with a quiet despair.

Dr. Zięba met me at the door, with the now familiar handshake and downward glance, and led me back into the study. "We had today the Solidarity meeting at my clinic," she said, placing two glasses of tea on the desk. "The discussion was about 'free Saturday.' Is that how you say in English?

"It is very difficult to be a director now in Poland," she confessed. "I'm afraid something is going to happen. And if it does it will be awful. I am old enough to remember how it was. We will have to be in at seven o'clock. We will only be able to go to certain places. We must — I don't know all we will have to do. And certain people — people of Solidarity — will go to the prison. And they are good people, these in Solidarity. They want to work and they want to change and they want to feel that they have a voice in what happens to them, to their country. But they are young. They can't imagine what it's like to be occupied. But then, a revolution can only happen with the young." These lessons turned out to be so interesting that I eventually decided to drop Wojtek, who, to my relief, seemed equally eager to drop me.

In February a new semester began. My emphasis in every lesson was on *spoken* English, and my goal was spontaneity, which suffered in these classes of thirty or more. I would quickly take attendance (mercifully shortened now that I could not only pronounce the names but also recognize the faces) and then I would walk up and down the aisle (or, in Room 26, back and forth in the front), looking for some item — a newspaper, a book, a bulging grocery bag — about which to begin a conversation.

At the end of every lesson in the book I would write down the new vocabulary words, plus some of the more important ones from previous lessons, on scraps of paper. Then I would ask two students to come up to my desk, hand each pair a list containing five words, and tell them to give clues to the rest of the class to make them guess the words. This strategy was well received (*Swear* — "What you do when you read *Trybuna Ludu*") and made me appreciate, perhaps for the first time in my life, the influence of American TV game shows.

As questioning is an important part of any language, I established occasional "press conferences." Two students (it was much less intimidating for them to work in pairs) would again sit at my desk, having just completed some historic endeavor, to face a roomful of instant reporters. The preoccupations of the moment always shone through. In my seven o'clock class, two students colorfully described their recent balloon trip around the world, while a third thoughtfully inquired as to whether, while leaving Poland, they had spotted any Soviet tanks along the border.

Katarzyna in my five o'clock class insisted that they be allowed a press conference with me, which I agreed to for the following lesson. The questions came unprompted, usually from the women, and revealed a certain preoccupation with my reaction to Polish life. "Why did you come to Poland?" asked Katarzyna. "What do you find most strange about how Polish people live?" inquired Agnieszka. "What did you know or think about Poland before you came, and what were you surprised to see when you arrived?" queried Tomasz. "What do you think of Polish youth?" "Will you stay in Poland forever?" My emphatic *no* brought roars of laughter. Of course, in these days even more than usual, Poland was the paramount subject of Poles, whose history has been so marked by occupation, insurrection, and war. Jan Lechoń protested in one of his vernal poems: "And in springtime let me spring, and not Poland see." Even today the more common Polish greeting among friends is not "*Jak się masz?*" ("How are you?") but "*Co słychać?*" (similar to "What's new?" but more literally "What do you hear?"). It betrays a fundamental concern for the public over the personal, and survives, it seems to me, from a long history of couriers, secret meetings, and censorship. Coming to learn something of the national ethos, foreign students find it, along with apartments, offered up in one way or another in half the conversations they engage in. Rarely is one's research in a country so effortless.

But by building their questions around Poland, my students were attempting to find out something about me without being impolite. At the same time, there was a touching modesty and sense of inferiority in their clear bewilderment that someone from a country as magnificent as America would come to homely Warsaw to teach Polish youths for złotys and learn their piddling language.

In the teachers' room, Piotr continued making endless toasts with Mazowszanka, despite Grzegorz's critical asides: "Mineral water! Hah! It's nothing but a joke. Just tap water with some bubbles added." One day we got on the subject of television.

"It's all lies," said Piotr, now his turn to be cynical, his glasses fallen on his nose. "Nothing but lies from beginning to end."

"But Piotr," Grzegorz insisted, "you don't watch it. How can you say?"

"It's lies. You don't have to watch it to know."

"Is *Anna Karenina* lies?" (The "Masterpiece Theatre" production had just begun, with the consensus of the ladies in the smokers' room that no English actress playing Anna could successfully embody the necessary Russianness.)

"Of course it's lies. It's fiction." He stuck his glasses back up again as if to emphasize his point.

"Well," relented Grzegorz, "ninety percent of television is lies."

"All of it is lies," insisted Piotr.

"Maybe ninety-five percent."

"Have you ever read the book?" asked Janusz.

"No, I have never read it," replied Grzegorz. "I think I can honestly say that I have read no more than two Russian works. I just can't do it. There's something about them. I pick a book up and start reading through it and then I get a terrible rash. I don't know what it is."

Nothing had come of the union's demands; the list had been removed from the bulletin board to make way for clippings. A few teachers brought in copies of the new Solidarity weekly newspaper, published officially but in limited editions, which they shared. Constant uncertainty, coupled with deteriorating conditions, was beginning to take its toll. Reconciling the invigorating climate of change with the unvarying daily routine was difficult. Despite all the talk of reform we still had the same drudgery of shopping and waiting for trams, the same senseless quibbling in the teachers' room. Though if the staff succumbed to depression, it rarely showed. Stefan was disappointed with the way things were going, but not distraught. He still had his research on body language. And he had a new student this semester, an Iranian, in whom he took some interest, asking him for books about his country and its return to fundamentalism. "You know, this revolution seems to be spreading," he said one day during tea. "Have you noticed how Islamic our own government is becoming? No meat. Higher prices for alcohol."

At the beginning of March I took on another private pupil. I had seen a notice in the U.S. embassy complex, placed by a Japanese woman, Mrs. Matsuda. I called from a nearby hotel (we had no telephone, despite having a doctor in the house) and received the encouraging information that my student would pay U.S. dollars (five an hour, which was enough, at the black market rate, to take Hania out to the best restaurant in Warsaw).

Rolna was a small dirt street lined with boxy one- and two-story private residences built in the shadow of Stefan's housing complex in the south of Warsaw. The Matsudas' house was sparsely furnished in Western style with wall-to-wall carpeting. A piano stood in one corner and a pair of French windows looked out onto a small yard.

Mrs. Matsuda was a pretty, petite woman with hennaed hair, who spoke English in a whisper often followed by giggles. Her husband, she told me, was a businessman who spent the week in Katowice trying to sell Japanese steel to Polish industries. ("This crisis makes my husband's work very difficult.") He returned to Warsaw on weekends. Her oldest daughter was also away, at a Japanese high school in London which educated, as stringently as in Japan, those children whose parents, usually diplomats and businessmen, had the good fortune to live in Europe. I quickly got the impression from Mrs. Matsuda that life on Warsaw's Rolna Street was, at least for her, unquestionably preferable to life in Tokyo. To begin with, a husband's presence only on weekends pleasantly diminishes a Japanese wife's duties. The house, she claimed, was larger than the one they had in Tokyo. (Their Polish landlord lived with his family in the basement.) The two Matsuda children still at home had their personal Warsaw taxi drivers to take them to and from school every day; the grade school, on Incomplete Street, was also Japanese. Mrs. Matsuda had her own car, a Toyota, which she drove to exercise classes at the American embassy and tapestry weaving lessons from a Polish artisan. She employed a Polish maid, who did the shopping and helped with the cooking and appeared during our lessons wearing a bright, plastic Union Jack apron to pour tea. It was curious to see the tradition of a country's wealthy class employing humble foreign help here completely reversed. The sight seemed to give Poland the mark of a Third World country.

I asked Mrs. Matsuda if she had heard of Wałęsa's claim that Poland could become a second Japan. She said politely that she thought it impossible. "Japanese people work very hard. I don't think Polish people want to work like that. My husband, when he is in Japan, goes to work at half past seven in the morning and comes home at eight or nine at night, sometimes twelve or one. I don't think Polish people are like that."

At Dr. Zięba's we moved our lessons out into the main room, which had a large front window facing west, a floor covered with attractive Persian rugs, and on the walls two original oil paintings, one with the telltale rip in the canvas. Against the far wall stood a long cabinet heavy with crystal and the expensive liquors that are the unsolicited trophies in every doctor's home in Poland. Sometimes Dr. Zięba would cancel a lesson to attend a medical meeting; the lesson on her return would be rich in highlights. Recently she had been at a meeting in Moscow of physicians of the Soviet bloc (what the Poles abbreviated to a sarcastic and moronic-sounding quaintness: *demoludy* — democratic peoples). There, she said, while all the others had been picked up by a bus at the hotel, a separate car had come to take the Polish delegation. In the same way, at the dinners, one large banquet table was always set for everyone else, while the Polish physicians sat at a small table off to the side. "They are a little paranoid, the Russians," she said amusedly. "This Solidarity business worries them."

Sometimes I would get to taste her patients' favors. "These are Witkowski's napoleons," she said one day, serving me the delicious pastry on her best china. "The first he has made since getting out of prison." When I asked the reason for his incarceration, she said, "His only crime was making too much money, something you are not allowed to do in Poland." (Others I talked to later were less convinced of his innocence.) "He began a café in Zakopane, then he came to Warsaw and he was manager of Hortex shop on Świętokrzyska Street. After that he was manager of Bazyliszek restaurant in Old Town. Then to prison. Now he wants to take the restaurant at Journalist's Club and make it the restaurant-nightclub, with music and the cabaret. But to do this he must get the kitchen equipment back from Bazyliszek. I don't know if it will work. He is the entrepreneur, the true entrepreneur, and this is not a country for the entrepreneurs."

Throughout March, the situation in the country did not change, it simply intensified. Teaching became difficult, as I would arrive at three to a teachers' room swelling with rumor and head off to a classroom of uncertain priorities and unconcentrated minds. Grzegorz began to talk of going to Chicago. Elżbieta approached me one day as if she were surprised to see me. "Aren't you fed up with things here yet, Tom? You know, it will be like this for at least the next ten years. And we're in the worst position. We're a lost generation. The only thing we can hope for now is that it will be better for our children."

At home, Jadzia complained in her animated fashion: "Nobody sees the path. Nobody sees the path." Leszek, who was active in his office Solidarity chapter, complained uncharacteristically that his work these days was "*bez sensu*" (meaningless). At the embassy, Krystyna told me that her husband, who unlike her was usually sanguine, had also become depressed and was looking for a position in the States. She noted that the debate within the embassy, while the food crisis worsened, was about whether to continue serving Polish employees dinner, or perhaps to restrict them to sandwiches and snacks. (The cafeteria food was for Krystyna, as for most of the other Poles, the main meal of the day.)

At the end of March, in the town of Bydgoszcz, police broke up a Solidarity meeting with clubs and sent a number of people to the hospital. A general strike was called for the following Tuesday. Having no foreknowledge of developments, Mr. Kuczma had scheduled a teachers' meeting for Monday afternoon with a visiting lecturer from England. The strike had not yet been called off when we gathered in the brilliantly sunlit Room 26. Even our visiting English lecturer could feel the tension. His talk was courteously, if distractedly, received, and further dampened by the chords of organ music wafting up from the practice downstairs for Sunday's service. Afterward in the teachers' room everyone gathered to exchange news feverishly before class. Miss Wiaderny, standing alone off to the side, caught my eye. "Mr. Swick," she said, "I heard one of your compatriots on the BBC today. Mr. John Updike. He read from a few of his works. I had never heard him before; he has a pleasant speaking voice. He said, 'And since I am an American, I must read something of Melville.' And," she said longingly, "he read from *Moby Dick*." More interesting than the fact that a radio program could so captivate Miss Wiaderny during this crisis was the fact that an American on the program could.

The Matsuda family fled to London the first week of April, on directions from the husband's main office there. They were comfortably put up in a hotel for four days, and then allowed to return to Warsaw. The ladies in the smokers' room found this highly amusing. Mrs. Iwanowska said she was "two hundred percent positive" the Russians would not come. Stefan said wryly: "They already lost one war with us in 1920 and they don't want to lose another."

"The Miracle on the Vistula," I said. Stefan had replaced the red-and-white Solidarity pin on his lapel with a brown one. It was a fine metalwork design, no larger than a clipped fingernail. "I notice your insignia has gotten smaller," I told him.

He looked at me with his vulpine grin. "Easier to swallow."

For Easter Hania's family sent me, as the only one with a passport in hand, to Vienna for shopping. I boarded the Chopin Express at Warsaw's memory-laden Gdansk Station with two empty suitcases and returned four days later with both of them filled with food and toiletries. Back at school I was surprised to find Stefan absent, for he was rarely sick. "It seems he had an accident," said Janusz. "I hear he will not be back for a while." That's all that anybody knew.

As Stefan did not have a telephone, I had to wait until the next morning to try to find out what had happened. My recollection, from the few times I had driven with him, was that he was a careful driver. But that offered little protection in a city where the national sense of decorum vanishes when one takes to the road. Warsaw's reputation for terrorist drivers was, like so much else, attributed to "the system," which, it was argued, had created a society in which the only place a man could feel in control and unbounded was behind the wheel of his car. Added to my apprehension was the inescapable fact that Stefan's car, a small Polish Fiat, was one of the tiniest and least sturdy automobiles ever designed. I could not forget, either, that his last words to me had had a slightly fateful ring.

On a rainy, late April morning, I arrived at Stefan's building, deep in the folds of the mesmerizing complex, and took the shaky elevator to the seventh floor. His oldest daughter answered the door and, when I asked about her father, quietly led me into her bedroom. There, on the daybed, Stefan lay perfectly still.

"Stefan. It's Tom," I said cautiously, moving closer to his inert body.

"Yeah . . . yeah," he answered sluggishly. "I . . . I was just taking a nap." He slowly pulled himself up in the bed.

"What happened? They said at school you had an accident."

"Yeah. I fell off a skateboard."

I could tell from the slight tone of humiliation that it was not a joke. I stifled my laughter as he was clearly in pain.

"We went to visit my nieces on Easter Sunday," he began. "Their father had just bought them a skateboard and of course I insisted on trying it out. The damn thing flipped over and my leg buckled under me. I lay flat on my side for several minutes and when I convinced them that I couldn't walk they took me to the hospital. The doctor examined me and told me I had broken my ankle, and that I'd have to spend at least the next month recuperating. By the way, it was a bloody American who invented the skateboard, wasn't it?"

He pulled back the covers to show me the cast, which went up to his thigh. Along the side, from ankle to knee, someone had written "Solidarity" in the familiar red script. "Body language," he said, noticing my attention.

We discussed, as usual, the situation. He expressed the feeling that the major problem now was people's "lack of morality."

"They have been destroyed so long by this system that they have no sense of right and wrong anymore. You see how the students cheat on tests. That's a minor thing. But people's explanation for any moment of weakness is that they must act that way to survive — it is the only way to get around the system. The fact that the system is itself corrupt seems to exonerate them, to make their corrupt actions right. Our society has to get its moral values back." Suddenly he asked, turning from the serious, "I trust you're going to the May Day parade tomorrow?

"You know, as long as I can remember, the First of May was a sunny, beautiful spring day. Now if tomorrow is like this it will mean that even God has turned against the Communists. And," he began, his eyes twinkling blissfully, "we will have yet another breakthrough."

On an exquisite spring evening two weeks later, standing on the third-floor balcony before my last class, and looking down upon the revolving traffic patterns in Savior Square, I learned from Elżbieta that the Pope had been shot. The teachers were unusually silenced by the news, pacing about and wearing expressions of shock and incomprehension. I thought, How much more can these people be expected to bear?

In the following days, their Pope recovered, but their cardinal's condition worsened. Cardinal Wyszyński, the primate of Poland, who had stood up to the Communists in the 1950s, and spent three years in prison, lay near death. Piotr brought in the latest *Newsweek*, containing a detailed map of the would-be assassin's international peregrinations. "Yes, yes," said Janusz, smacking his lips. "There must have been some source for the money for such trips, some partnership with a superpower. People say it must have been a very super power that wanted him to carry out his mission."

"Things are not good," Dr. Zięba began our last lesson of the month with what was now her habitual declaration. "Cardinal Wyszyński has died." She told of how, earlier in the week, she had been called with other hospital and clinic directors to a meeting at the Ministry of Health. There they had been told to keep a certain number of beds free, and to get drugs, medicine, and equipment ready in case of an emergency. She had received a similar command only once before — in the days preceding the threatened general strike in March.

Then she told me of a visit recently from an old patient. "I have been a doctor for many of these important men," she said matter-of-factly. "And they always change. But I don't. So I get to talk to many different ones. When this man first came to me, right after falling out of favor, he spoke with such condemnation of the government that I always closed the door. I was afraid for these views to be heard — they were so unusual for the time. When he was still the 'big man' I would walk him to the door of the clinic and then, when he came to me in the 'between period,' I would still walk him to the door. And he asked me why I continued to do this when he was no longer important. And I said to him that I do not change — others may change but I do not change in my actions toward them.

"About two years ago, again, he asked me why I continued 'to demonstrate' about him, and I said: 'You know, someday if you get back in favor, you will remember me and I will have a protector.'" She laughed. "And now, because he was the first to criticize Gierek, he is coming back into favor. There was a big article in *Trybuna Ludu* about him, and when he was in the other day I said to him, 'Now tell me, is this article good for you or bad for you?' And he said. 'It's good! It's good!'

"He asked me recently why I was so angry. I told him I was tired of trying to work, to be a director, in a clinic where there was no money, no facilities, shortages of everything. And he said to me, 'Be patient.' Patient, yes? 'For one more month.' Why one more month, I don't know.

"This is terrible time. But I have lived through others." This, too, she said matter-of-factly. "I lived through the war, the occupation, the Stalin period. That was truly awful. Many people were in prison. It was very difficult for me. My father was in England and you were discriminated against if anyone of your family was abroad. I couldn't get a stipendium. I couldn't get a place in the students' house because my father was in Great Britain. In those years students would receive once or twice a month food packages from America. These were very helpful, with fish and things, that you could almost live on for a month. Everyone got one except me, and any others whose families were abroad. Sometimes, of course, my friends would share things with me, but I didn't like that. It was very difficult for me. At university I had to clean the house I had my room in for to pay the rent. And I remember going home between lectures and holding a book in one hand, stirring the soup with the other, and wiping the floor with rags under my feet all at the same time.

"Many people are leaving Poland now," she continued. "It is good that others stay — they can only stay if they have a hope to change, to work for something better. If the Russians come, the young people should leave. I won't leave. I will stay here to the end, but the young people, they should leave."

Changing trams on the way home, I saw, for the second time in two weeks, crowds gathered around the church on Narutowicz Square. Two red-and-white Polish flags, with a thin black ribbon tied to the top of each, flew on either side of its large front door.

A few days after the cardinal's funeral, I stopped in to see Stefan. He was in good spirits, getting around the apartment inexpertly on crutches and playing with his daughter's new hamster.

"I watched it on television," he said, after I had described to him what I had seen in person. "There were several significant things. First of all, the fact that an Italian came here, from the Vatican, and said Mass in Polish. That was a sign that we are still, and always have been, tied to the West, to the Greco-Roman tradition or whatever you want to call it. But more than that it was a demonstration that the center of Catholicism had shifted, if only for a day, from Rome to Warsaw.

"The other thing, which was extremely fine, was Wyszyński's last testament, read from the crypt of the cathedral. To lead the government representatives into church, and to make them stand there, listening to his philosophy — speaking to them from the grave as it were — was like a last joke on the authorities."

The school year drew to its regular close one week later with Miss Wiaderny's tests. The students huddled close to one another, the brightest ones attracting entire phalanxes, while I sat behind my desk pretending to read a month-old copy of *The New Yorker*. "O.K., Jacek, that's enough," I would yell, catching a rubbernecker. "Go sit in the chair in the back." And Jacek would saunter back without a hint of disgrace, only annoyance.

Often I would look up from a page to survey my dominions, examining the familiar faces in a way I never had time to do when teaching. And I would look out over them collectively, Polish youth, in their jeans, scuffed shoes, and open-collared shirts; the girls, many of them, with their hair pulled back into braids or ponytails; the boys, almost all of them it seemed, with a thin brown slick combed from left to right. Their leather satchels hung across the backs of their chairs, sometimes a plastic bag of cucumbers sat at their feet, as they pulled cheap ballpoint pens across their papers. With something, I suppose, of the parent watching as his children sleep, I would gaze down at them — momentarily hushed and unaware of my observance — and wonder about, despair for, their horribly uncertain futures.

In September, following a vacation, I returned to Warsaw. The great gray building still loomed over Savior Square, the walls, if anything, slightly darker from the exhaust of a summer of circling automobiles. I walked past the biblical inscriptions, up the soon-to-be-busy staircase, and into the teachers' room, where, against the window, a fresh bottle of Mazowszanka awaited the thirsts of a new semester.

Of the teachers at our end, only Piotr and I remained. Maria had quit, and Grzegorz had gone to Chicago as he had threatened, where he was now painting houses with a cousin. Janusz had taken a vow of silence for a year and entered a monastery. ("That seems to me a logical result of having taught for five years," said Stefan.) Stefan, sadly, had feuded with Mr. Kuczma over sick leave, and now, in a lamentable waste of talent, worked as a translator for the Malaysian embassy. They were all, for the most part, replaced by earnest, dedicated, dull young women graduates of the university English department. How different, I thought to myself sadly, from a year ago.

Though it seemed impossible, the food crisis had worsened over the summer. Our first day back at school, we received — along with our meat cards, sugar cards, rice cards, and butter cards — ration cards for cigarettes and vodka. A recent photograph in a magazine had shown a table set with nothing on the dishes save for ration cards.

Food packages began arriving at the school, sent by both Methodist and non-Methodist churches throughout Western Europe. We would line up outside the library to get our portion of butter, rice, canned goods, and sweets. One evening we entered to find Mr. Kuczma cutting thick slices from a large cheese wheel sent by a diocese in Holland, while Mrs. Kuczma wrapped and handed them out — a scene that nicely reinforced for me the mom-and-pop-store image of the school.

Jolanta had returned from her studies in the States and taken on some classes. She sat with the ladies in the smokers' room. I watched her laughing heartily at their jokes and finding solace, I suspected, in knowing that, despite hardship and privation, this indomitable mirth still thrived. "Yes, they're funny," she said, when I asked her about being back. "But they're all so cynical." Her face was pinched with disapproval. "You cannot say anything to them without their winking an eye or shrugging a shoulder. There is nothing that they can believe in or accept with hope."

Autumn was, as always, cold and wet. The city had not yet turned on the heat for its apartments, and we now found extra reason to gather in the kitchen. Jadzia, who had spent most of the summer at the spa in Konstancin, had returned to us even more weary and depressed. Her son came from Lodz and they argued at supper in front of his daughter. "It's worse now than during the occupation," Jadzia fulminated, as if he were responsible. "Then at least we had our ration cards and got what we were rationed."

"But there were still Germans, Mama," Andrzej replied. I wondered how he explained it to his daughter. Our four-year-old neighbor was already wise enough to say to his mother, when they went into the shops, "Mama, there isn't anything."

I resumed my lessons with Dr. Zięba and Mrs. Matsuda. Dr. Zięba brought me greetings from America. To hear her tell it, her August trip had been a phenomenal success for which I was solely responsible. With the exception of Dallas cab drivers, she had understood everyone. She had been surprised by the number of Americans with Polish backgrounds, and touched by how often they had come up to her to ask of the situation in Poland, and to offer what assistance they could.

After my hour with Mrs. Matsuda I wandered over to the housing complex to see Stefan, home from a day at the embassy. He led me into the living room, walking with a slight limp, and then went into the kitchen for something to drink. He returned with two large brown bottles of Pulaski beer, which, he pointed out with bemusement, were imported from Hungary.

"So, how are things at the Methodist school?" he asked, settling down into his chair.

I told him of the uninspiring company, and of how much I missed his conversation. "Well, you still have Miss Wiaderny, don't you? Or," he began, his lips starting to lengthen, "has she gone off to America too?"

"Do you miss it?" I asked him.

"No, not really."

"How do you like the work at the embassy?"

He paused, making a slight grimace, before answering. "Most of it is translation. There are about ten Poles — 'the local staff' — and about the same number of Malaysians. Almost none of them bother to learn Polish, so they're dependent on me. Their English is often quite difficult. And there's such a hierarchy. Rather than walk across the hall, they'll call me on the telephone.

"Well, every day I have to translate *Trybuna Ludu*, my favorite newspaper. Last week they were very interested in this plenum, so that took a long time, going through all the talks and procedures. It's a good thing I don't have a telephone, because they tend to call the locals up after the evening news and ask them what it was about. The only locals who have telephones are a couple of the drivers, who speak very little English. One guy told me he was once called out of his shower to watch some report on television.

"The most crucial part of my job is to translate, type, and make copies of the daily television program. The ambassador insists that he have it on his desk by twelve o'clock every day. I have nightmares about making the deadline. Once I asked one of them if he wanted the version for color TV, and he said yes. I gave him a copy of the same thing. It took him a while to get it.

"Then of course, some of the work is social — calling tailors and arranging fittings. I always have trouble explaining things to them — such as when one of them pays extra for a suit to be made in three weeks and then gets it after two months. You know, they're Western in this sense, their country is developing and they often act superior and make fun of the situation here. I don't let it bother me.

"Sometimes we're invited to dinners, with native Malaysian foods, very spicy dishes, everyone dressed in native costumes."

"That must be nice for you," I ventured.

"It's terrible. They're Muslims and they don't drink."

He continued. "But it's fun to get beyond the facade of diplomatic life and see what a sham it all is. We get a lot of mail from other embassies, all written in Polish, no doubt by their local staffs. For example, a letter will come in saying, 'We humbly take this opportunity to inform the most honorable ambassador from Malaysia that our own honorable ambassador will be away from his duties in the Polish capital for three days the week of September twenty-fourth.' By the time we get it and translate it, he's already back.

"Or something from the North Korean embassy that

came in recently. It said, 'We have the great honor of informing his majesty the ambassador of the National North Korean Day. Because of a necessary cutback in funding, there will be no reception this year. But in lieu of this we would most gratefully accept the ambassador's presence at a special screening of *The Brave Nurse*.'"

I spent more time than ever going to my private lessons because of the degeneration of the transportation system. One constantly heard stories of all the disabled buses for which there were no parts. I was already bundling up again for the stultifying waits. The air was chilled, damp and heavy with mist and soot. Pyramidal piles of coal sat dumped on sidewalks before concrete tenements, waiting to be shoveled into cellars and fed into furnaces to blacken the sky further. One night after school, waiting for an overdue tram with Agnieszka and her boyfriend, I asked if we could write a letter of complaint to someone.

"Well," said the young man helpfully. "You could. Of course you could. The stamp is no problem. Two złotys for the stamp at any post office. The envelope is a bit of a problem, though. You may have to glue it yourself, as they rarely stick these days. And good luck finding the glue. And, while you're at it, good luck finding the paper. But once you get the paper, sure, of course you could write a letter."

My love of Warsaw trams — their old-fashioned headlamps, their pale red cars, their nudging movements — was inextricably tied to the frigid, semiconscious ecstasy I usually felt on seeing one. They cut through the vaporous evenings, their frail wattage refracted by the dimness, and rumbled comfortingly down embedded tracks (the only thing in Poland, it seemed, that never wavered from its course).

Riding the trams these days I was always struck by the faces I saw. They did not so much exude tension (the emotion attributed to them by the Western press) as fretfulness. I had seen this same aspect, this mating of worriment and exhaustion, as well in the States, riding the subway under Manhattan, with this difference: there it expressed, no matter how painfully, only a personal misery; while here, in that one face — multiplied a hundred times in the course of a single journey across the city — was a whole trauma and despair for the fate of the nation.

I still took my weekday meals before school in the American embassy basement, usually meeting Krystyna. Her husband had gotten an assistant research position at an American university and had gone on ahead of her. She was now applying for passports for herself and the children. Some new graduate students had arrived. Gregory was a genial, bearded, radical-looking political scientist who threatened the monopoly of another graduate student who had been tracking Solidarity from the start. Not only were they after the same story, but they were from the same university. "Before I came," Gregory told us, "Henry said to me, 'All right. You can come. But just stay out of Warsaw. That's my territory.'" It struck me as ironic that their subject was Solidarity.

My bakery on Mokotowska Street no longer made *pączki*, so instead I bought a small, circular cake, lightly iced, with a delicious pool of yellow custard in the center.

At school Piotr had become virtually impenetrable,

retreating behind his fallen glasses and unchanged Mao jacket with the Solidarity button above the pocket.

Once, discussing the shortage of gasoline, Mr. Romanowicz queried down to our end of the table, "Mr. Nasterski, I believe you have a car?"

"Well, not really," replied Piotr with a victorious smile. "That is to say, there is a car that I use but it is not exactly mine." After which he was left to atrophy in peace.

I began spending more time with my students, often not going back to the teachers' room except for tea. The new year had begun with most of the same faces (as well as sweaters) stretching for rows in front of me, and a few new ones sprinkled about. My relations with the regular students had been fortified from our having struggled together not only through two semesters, but also one year of Polish history. Once, when I announced a test in two days to my five o'clock group, Katarzyna insisted that they give me one in Polish, which they presented to me at the next class ("This isn't fair," I said, "you all have somebody to cheat off of"). They returned it, properly graded, at the following lesson.

When a lesson was going well, I was filled with an unparalleled contentment. It was not only for my orchestration of thirty-odd voices in a fifty-minute class period, but for my having established a place in a once intimidating world. In the lulls between classes I would sometimes reiterate, as if to remind myself, that I was in Eastern Europe. Poland. Warsaw. Nothing should have seemed more strange, yet nothing felt more natural. It was home to me.

As much to keep up my interest as that of my students, I had begun the year by bringing my new tape player to class. It was a Polish product, dubbed Marta by the manufacturer. I pulled it out of my book bag in my first class with a certain pride, though the students unanimously denigrated its quality, assuring me that it would not last long and suggesting a critical disappointment that I, of all people, would resort to Polish technology. Nevertheless, it served us well.

Visiting over the summer, my parents had brought me a tape of Woody Allen's old nightclub routines, which I played once in class with such success that it became a standard feature. I had to exclude the ones that dealt with sex (owing to the nature of our institution and the age of some of my students) and those with arcane American frames of reference (Kate Smith, Willie Mays, the Dewey Decimal System). Surprisingly, that still left a good number. Before each Friday class, the day I brought Marta, I wrote on the blackboard the unfamiliar words from that evening's sketch (ransom note, flannel underwear, Berkowitz's). Then I played it one sentence at a time. Allen's speech in many of the monologues is remarkably crisp and distinct, and not always as rapid as one might expect; my quickest students frequently understood a sentence immediately. An extremely satisfying sight was an entire class cracking up at a punch line. The students knew Woody Allen from his recent movies, which had been well received in Warsaw, and these comedy routines often transformed their faces on dismal nights. I liked to think of them going around Warsaw repeating to themselves, "I shot a moose once. I was hunting — upstate New York — and I shot a moose," a sentence which, however silly, successfully combines two frequently used aspects of the past tense.

I still worked tirelessly on their pronunciation, but knowing it to be my last year, I began to spend a class now and then talking about "American culture." One day I devoted to aphorisms; the English majors knew of Shaw and Wilde; I introduced them to Bierce and Mencken. They, in turn, provided me with some examples from their writers, like Lec and Słonimski. Then I added Europeans. They showed no appreciation for Rousseau's "Poles! If you cannot prevent your neighbors from devouring your nation, make it possible for them to digest it." In fact it prompted one usually quiet girl, Agata, to ask in the most sullen tones why Americans told such humiliating jokes about Poles. Everyone in the class echoed her hurt. I replied that they were only a fraction of American ethnic humor — that the same Polish joke in Chicago became an Irish joke in Boston — though, looking out at these Poles studying English at eight o'clock on a Friday evening, I had to wonder myself.

My students were curious about American school life. They expressed amazement that I had had only five courses a semester in high school; they were required to take a dozen, among these, physics, biology, chemistry, mathematics (including calculus), history, geography, Polish philology, and Russian, as well as another foreign language. "This is why we cheat," explained Jacek. "There is no way I can know so many subjects."

Institutions like cheerleaders and elections for "best dressed" and "most likely to succeed" struck them as preposterous. "And you tell Polish jokes!" said Ryszard pointedly.

To my advanced classes I read Thurber stories. In "University Days," I carefully avoided naming the dim-witted tackle, Bolenciecwcz. Ignorant of that, they howled with laughter.

My six o'clock beginners, now approaching intermediate status, were still my most easygoing. They regularly came up to talk with me after class. One young
man complained that the American embassy had refused him a visa. (When I told Krystyna this, she said
the recent average was four visas granted out of every
120 applications.) Magdalena, whom I frequently ran
into with her boyfriend, told me that her thesis on
Mallarmé was going well except that she had run out of
paper.

At tea Piotr leaned back in his tilted chair, his newly
sheared scalp propped against the wall, his eyes closed,
his hands clasped, the only sign of life the subtle rising
and falling of the Solidarity pin on his Mao jacket. Mr.
Romanowicz announced that the peasant woman who
had provided his building for years with pork and veal
had arrived from the country with the news that their
commerce was being terminated. "You only give me
money," she had said. "What can I do with money?
There are no clothes, no soaps, no food." In the smokers'
room a bartering system had taken form, so that anyone
who had been able to find a nonrationed item bought it
in bulk and then brought it to school in hopes of trade.

By November, rumors of an impending state of emergency became more frequent. Jadzia continued to fume
that "Nobody sees the path!" and practically convulsed
when the government blamed Solidarity for the chaos.
"And what do they think has been going on for the last
thirty-five years!" On television one night an appropriately uplifting show appeared: "Winter 1981–82 —
How to Survive."

III
War Months

Months in our history play an important role. Perhaps no other nation has as many months of importance. There are thus, "Polish September," "Polish October," "Polish December," "Polish August," "January" as well as "November."
— Antoni Słonimski

ON THE WAY to school I found a large crowd in front of the Solidarity headquarters on Mokotowska Street. Loudspeakers stood in the upper-story windows directly above the entranceway, members wearing armbands handed out communiqués in the street, and young men with megaphones paced up and down the steps, pleading with the crowd to make way for the student firemen who were starting to arrive, in their natty blue uniforms, for a press conference. They were greeted by hearty applause and cries of "Bravo, boys!" The firemen had just come from their training school, which they had defiantly occupied the previous day and night while growing reserves of police and ZOMO — the special police unit made up in part of criminals — assembled outside. I took one of the communiqués and opened it in the teachers' room. It was printed like a theater advertisement: "Attention! Young People! New, Hard-Hitting Program. In Appearance, the Famous ZOMO-BROTHERS. For All Bigger Groups. Organized by Your Government."

7 December

GOT MY VISA renewed today. On the tram back, with the snow falling over the Vistula, I was granted a beau-

tifully colorless view of the river and the Old Town sky-
line — the muted, gray-and-white-sloped roofs with
sweeping half drifts of snow, the white steeples, and in
the distance, on the bridge upriver, a train passing, its
cars lit and moving like identical boxes through the
snowflaked mist.

A defeating night at school. Either they failed to answer my questions or I failed to answer theirs. At my
five o'clock class Agnieszka burst in from a strike and
barely got her coat off before giving a five-minute run-
down in Polish of the situation. Things are getting
tense again. Received Christmas packages at school:
cake mixes, chocolate, coconut butter, raisins, nuts,
marzipan, salami, corned beef, and condensed milk
donated by some Western country.

At home, more talk of the situation, and what to do
if a civil war erupts. Leszek said the first thing is to get
enough food in reserve. In such a situation, there could
be hunger in Warsaw. He added that all foreigners
might be asked to leave within twenty-four hours. He
also suggested that I make a copy of all my documents,
remembering, he said, what the Russians had done
during the last war. "They'd ask for your documents.
You'd hand them over, they would tear them into
pieces, stamp on them, and then do with you what they
wished. Who are you then? What's to say you are who
you say you are? My uncle was sent to Katyń. . . . The
best is to prepare for the worst."

8 December

SOMETIMES THE FACES on trams, looking out from those
gray, rain-streaked windows, remind me of the contor-

tions of the mentally deranged. Two today — one a man with a long sausage nose and a silly, woolen hat with earflaps; the other in a plain wool hat, his eyes flattened behind goggle-shaped glasses, his lips parted in a grimace, his long, tobacco-stained teeth rising out of reddened gums.

English lesson with Mrs. Matsuda this afternoon. She says Polish people must work. Now they don't work, they just stand in queues. In Japan, she says, you cannot arrange personal affairs during working hours: you cannot use the telephone except for business. "My husband's secretary talks to her mother, for a long time, on the telephone. My husband gets so mad."

Saw a few crates of yogurt in the "supermarket" today, each plastic container punctured or soiled, the contents drained to a liquidy half, the juice spreading in an orbit on the muddy floor. I picked one up that still looked mildly appetizing. The lid crawled back and a mixture of milk and dirt ran onto my fingers.

Mleczko cartoon: "Give me a half kilo of whatever there is."

Mleczko prostitute: "What's all this talk about democracy? For the last ten years I've been giving it to everybody."

10 December

LESSON TODAY WITH Dr. Zięba. She had been to a medical meeting in France and told of the opening ceremony. All the physicians were seated in a great hall for the introduction of the foreign delegates. When they came to those from Poland there was a loud burst of applause. To acknowledge this, her colleague rose and made a brief statement about the importance of such meetings, the sharing of ideas, the solidarity of the scientific community. At the sound of the word *solidarity*, she said, the entire assembly chanted as one "*So-li-da-ri-té! So-li-da-ri-té!*" until the whole room reverberated with the cry.

When I told Hania, she said: "We're so popular because we have a crisis?"

12 December

WOKE LATE AND spent the day correcting tests. I'd asked my students to write letters to imaginary pen pals in the United States, telling about their lives in Poland. I learned that one girl works for the "Paid-in-Advance" office of LOT airlines; another for *Trybuna Ludu*, calling her job "nothing important." A great number worry about school exams and plan winter ski trips. The recent strikers tried to justify their striking. One girl related almost the entire history of Scarlett O'Hara. Many are concerned about the current situation:

Dear Gilbert,
Excuse me the fact that I haven't written but our life in Poland became so full of experiences of all sorts that it is difficult to take breath, to stop living like somebody crazy. On the other hand, there is actually an occasion that didn't appear so far, to analyze our social and private life, its organization and aims. The results are not very hopeful, because we criticize the existing state of things and we can't give a coherent or practical proposition for the future. We know one thing: that the future has to be bright and happy, but our life becomes more

and more difficult and — as a result — discouraging.
I'm young and I think my generation has no perspectives,
in the material sense, for the rest of the life, but it has
some ideas, some great ideas, yet. Our life depends on
politics every moment, on this so-called great politics that
is not great at all, it is the most cruel and thoughtless all
the time. In this context I consider that poor Poland is an
unusual country that fights for the truth and happiness
of every humble human being.

> *Yours,*
> *Ewa*

My dear friend Ludmiła,
I am writing this letter in a queue for shoes. I have stood
here for seven hours and I am very tired. This letter is my
only amusement in this sad life. For seven hours I think
only about shoes. Please understand me! I have only one
pair of shoes and they have a hole. In Poland now people
are standing in the queue even if they don't know what
is in the shop. Often we are standing for nothing — it
doesn't mean that we are standing for fun or sport!
It's stupid, I know, but it is our only chance to buy
something.

> *Love,*
> *Grażyna*

Dear P.,
First I wanted to write about the political situation in our
country, but now I know that isn't important. The situa-
tion looks like the death agony of this system. Our govern-
ment makes a lot of mistakes. But it is snowing, and even
socialism looks better under snow.

> *Cezary*

13 December

MARCIN, our across-the-street neighbor, woke us up
with a knock on the door this morning to tell us there
was a "state of war." He had recorded Jaruzelski's early
morning message and now gave us the tape to play.
Our new telephone is dead.

About eleven o'clock I went out to see if the buses
were running. At the corner a taxi driver pulled his
cab up onto the curb, stepped out, and quickly pasted
two poster-sized "proclamations" on the wall of the
apartment building. Immediately a crowd gathered —
reminding me of some old French occupation film —
to read the contents. The posters contained a list of the
measures that had been taken: strikes, public meetings,
sporting events, and entertainments were all forbidden.
Church services were not. (Later in the day somebody
suggested that Solidarity proclaim itself a theological
study group.) Also included was a list of measures that
could be taken — among them, closing the borders —
if it seemed appropriate "for the peace and welfare of
the nation."

At two Hania and I went over to Marcin's apartment.
The television was on, showing men in military uniforms reading communiqués. Everybody was at a loss
as to what to do, how to act. Marcin said the best thing
was to sit at home; Warsaw, he added, was the safest
place to sit.

The usual nightly newscaster came on, wearing the
same plain military jacket as the others. This brought
howls of laughter from all of us. We learned there was
to be no movement in the city from ten P.M. to six A.M.
Marcin and I played chess.

Around midafternoon, after the third game, Hania and I left to get a taxi to Stegny, a housing complex across town where Jadzia was staying for a few days. The driver took us down the airport road until we ran into a blockade. Soldiers in fatigues stood in the middle of the avenue, directing cars to turn back, while in the island a rifle-snouted tank sat, a soldier's helmet poking from the top. I remarked that it was the first time I had ever seen a tank activated for use. We drove down Trasa Łazienkowska and found the setting repeated. We finally got through by another route.

Dinner was already on the table. I left a tiny piece of fat on my plate which caused Jadzia's sister to comment: "You don't waste things now. We learned that during the war. You ate then every crumb of bread and you wiped up every spot of grease. The same now."

The newscaster was back in his military tunic, along with another man, reading an interminable list of powers — we left at number forty-one — now enjoyed by the military government. They can ask to see your documents at any time, they can put you on trial in their own courts, they can make you work longer hours, they can move people into your apartment if you have extra space. Jadzia said in a rage: "They can do anything! Absolutely anything!" All schools were given their Christmas vacations a week early.

In Leszek's car on the way home we caught the BBC and heard Tim Sebastian reporting that during the night soldiers had taken over the Solidarity headquarters on Mokotowska Street, confiscating money and documents. During the process they had had to hold off an angry mob, some of whom shouted "Gestapo" at them. By morning, he said, Soviet-built tanks had rolled through the north of the city. The army now holds the bridges and controls all major roads out of the capital. Soldiers patrol the city, bearing carbines and machine guns. Various Solidarity leaders have been arrested, but not Wałęsa. Perhaps it was hearing it all for the first time in English, or in the unique presentation of Western reporting, that made me feel more frightened than I had all day.

At home we got the broadcast from London in Polish, and heard that the workers at the Ursus tractor factory outside Warsaw were calling for a strike on Monday — tomorrow. Leszek said that if there is a general strike it will mean an occupation of buildings. He is prepared to join. He suggested knocking out the television cameras at the intersections of downtown streets (I hadn't known such cameras existed.) He is taking a supply of food and clothing with him tomorrow in case.

I see little tonight to be optimistic about in this emergency state save for one overused cliché of national character: Poles are good in emergencies.

14 December

OUT BY NINE this morning to see if the closing of state schools affected ours as well. Hania told me to be careful. Got on a number 2 tram that took a surprise turn on Niepodległości Avenue, the intersection heavily congested with soldiers. Boys mostly — two of whom fiddled with a rifle hooked onto another's back — all of them looking innocent and frozen. Young faces pinched by cold, bright ruby noses and ears under square fur military hats, black fur collars folded down on their khaki green coats, sleeves thick with woolen layers, making their arms stick out from their bodies like scarecrows. The same with gloves — stubby, gray fingers pointing out in all directions.

The school was locked, as usual in the morning, but with no sign of cancellation in the window. Next door I passed by the Solidarity headquarters, guarded by soldiers. Went to the American embassy and ran into Krystyna. She was in a terrible state, though said they promise to speed up her visa process. Together we walked to Gregory's apartment.

His landlady led us back to his room, where he sat in a T-shirt under the yellow stream of light from his desk lamp, toying with the batteries from his tape recorder. He told us about his weekend, getting "great" pictures of the break-in at the Solidarity headquarters Saturday night. He seemed tormented by the thought of all that was no doubt happening now without his knowledge. "I'm wondering what went on at the Lenin Shipyards, at Ursus, at six o'clock this morning."

"I'm not," said Krystyna.

"Are you kidding? At six o'clock this morning hundreds of thousands of workers reported to factories, to mines. What the hell happened? Did they just go in and work like nothing happened? Did they strike? Did they resist? I'm going to Ursus this afternoon."

"They won't let you in."

"Of course they won't. They never do. I'll stand outside the gate. Get there at two for the second shift. See the next massacre."

"God, I hate people like you," said Krystyna. "For you it's all sensation. Get your pictures, get your story. You just want something to happen."

"No I don't. Honestly, I don't. But I don't want Solidarity to stop, to give up all that it's gained. Look, I do this for the Poles. When I was taking pictures at the raid, people were telling me, 'Take that picture! Get that! I'll give you cover.' When I put the camera away they yelled for me not to stop."

Krystyna was so shaken up she did not offer a good argument. She said she was thinking of sending the children alone to her husband because she was no longer in any state to handle them. "Once when I was five I saw my mother cry," she said, "and I have never forgotten it. Now Adam sees me crying every day." Her eyes are red and tired; today not only her hands, but her arms were shaking visibly. Gregory gave us tea; pressed biscuits on me, a tranquilizer on Krystyna. Before we all went out, he rubbed Vicks petroleum jelly on his cheeks, lips, and forehead.

We walked to Constitution Square and passed a small stand that sold tree ornaments. "Oh, God, Christmas is coming," Krystyna said. "What a time for Christmas." I left them to take a bus down to the university. What busloads! Grim, indignant, silenced masses, a different race from those who entered and rode them last week.

Back to the school before three. The charwoman let me in, telling me there were no classes, but that I should wait for the director. Eventually about ten of the teachers arrived — there was smiling, and a rather natural atmosphere, though none of the spontaneous laughter of the teachers' room. Several asked me if I was leaving. "Oh, I would," Dorota said. "You see what's happened now. There's no hope left." Elżbieta said her husband, who is in West Germany, was supposed to come back for Christmas; now she hopes he won't, but there's no way of contacting him. She fears he will not be allowed out again, or, in an extreme case, may even be drafted. Mrs. Iwanowska said to me: "Now you see, Tom, what it is to be helpless." Elżbieta commented: "Yesterday I watched television and I cried. This is the way Poles speak to Poles? I cried and cried, I was so upset." "Merry Christmas," someone said later. "What's merry?" came the reply.

On the tram home I found a fresh communiqué from Solidarity pasted on one of the back windows, calling for an immediate general strike throughout the country. There is now a penalty of up to five years in prison for distributing such materials.

15 December

TOOK A BUS down to Nowy Świat, hoping to kill some time in the reading room, not knowing that they had been closed also. For all his desire to make people work, Jaruzelski has laid off a massive number of people: teachers, film projectionists, athletes, actors, directors, journalists, printers, all those in theater, and many of those in radio and television. (There is only one TV channel now, instead of two.) Our neighbor said yesterday that nobody did anything in her office on Monday.

I walked down Nowy Świat in the direction of the Old Town, finding what looked like a file of spectators lining Krakowskie Przedmieście Street. Walking closer, along the walls of the Academy of Sciences, I came upon an untidy gathering of military wagons parked between the entrance to the academy and the statue of Copernicus, who, appropriately, sat with his back to them. The wagons, and the ZOMO troops that stood outside them, attracted the gaze of a vastly growing crowd on both sides of the street, and a brash group that pressed close by. I was part of this outfit. It was bitterly, painfully cold. We saw, at first, some students, or young professors, being led out into a wagon that appeared already full. Bare hands waved out of the small cracks at the tops of the windows. Some people approached with coats and handed them through the cracks. There was growing anger among the crowd surrounding the scene. Chants of "Ge-sta-po! Ge-sta-po!" rose and fell, as did verses of the national anthem. There were moments that made my heart jump. Another wagon pulled up next to the others. A woman walked toward the captive students (they had been striking inside, hence their removal) with cigarettes held aloft as an offering, only to be halted by one of the guards and turned back. New reserves of police cars, with sirens blaring, careened into the street. They were pelted with snowballs and insults. Then I saw one of my students, Joanna, in her big brown fur coat, pulled from the building and deposited into a waiting wagon. The street was now completely closed to traffic, and in a moment ZOMO reserves, four or five in a row, moved toward the restless crowd with nightsticks. We moved back in the direction of the university, some went into Holy Cross Church, only later, I believe, to be evicted. "It's winter and they are heating things up," someone said. On the balcony of the Prus bookstore, employees looked down on the lamentable scene, as they did likewise, across the street, from the Geographical Institute. I stood near some elderly women, their eyes wet with tears. "It's like the occupation again," one said weeping. "Then the Germans took our brightest.

Now our own are taking them. It's Pole against Pole. Pole against Pole," she repeated in a heartrending tone. The street was still empty, save for a patrol car full of policemen, one with a megaphone of instructions to clear the area. White, untrampled snow slowly began to coat the street; soldiers in groups of three or four marched on both sidewalks. One troop carried bayonets attached to their rifles, the long steel blades shooting coldly upward.

In the evening I went to visit Stefan, who was in unbridled high spirits, celebrating. "You see, this is really the end of the myth of socialism. They've lost. There is nothing they can do to redeem themselves after this." We traded rumors, Stefan claiming that they are striking in the Lenin Shipyards and threatening to blow up the place if the army attacks.

We ate rolls with butter and cold cuts and drank Żubrówka (Buffalo Grass vodka). Stefan said he was idle at the Malaysian embassy, with few papers to read and, of course, unable to make or answer telephone calls. His daughters played on the floor in front of the television set, which showed a documentary on the life of Lenin. Their mother came and turned it off abruptly and scoldingly: "Those people killed masses of Poles!" On my way out I passed Marysia's hamster in the hall. "He's getting big," I said. "Yes," said Stefan, laughing, "he'll be meat for the winter."

16 December

WENT OUT AT nine again this morning, into an eerily still and foggy world. I could not see, at that hour, a block in front of me, and thought, What ideal weather for a military junta. Stefan, with wonder, said last night of Poland: "A sizable country in the center of Europe that all of a sudden disappears — no telephones, no communication, nothing." And this isolation was intensified today by the weather: a winter fog enveloping us so that we could not see a tram two blocks away (let alone dream of neighbors to the west) and a brittle, unmitigating cold that seemed to freeze every movement. Such a feeling of so many people being so helplessly cut off — the frost and fog adding to the disconnected telephones — I don't think I have ever known.

Had less success roaming the streets today, not because of the fog but the cold. After ten minutes my fingertips would lapse into pain and my toes as well. Constantly had to pop into shops and pretend to look at things, though to dissemble was not easy, for there were not always things to look at, and when there were my glasses were usually too steamed to see them. At about four I could no longer bear the cold — night had fallen and the streets were full of dusky, unidentifiable forms — so I went into the Café Corso in Savior Square. Ordered tea and spaghetti, and was surprised by the first slice of lemon I had seen since October. The main course was accompanied by a large plate of pickles, a tomato and onion salad (the tomatoes, rather like myself, pale and frozen), and cubes of marinated pumpkin. While eating, I noticed in the mirror of the bar — squeezed between the lighted advertisements for Marlboro and Rémy Martin — the merry-go-round blue lights of a Polish *milicja* car. Turning, I saw from the window an entire defense parade come out of No-wowiejska Street, half circle the square, and head up

Marszałkowska Street. It had already been going five
minutes when I paid and went out to observe it close
up. All traffic had been stopped: trams were lined up
one after the other; pedestrians, unable to interrupt at
the intersections, had formed groups large enough to
be illegal. There were primarily four types of vehicles:
armored cars with guns atop; square army wagons with
grilled windows, some empty, some full of soldiers (and
seeing their helmeted outlines through that cold, in-
hospitable night air, huddled in darkness in the back
of a wagon, one wondered what thoughts were going
through their heads); jeeps; and the small blue vans of
the police. They rolled for another fifteen minutes —
in all, more than one hundred vehicles — and, unlike
the crowd at the Academy of Sciences, this one stood
rapt. People stared in stunned silence at this raw military abundance in a land of fundamental shortages. No
one knew where the vehicles were headed — some said
later that it was just a "show of force" — at this first
darkened hour of the day, when the city unloads its
workers toward their homes.

In the evening, a small gathering at Marcin's to discuss the day's discoveries. (One thinks of all the discussions that must be taking place in living rooms and
kitchens all over the city, all over the country now.)
Marcin said at Ursus a tank was placed in front of occupied buildings, and the mood was one of fear, not
defiance. I was told by a sad-eyed, middle-aged man
that "in America people do not really know what
'evil' is."

Got home before ten (the curfew) and listened to the
radio. Radio Moscow clarified the situation: the government's move came only hours before the nation fell

into a catastrophe; hostile, antisocialist forces had declared a desire to seize power. (I prefer Timothy Garton Ash's analysis that Solidarity almost against its will
was being "sucked" into power because of the "vac-
uum" left by the government. Kuroń, he reported,
viewed this inability to take power as an advantage for
Solidarity, for they were immune to its corruption, unlike the movements of so many other failed
revolutions.)

Turning the dial of the radio, I caught a vaguely familiar voice speaking with terrible urgency in English,
and hardly had time to wonder, "the Soviet Union?"
"Wałęsa?" before hearing "the Oakland Raiders" and
recognizing the voice of Howard Cosell.

17 December

KRYSTYNA HEARD a child on the bus the other day ask
his mother about the tanks standing along the route.

"Mommy, whose tanks are they?" he asked.

"They're our tanks, dear."

"And who are they against?"

"Well, they're against all of us."

"But wouldn't it be better if they were German tanks,
or Czech tanks?"

Today the Polish press reported that seven people
had been killed at the Wujek mine in Katowice. It is
devastating news. We have gone, in the year and a half
that I have been here, from commemorating with heroic monuments and uncensored words the workers
killed in past demonstrations, to killing workers again.
And one despairs to think how long it will take to com-

memorate these most recent martyrs, and for what reason? — if the same sinisterly false and brutal cycle is
only to be repeated again and again.

18 December

SAW KRYSTYNA THIS morning; still in a poor state. Her
son, Adam, always enjoyed watching the weather fore-
cast on television, especially the maps they showed —
first of Europe and then of Poland — labeled with the
appropriate currents and degrees. Now he is very disappointed because the newscasts are interminable and
there is virtually no weather, at least no maps, merely
an "anchor soldier" reading some temperatures. "The
Flintstones" has been on every day since the beginning
of martial law.

Krystyna was with Adam on a bus — packed as usual
— when it passed a caravan of military vehicles. Boom-
ing forth out of the silence from the back of the bus
came a man's voice declaiming: "Communism will
never succeed in Poland. The whole nation is against
it." More silence, and then again: "Communism will
never succeed in Poland. The whole nation is against
it." Adam turned to his mother and asked, "Momma,
why will Communism never succeed in Poland?" And
Krystyna replied in a quieter, more maternal tone,
"Because the whole nation is against it."

Someone identified as a "literary man" read a message on television last night, pleading with the people
for reconciliation. Krystyna has a friend who lives in
the man's building and who told her that soldiers were
stationed in his apartment all week to make him produce. An original cure for writer's block.

19 December

WENT TO SEE Jolanta to go with her to the school Christmas party. She gave me tea; told me the ruling desire among her male friends right now is to leave the country. Single American women are in demand. We donned our cold-weather gear — a lengthy procedure — Jolanta with a smile, swinging her bag around to her front and saying, "I'm wearing it military fashion now."

We walked on Marszałkowska Street under a heavy snow, passing steadfast men carrying Christmas trees home. I thought of Peguy's prediction that "the revolutionary of the twentieth century will be the father of a Christian family." We passed many people on this last Saturday before Christmas, but the mood was understandably solemn. There were no lights, a few stands selling tawdry ornaments, and no music. We went into Cepelia, the state shop of folk art, looking for the primitive wooden figures — usually of saints and religious personages — that are beautifully carved by hand in Poland. Only two remained; the larger of these was an uncharacteristic statuette of two soldiers caught in a fraternal embrace, one with a white eagle on his helmet, the other with a red star. We did not buy it.

At school, almost all of the forty teachers were gathered in the teachers' room. The long table was set with pitchers of tea and plates of cookies and decorated with pine wreaths and candles. At each teacher's place sat a bar of West German chocolate and a bag of toffees. A cassette player played carols — "What Child Is This?" and "Joy to the World!" — which sounded more moving to me than they ever had. Again my respect grew for these people — who before this season so rich

in meaning for them had experienced the most pro-
found disillusionment of their generation — here talking, joking, expressing concern for one another's
families, continuing life as it must be continued. "Welcome to the New Poland," Elżbieta said to me heartily.
Another teacher said: "President Reagan says he sup-
ports the Polish people, and the Polish nation, but not
the present government. Isn't that beautiful?" Mr.
Kuczma addressed us as he always does, in English:
"I'm glad so many of us could gather here today to exchange our best wishes for the holiday. It's unfortunate
that we could not have our usual Christmas program,
but the present situation in our country did not allow
it. But despite all the things that we are made to" — he
paused here, searching for a word — "experience in
our country, I am pleased to see so many of you happy
and well."

20 December

DINNER WITH JADZIA in Stegny. Andrzej had come from
Lodz. We sat at the table in the small, bare living room;
rolls of thick wool blankets placed at the bottoms of the
windows kept out drafts. Andrzej said of Wałęsa: "He's
finished. It's already post-Wałęsa. He's like Dubček now.
His best chance is to get out, live a happy life abroad,
and write his memoirs."

Of Solidarity he had nothing original to note. "They
brought it on themselves. They got too arrogant toward the end. There was a chance for a great thing to
happen, and they have to do this shit."

From the windows we watched the occasional army
wagon going down the road, their yellow lights turned

on in midafternoon under a brooding sky. We sat
around the quickly finished meal in somber thought.
Jadzia said that there were Russian soldiers participat-
ing in the maneuvers.

"Momma, don't spread such stupid lies!"

"How do you know they're not here? They must
be here."

"Happily, they're not yet."

About coming for the holidays, he said he would
have to talk to his wife. "She's frightened," he said.

"Frightened?" asked Jadzia critically. "Of what?"

"Momma, she knows what I think and what I say and
where I work." (Hania told me he is a sort of free spirit
in the headquarters. For example, he hates the current
inspection of identification papers — it smacks to him
of Nazism — and he hands his over with a sharp *Bitte*.)
"And she's tired."

"Tired. That I can understand."

"They're all tired," said Andrzej. "These women who
work, and who have families, and who have nothing to
give them to eat, and who have been going through the
same thing month after month. I see them crying, crying. They've had enough. They've had it up to here."

Gosia interjected at one point: "My boss said to me
the other day, 'Is it really cursed, our Poland?'"

Marcin says: "Now I believe nothing. I don't believe rumors. I don't believe propaganda. I just don't
believe."

22 December

WENT TO THE embassy today and passed by the desk
of the Polish security guard who is assumed by every-

one to be planted by his government as a spy. There was a book opened on the desk: Michener's *Chesapeake*. I thought to myself, This emergency state may last some time.

There were about fifteen compatriots, known and unknown, gathered for information. One young couple from the state of Washington. They had both been teaching at the economics school and now said they were leaving. Their Polish adviser was insisting on it, though they hated to. The material difficulties are hard, but the spirit of the people makes up for it, they said. They told a story that when one of the Polish instructors heard that they were leaving, he led them into his office, closed the door, pulled open a drawer of his desk, and took out a box of staples. He then extracted two Solidarity pins that had been hidden underneath, and presented one to each of them as gifts.

They offered to take letters and mail them as soon as they got to Vienna; I quickly wrote a reassuring note home. Despite the extreme circumstances, the embassy has refused to send our letters through the diplomatic pouch, unlike the French embassy, which has opened its pouch to every citizen of France who currently finds himself in Poland. Mine have gone with the Dutch mail, graciously taken by our friend Aneke, who works at that embassy.

23 December

MET DOUG IN the embassy cafeteria for lunch. (If they don't carry our mail, at least they sell us food.) He is here for a year working in a Polish economic institute. Said that on Monday strict rules were laid down — one

must report to work on time; if late, it will count as a
day of absenteeism. There is to be no leaving the office
during work hours; if one must leave, he is obliged to
sign out and state the reason for his departure. "So,"
he said, "I guess it was on Tuesday, we were all sitting
around doing nothing and somebody came in and said
'There's carp!' and everybody said 'Carp!' and dashed
out of the office."

25 December

LAST EVENING Hania, Gosia, Leszek, Jadzia, Frederique — a friend from the Swiss embassy — here for
Wigilia. We began the meal traditionally by offering
each person a piece of our wafer and wishes for the
coming year. "Let us hope," Jadzia said to me, "that
General Jaruzelski will not cause us any more dolor
than he already has."

During the dinner the radio, which had been playing
carols, broke in with General Jaruzelski's address. Jadzia
cried, for the benefit of Frederique, in French, "Shut
him up. I will not put up with that, especially not on
Christmas Eve."

On television there was a children's puppet show of
the biblical story of Christmas and a smoothly filmed
documentary of soldiers' vigils, with lonely recruits
telling us with white puffs of breath their thoughts of
home, while in the foreground licks of fire flashed up
from their garbage bin hearths. The first Western film
since, as everyone now calls it, "the war," was offered at
nine-thirty: Hitchcock's *Rebecca*, a puzzling choice on
this night of holy wonder. "Not really," said Leszek.
"They think they can tempt people from going to
church."

Midnight Mass at our neighborhood church was packed; a soldier, in uniform, with his carbine still tied to his back, joined the communicants before the altar.

27 December

DANUTA, HANIA'S FRIEND from boarding school, visited us this evening, having gotten special permission to come from Lodz to see her parents. She was, as always, in good spirits, though her husband, she told us, has been fired from his engineering firm. He went to work one day last week and found nobody would talk to him. When he finally asked a colleague what was up, he was told, "'You better go see the director.' He was not a real activist," said Danuta, "but whenever there was a Solidarity meeting at work, he was the one who organized it. The ironic thing is that just last month he received an award for one of his designs. Of course there's no chance of his getting any other job with a state enterprise. And the private ones don't have any materials to work with. I suppose," she said, laughing easily, this mother of three, "we'll end up raising mushrooms." I was fascinated, as much by the story, as by Danuta's style in telling it, which was completely free of rancor. Rather than railing at the injustice of the dismissal, she delighted in its absurdity. She comes from a well-educated Catholic family, and like other people of this background whom I have met here, seems above bemoaning the vicissitudes of life under a corrupt and earthly regime.

28 December

WENT TO THE Forum Hotel for lunch today. The restaurant doors, which a few weeks ago were locked with a

sign declaring FOR HOTEL GUESTS ONLY, were now wel-
comingly open. Three tables were occupied. The place
seems not the same without the Arabs. (The resump-
tion of air service last week included almost exclusively
flights to Damascus, Cairo, Tripoli.)

After lunch, waited for a C bus, there in the heart of
the city, my back neatly turned on the Palace of Culture. There was a fine gloaming of a winter's afternoon: the sky lay in variegated sheets of pink and bluish
gray and the creamy intricacies of the Jerozolimskie
Avenue facades stood out in a highlight of icicle and
snow, looking today as noble as the noblest of wintry
northern European street scenes.

Home to find Gregory waiting on the dark stairs.
(All the joy of unannounced visits from friends has returned with the disfunctioning of telephones.) He is
full of insecurity. Said he goes around to people's
apartments and everybody's feeling bad, and he feels
bad too, but they tell him he doesn't know, he can't feel
as bad as they do, he's an outsider, he can always go
home. So he's excluded. His reaction, he said, since
they don't allow him to feel as they do, is to live as they
can't. "I went to Pewex," he told me, "and for the first
time since I've been here bought some things in the
American embassy commissary."

In the evening, over to play chess with Marcin.
(When our games last past the curfew, as they frequently do, I dash across the street home like an escaped convict.) Before I went out, Leszek asked me if I
also liked card games. "They, too, provide an excellent
mental relaxation," he said. "During the war, in Hitler's
Germany, to graduate from officers' training school
one had to know how to play at least two card games. It
was a very good idea. If you were at the front, and

there was no action, you could go crazy just sitting and waiting. But if you had a game of cards to play, it would take your mind off the immediate surroundings and work as a wonderful relaxation."

29 December

WENT TO SAY good-bye to Mrs. Matsuda today, who, with her children, is being recalled to Japan. She was very troubled by this unexpected exodus, and said that in London, their first stop, she is going to "speak the truth" about the situation in Poland, and tell her government representatives that there is no danger in staying here. "I have lived here for six years," she said. "I like Poland. I like Polish people. I have not had coffee for two weeks. In Japan, when you wish something very much you give up eating or drinking the thing you like most. So I do not drink coffee for two weeks, because I wish that things will get better for Poland."

Hania went to Mr. Matsuda's office the other day, as we had been out of contact. He was not there, but she spoke to his secretary, a Polish woman in her ninth month of pregnancy. Her husband is in Italy, and she hasn't heard from him since "the war." (He was supposed to have been back by now.) She doesn't drive, because of the dangerousness of the slippery streets, and stays alone in the apartment, without, of course, the use of a telephone.

Then went for my first lesson with Dr. Zięba since the war. She told me of a friend of hers who works in a factory supply room. She told Dr. Zięba that she used to receive eight hundred items a day on the conveyor belt, now she receives fifty or sixty. "She says that people come to work, but one woman will do this [she screwed an imaginary item clockwise] and the next woman will do this [she screwed the imaginary item counterclockwise]. Most items have to go back through again and again. When one gets through successfully, it is an accident. And this is all done without conference, without strategy. They all of them do it alone, in self-protest."

At home in the evening, more friends over, making light of the situation. There has been a tremendous outpouring of jokes. "What's the government's biggest problem now? What to do with those who survive the winter." "What is the lowest rank in the army? Television commentator." "Do you know the three famous military leaders? Horatio Nelson [hand over one eye], Moshe Dayan [hand over the other eye], Jaruzelski [hands over both eyes]." "Did you hear Jaruzelski is going to change his name? Yes, to Zomosa." There is no school yet, but there are school jokes. "The teacher asks Jacek to name three men who are responsible for bringing Poland into a crisis. Jacek says 'Gierek.' The teacher says 'Very good. Who else?' Jacek says, 'Olszowski.' 'Very good,' says the teacher, 'who else?' Jacek says, 'Jaruzelski.' The teacher, stunned, says, 'Jacek, how can you dare say that our dear general brought Poland into a crisis?' A classmate, Anna, raises her hand and says, 'Jacek always reads three lessons ahead.'"

31 December

A QUIET New Year's Eve at home. Few voiced meditations on the year just passed. Jadzia, who has moved back in with us, shook her head sadly and said, "Terrible, terrible."

"Momma," Gosia prompted her cheerily, "you are living through an interesting time."

Jadzia looked at her and said, "That we suffered all these years to arrive to this."

Life in the new year did not return to normal; rather it acquired another, stranger normalcy.

Institutions reopened and I returned to the Methodist School to resume my classes. I was as pleased to see my students as they were surprised to see me. "You're still here!" Katarzyna and Ryszard blurted out with laughter, as I walked into my five o'clock class. I returned their letters to them, which I had corrected, it seemed, ages ago, and asked if there were any questions. "Yes," said Krzysztof. "How long are you going to stay in Poland?" I was somewhat surprised to see them in such good spirits; at first I assumed it was their youth that kept them from appreciating the seriousness of the last few weeks, but later I saw a similar lack of moroseness in older Poles as well. When I commented on this to Hania, she asked, "What are we supposed to do? Sulk?"

The present circumstances had ushered in a whole new, partly martial language, the words of which my students now eagerly asked the English equivalents of. "*Stan wojenny?*" Tomasz called out (literally, "state of war," which is what had been declared). "*Godzina policyjna?*" asked Wacława (curfew). "*Internowany?*" (interned). "*Spekulant?*" (speculator). Hearing these solemn staples of the military-clad anchorman on the evening news, now shouted in familiar confines, made the students laugh.

I asked them what they had done over the unexpectedly long break.

"I had an experience with the Polish police," said Tomasz, "and then I started working."

"You'll work until the university reopens?"

"Nobody knows."

"Only one person knows," said Agnieszka.

"Who?" I asked.

"Brezhnev," she said casually, to more uncensored chuckles.

After my last lesson I ran into Mrs. Iwanowska getting her coat in the teachers' room. "It wasn't a nice Christmas this year," she commented to me. "Not at all." Then, without a trace of pity, rather as an unbiased historical fact, she said, "We are truly an unfortunate country."

The next day of classes we were informed that there would be a teachers' meeting on Friday. "I wonder what that will be about?" said Piotr. "A guest from the military, perhaps?" I noticed that his Mao jacket was now bereft of its Solidarity pin.

The Matsuda family had returned to Japan, but I continued my lessons with Dr. Zięba. She complained that the disturbing thing now was that nearly every day she had to answer questions. "How many from my staff were Solidarity members? How many of them were heads of departments?" I asked her who conducted the inquiry, and she said someone from the army council.

"He asked me if there was ever any opposition against me as a director. I said no. He said, 'Are you sure there wasn't any?' I tell him again no. He said he knows of one incident and asks me if I remember. And you have to wonder: How does he know this, this officer who has never been to my clinic before? He laughed, and said, 'We know everything about you.' Now I know that someone from my clinic has told about these things. And that is what is bad. From now on I must suspect everyone; I will look at them all with new eyes.

"You must know the special atmosphere of these meetings," she said. "It is not tense. They smile and laugh and talk smoothly and then every now and then" — she pushed her hand out and turned it sharply — "they twist into you."

No soldier appeared at the Friday teachers' meeting, though Mr. Kuczma, in a grave tone, ordered that there was to be no union activity whatsoever and no discussion in the classrooms. "The students come here to learn English. Nothing else. So we are to teach them English. And nothing else." It made me feel uneasy about my talks the first day back. He added that all students must have their registration cards with them at all times.

Life took on novel, though quickly assimilated, patterns. State-run firms were under army regulations. When I asked one of my students, a LOT (Polish airline) employee, where she had been for a week, she replied winsomely: "I've been militarized." Other students would ask to excuse themselves from class to attend Mass: for the interned, for the nation, for Piłsudski. The curfew inspired among young people a practice of sleeping over after parties. The price increases inspired a macabre humor about the elderly. "Did you hear senior citizens have been banned from Warsaw parks? Yes, to prevent them from eating the bark off the trees." Events became divided into *przed wojną* and *po wojnie* (prewar and postwar). At home, letters that had once been delivered opened, accompanied by a feeble note about damage upon arrival, now bore a straightforward red stamp proclaiming: OCENZUROWANO. One I received carried the more winning message: NIE OCENZUROWANO. Our tipsy mailman, also militarized, arrived in a new tall fur hat with a gold eagle nestled in the front and a blue military frock coat, as elegant as I had ever seen him. Telephones returned to working order, but, like the mail, with a confessional note of censorship. In the initial seconds of any conversation, one heard the mechanically repeated message: "*Rozmowa kontrolowana. Rozmowa kontrolowana.*" (The conversation is being controlled.) Movie theaters reopened; our neighborhood cinema played *Picnic at Hanging Rock*, which Hania and I went to see immediately. With its sun-scorched hills and white lace dresses, it seemed no more inconsistent with our daily experience than the Soviet film at the Friendship Theater: *Life Is Beautiful.*

A few newspapers returned to share space on the newsstands with *Żołnierz Polski* (*Polish Soldier*). The first issue of *Życie Warszawy* which I bought carried a front-page story with the headline: "There Will Be More Cement." On the back page, in the column, "In the Kitchen and Around the Table," the unenviable food writer addressed one of the few things left — *płatki*:

> Everybody knows that a horse is beautiful and strong only when it is fed oats. And so, as well, mammals. Do oats work differently on us? No! After oats we have beautiful, luxuriant, shiny hair . . . healthy, robust young skin and complexion, and a regular stomach (also something important!). They do not threaten us with ulcers or stomach cancers or duodenitis, and in general we beautify ourselves.

There followed recipes for Cutlets with Sugared Oats and Macaroni and Oats.

One constantly heard stories of vetting and life in the internment camps. Dr. Zięba told me of a friend, a television journalist, who had recently had her *verifikacja*. She was brought before a commission of three and questioned for over an hour. At the conclusion, she was asked to sign an oath of loyalty. It was the first time during the entire questioning that she became angry. She said that the fact that she had been to the West and had returned to Poland proved her loyalty far beyond any signature. And so she refused. They let her go with pay. She is one of five in a family of six working people who have been laid off but are still receiving salaries. "You see what a rich country Poland is?" asked Dr. Zięba. "What other country is so rich to pay so many people not to work?"

News brought back from the internment camps varied. There was much talk of frigid cells, illness, lack of food and medicine. St. Martin's Church in the Old Town began a collection of blankets, clothes, and foodstuffs for the inmates. One of our neighbors went to visit her son, who had been given the fateful assignment of night duty at the Solidarity headquarters on Mokotowska Street on December 12. He was at Białołęka, perhaps the best known of the Warsaw area camps, and she was allowed one visit a month. They met in a room with other prisoners and family members, each group seated at a desk furnished with a microphone, while various policemen surveyed the scene. There were, she said, occasional outbursts. She had suggested to her son that, when freed, his best option would be to go abroad to their relatives in France. He exclaimed loudly: "I am a Pole. I was born in Poland. I was raised in Poland. Poland is my country. I will live in Poland until my death. If I don't have work, if I don't have bread, it doesn't matter, I will never leave Poland!" Others, no less patriotic, would take advantage, when it came, of the offer of freedom at the cost of exile.

He had told his mother that the conditions at the camp were relatively good. The internees walked an hour every day. They had radio speakers in their cells, and some were allowed small transistors. Though they all complained of not getting enough to eat. (Knowing what food was like at home, I shuddered to think of it in prison.) They were not, he said, restricted in their contacts with other internees. They had long talks, card games, foreign language lessons. The three languages taught were English, German, and French; a few people took over the instruction of the others. One day was designated English day, another French day, another German, during which all the internees taking the lessons were to speak nothing but that language. Apparently, they followed this rule rigidly, especially when addressing their guards.

Despite the concern about vetting, none ever took place at the Methodist School and, despite the virulent anti-American campaign, no one ever came to question or observe my teaching there. At the beginning of February, Krzysztof came up after one of our five o'clock classes and consoled me. "Our government is saying a lot of bad things about America," he said. "'Oh, America. America is very bad.' But it is just the government. The Poles, the average Pole, likes America and Americans. Because they want us to be free."

A high school student, Jacek, asked me if I had a copy of Orwell's *1984* to lend him. "Our English teacher tells us Poland is just like that now."

Packages arrived at the Methodist School with an ever greater frequency and variety. "A gift from the Icelandic nation to the Polish nation," read the label on a five-pound container of herring which each of us received, courtesy of the Icelandic Institution of Church Assistance, the Icelandic Catholic Church, and the Icelandic Union of Working People. At home, as well, packages arrived from family and friends, one of whom, in southern Maryland, had neatly used as stuffing paper a week's worth of *Washington Post* reporting on the imposition of martial law (a gesture that won admiring respect from my Polish family and friends).

Hania's aunt Bocia still came regularly with fresh fish for the cat. One afternoon, while Hania was out and I was lying down, Bocia knocked at the open bedroom door and asked if she could have a word with me. She took her mincing steps into the room and sat daintily at the foot of the bed. A cigarette protruded from its yellowed plastic holder. It was perhaps the first time that we had ever been alone to talk, which made my natural uneasiness in her presence all the more complete. She prefaced her remarks by pointing out that I surely knew how close she felt to Hania. (Indeed, she was not only an authentic aunt, but she had been Hania's sole guardian for the first five years of her life, while her mother languished in prison for political reasons.) It was in knowing how much she loved Hania, she said, that I would be able to appreciate what she was about to say to me. "You see, Tomasz, what things are like here now," she said sternly, using Polish instead of French to be sure of her meaning. "There is no hope for Hania here. Nothing is going to change. She will just waste away here. You should both go back to America now. Take her with you away from this." She went on in this way for several minutes, and when she was certain that I understood, rose from the bed unsteadily, shaken by the selfless, dutiful sending off of her beloved niece.

With the waning of winter, some of the harshness lessened. Krystyna finally got her passport and went off with her children to join her husband in America. Replacing her as Polish teacher at the embassy was Piotr. I found him one day sitting all alone in the library reading a magazine, his grazed head set just inches above the page, his glasses fallen on his nose, his Mao jacket enveloping his frame. Glimpsed through the two sets of glass doors, he seemed to be in a sort of quarantine, calmly if suspiciously ensconced in the eye of the storm. I wondered how his militant teaching methods would be received, though with my attitude toward American embassy personnel firmly established, I could not help but think that the two of them deserved each other.

Andrzej still came regularly from Lodz to see his mother, while, through all the crises and turmoils of the last two years, the other son failed to appear once from Kielce. Nevertheless, Andrzej's superior devotion was not always rewarded.

"The factories aren't doing anything," Jadzia complained to him one evening in April. "They don't have the materials to do anything with."

"In Lodz the factories are still running, Momma."

"Yes!" shouted Jadzia. "With materials from the Soviets, producing goods for the Soviets!"

"*Mommmma!*" he cried, exasperated. "Where do you hear these things? Radio Free Europe?"

"No. They don't let me catch it. But there are others I can get."

"BBC. Voice of America. They're full of lies, too."

He was in an especially unpleasant mood. His new avocation — carpentry — was going badly, and he had resigned himself to longer service in the party; as a result, he fell more than usually prone to its defense. He insisted, for instance, that the party had won.

"How can you say that?" challenged Hania. "When practically the whole society is against it?"

"And who has demoralized society for the last thirty-five years?" asked his mother. The subject was dropped in deference to Jadzia's heart.

"It's a different atmosphere in Lodz," Andrzej said. "There the people are tired. They live in fear, simply. Their most fundamental fear is their work. They're scared to death of losing their jobs. The second fear is of not getting the basic necessities of life: food, clothes, washing products. This is what their life is like now. Yes, Panie Tomku," he said, looking to me as if to someone incapable of understanding, "the future of this country doesn't include anything pleasant."

The others went off to the living room, and Andrzej continued talking to me, smoking his cigarette. A softer, somewhat professorial look passed over his small, dark, pessimistic face. "We Poles are lacking any rationalism," he said. "What you see is a tremendous emotionalism, but there is never any rationalism, thinking things out. We don't think anything out. Now we need more than ever a sense of unity. We mustn't revolt, but build." These remarks reminded me of a line I had recently come across in reading the nineteenth-century poet Cyprian Norwid: "I am from a nation," he wrote, "in which for nearly a hundred years every book has come out too late, and every deed too early."

"Panie Tomku, would that Poland were a normal

country," he mused, "and its citizens as well. I mean, I wish we could sit here and discuss the football match, the weather, Faulkner or Hemingway. But we can't, or don't. Instead, the situation forces us to keep on harping on the same things — politics, what tomorrow will bring. It's a shame.

"Poles like to blame all their difficulties on the partition, the foreign domination," he said. "'Look, we were lost, cut up between Austria, Prussia, and Russia. *My biedni Polacy*! (We poor Poles!) What can we do? Look!' We like to think we are unique in this, but we aren't. Other countries suffered the same things: Greece under the Turks. 'Oh!' but we cry. 'We, we Poles!' It's an easy thing to say. Very easy.

"Another important characteristic: we have no sense of humor about ourselves. We cannot laugh at ourselves. Oh, we can laugh at others; we can mock the Russians; we can roar at the Russian teacup with the handle built inside. But let someone make the same joke about us and we object indignantly. We can't look in a mirror, stand back, and laugh at what we see. But," he concluded, smiling, "in the final analysis, Panie Tomku, we're fine. Funnily fine."

IV
Great Night

WIELKANOC (Great Night) is the Polish word for Easter, and the other days of Holy Week are also "Great." On Great Friday afternoon, Leszek, Gosia, Hania, and I went to visit the "tombs" in the Old Town churches. It was at St. Anne's, the Academic Church (where I had stood to watch the cardinal's coffin passed across Castle Square a year before), that the tradition of tombs began. Clandestinely and at great risk, Polish artists came every Great Friday of the German occupation to decorate in a personal way the grave of Christ. It was a time during which the Easter message of suffering and resurrection carried an irresistible meaning for Poles. As with so many Polish religious traditions, this one has not only continued, but flourished.

We took our place at the end of a long queue stretching out of St. Anne's, from which point we could see queues for the other churches traced across the square below. The early April sky would turn dark with thunder-clouds, sending down on us thick wet flakes of spring snow, then would open up to an intense, wintry blue. "Like a kaleidoscope," the Poles say, and I remembered Jadzia's warning earlier in the week: "Whenever Easter and Passover coincide, the weather is miserable." As novel as it was for me to be queuing to look at church crafts, it seemed at the same time the most appropriately spent Good Friday I had ever known.

At St. Anne's we were led past the tomb, like mourners paying our last respects, after a half hour's wait. It consisted of a plaster white column topped by a gold cross draped in black, atop which sat the Polish eagle, crown intact. A crown of thorns circled the column with three ribbons wrapped in it, two black and one long red-and-white one that trailed down to the floor to decorate the slain body of Christ.

St. Martin's Church, on the next street, displayed a tall, thin wooden cross, from the left arm of which hung an anchor, symbol of the wartime resistance movement, and from the right arm the dates "'56, '68, '70, '76, '80," written in chalk — with a space left for the inevitable one to follow. People approached the cross, stood for a minute or two in silence, and then passed on.

Great Saturday is the Polish day of "blessing the baskets." Jadzia and Hania made one up at home with the necessary ingredients: bread, kielbasa, painted eggs, salt on a little dish, with sprigs of dill and parsley planted throughout, and a white linen cloth to cover the top. What a pretty sight that wicker basket of peasant fare was to someone brought up on synthetic green straw and pink marshmallow chicks!

Hania and I took the basket to our neighborhood church. Inside we inched our way toward a table rapidly filling with paschal offerings. From a distance the baskets had looked almost identical, but here, under closer examination, they were visibly varied, with eggs of diverse artistry, lace intricacies overlapping some sides, bright green shoots of dill, and the occasional lamb standing honorifically in the center.

The priest read a few prayers, took up a brush, dipped it in holy water, and then waved it vigorously up and down the length of the table. He invoked the customary wishes of the holiday, ending with the unusual benediction (to me at least) of "*Smacznego jajka!*" (Tasty eggs!). I was to hear it in the next few days as a common Easter greeting among friends, along with the even more improbable *Wesołego jajka!* (Merry eggs!).

On Sunday morning, at four o'clock, I went alone to attend the cathedral Mass. I walked through our silent, empty neighborhood and had that rare sensation of feeling that I was the first person up in the city. All was dark. Once on Grójecka Street I took a spot midway between the tram stop and the bus stop. At last a taxi approached and I waved it over.

"So early?" the driver asked.

"To the Resurrection," I said. "One must get there early."

As usual, however, I had overestimated the difficulties of arriving on time, and found myself locked out of the cathedral on a blustery and ill-lit Świętojańska Street. I prowled the hallowed quarter for a while and, when I returned, joined two small elderly women who banged with undue ferocity upon the portals. They opened shortly to take us in, unveiling an impassive young priest, who commented: "You could have still slept."

The procession was long and impressive. It was led by a crucifer and a priest carrying a small statue of Christ standing. Then five banner bearers, the banners like dusty sails atop their lengthy poles. All were upright except for one slung over the shoulder of a long-haired young woman in a white robe. Rows of priests followed. Behind them came a group of six hoary elders in black suits, gray silk ties, and white gloves, each clutching the wooden pole of a six-pointed canopy of cloth. Beneath the canopy, the bishop walked, bearing, with his elbows

pointed outward, a heavy gold cross. A formal gentleman hung on each arm in a posture of support.

They were followed — as winter then to spring — by
a dozen young girls in Mazowsze folk dress: flowered
vests and thick cloth skirts of bold red, green, and orange
stripes. Then came a troupe of six little girls in white
dresses and floral head wreaths. Their leader carried a
small basket of dried flowers, and every six or seven
steps would turn and gamely toss the cuttings at her
charges, strewing the stone floor with petals. The girls,
at each toss, would fall quietly to one knee.

The Mass lasted two hours and contained one hymn
familiar to me from the Episcopal Church, "Jesus Christ
Is Risen Today," sung more slowly and with more so-
lemnity than I had ever heard it. At the dismissal, we
were asked to remember those who could not be with
their families this holiday. There was no need to explain
this reference.

Easter breakfast was at Leszek's apartment in Mokotów. His wife was away for the holiday, and he had taken
advantage of her absence by inviting us all, though
Jadzia, out of a sense of propriety, stayed home. Hania,
Gosia, and I arrived and found the novice host hurriedly throwing on his tie and jacket as he answered the
door. This done, he led us into the apartment. It was a
Gomułka of thirty-five square meters — small for any
family; claustrophobic for two teenage children and a
husband and wife who don't communicate. Yet given
charge this day, Leszek added an appealing domestic
quality to his impeccably gracious manner. He offered
us a choice of cakes — *babki* and *mazurki* — that he and
his son had baked and that now sat on stony slabs atop
the piano. Here, amongst the *mazurki*, I found a small

slip of paper slightly larger than a postage stamp. The top half carried a black-and-white depiction of the Pope, the bottom half the words: "Solidarity wishes you faith and hope in these Easter days of 1982."

"Solidarity lives," said Leszek, noticing my wonderment."

"Where did you get it?" I asked.

"From colleagues at work," he replied nonchalantly.

Gosia passed around a plate of quartered, hard-boiled eggs. When each guest had a slice, he offered it to his neighbor, who took a bite, then kissed the other three times on the cheek (occasionally leaving a smudge of yolk) while extending all good wishes. Then the receiver of the egg would offer his own, and in this way the process was repeated around the room. It was identical to that of the wafer at Wigilia, though I found the egg somehow gave it an ingenuous appeal.

Great Monday is a holiday throughout Poland and, as on All Souls' Day, businesses and offices are closed. Traditionally it is the day of Śmigus Dyngus, when it is the custom for young boys to douse girls with buckets of water. (One can find postcards with colorful woodcuts of youthful peasants cavorting about a well.) Most Varsovians claim that the drenching is carried on now only in villages, though Hania, a year or so before, had had a small bottle of perfume emptied on her as she made her way to her morning tram.

All weekend the citizens of Warsaw had been expecting another incarnation of sorts — Solidarity's. Walking in the Old Town on Great Friday, we had seen a notice, taped to a wall, of the first underground radio broadcast, planned for this evening. By Sunday, similar notices had appeared in most of the churches. At breakfast when Hania mentioned casually that the broadcast was tonight, Jadzia cried, "At nine o'clock on frequency seven!" and nearly toppled her tea.

In the evening Hania and I went to dinner at Aunt Janusia's in Mokotów, where, though we had no way of knowing it then, there was to be the best reception of the broadcast. Some of her family had come for the holiday: her daughter, Helena, a stern, matronly woman; Helena's husband, Władek, a tall, bombastic gentleman with an elegant white mustache; and their son Łukasz, who lived with his wife and four children in a small town near Poznan. At eight we sat down to *bigos*.

"Real Polish *bigos*," said Uncle Władek, advertising the dish to the foreigner.

"Ha, for these days real," said Helena.

"Real Polish wartime *bigos*," he corrected himself, and executed a head bow in deference to his wife.

"Łukasz, how's the food situation where you are?" asked Hania.

"Warsaw is plentiful by comparison," he said. "All we have in the shops are shelves of vinegar."

"So that's where it is," said Hania.

"There's little food. No shampoo."

"What about toothpaste?"

"Toothpaste? It's not a necessity," he said, then added, laughing, "if you don't eat, what do you need toothpaste for?"

"Things are not so bad that people are starving," said his mother sharply. "Not so bad that we need handouts from the West. I bristle with rage when I see those trucks coming into Warsaw loaded with food. We don't need their goods," she said in a tone of indignation. "I would rather eat Polish blueberries than Swedish salmon any day."

Uncle Władek and Łukasz began checking their watches a good twenty minutes before nine; at five to, we all moved into the adjoining room. Władek fiddled with the dial of what looked like a prewar radio; Łukasz manipulated the antenna; his mother, seated in a corner, took up her knitting; Hania and I settled down on the couch. There was a terrible burst of static ("Just like during the occupation," said Uncle Władek fondly) before a female voice came through that we knew as "ours." She gave instructions: If you hear well, blink your apartment lights three times; if you can hear moderately well, blink them twice; if you have difficulty hearing, blink them once. Łukasz ran to turn off all the lights, then blinked them three times. We had a view onto a back lot, so could not gauge the response, though later we were to hear that the large ten-story apartment complexes to the south of us had twinkled like space stations.

The words, coming through distant yet clear, had a mesmerizing effect on us. Aunt Helena looked up from her knitting with a triumphant smile, and wordlessly we gazed from one to another with marvel. Łukasz stood motionless in the middle of the room, his one hand extended in a gesture of silence, though no one had spoken for minutes. It didn't matter that barely any news was reported. (The announcer turned the segment over to a balladeer.) It was a news broadcast in which the biggest news was the broadcast itself. For days after people talked not of what they had heard, but that they had heard (and how well they had heard), and not of what they would hear, but that they would hear, again. A brave voice from a secret and widely hunted chamber had been transmitted over the city's airwaves and had spoken to the suffering of resurrection.

V
The August Pilgrimage

Forth, pilgrim, forth! Forth,
* beste out of thee stal!*
Know thee contree, look up,
* thank God of al;*
Hold the hye way, and lat thy
* gost thee lede:*
And trouthe shal delivere, hit
* is no drede.*
*   — Geoffrey Chaucer,*
*   "Balade de bon conseyl"*

ON A MILD EVENING at the beginning of August, Hania and I took the bus downtown to St. Anne's Church on Castle Square. We had received a call that a group of pilgrims — a half dozen of whom were to stay in our apartment — had arrived from France. A few days later, on August 5, we returned to the church with my bags for loading. I had a sleeping bag and two knapsacks; the latter contained changes of socks and underwear, a second pair of shoes and pants, three shirts, two sweaters, a foldable raincoat, an inflatable mattress, an umbrella, and toiletries. There were also some cans of corned beef, sticks of kielbasa, and, due to the kindness of the French, La Vache Qui Rit cheese in neatly packaged wheels. The omission of a tent can only be ascribed to an optimistic and wholly unrealistic yearning for the days of Reymont's *Pilgrimage to Jasna Góra.*

Władysław Reymont (1867–1925) is best known for his novel *The Peasants,* which helped earn him the 1924 Nobel Prize in Literature. Yet one of his first, and still lesser known, works is a small book written of the pilgrimage to Częstochowa (Jasna Góra is the site of the shrine within the city), as he walked it in 1894. The critic and translator Franck L. Schoell wrote of it in his French translation: "These simple notes of the road, nervously scribbled on the knees by the young writer . . . are, in reality, one of the most beautiful works of Władysław

Reymont and . . . one of the most joyous of Polish literature at the end of the nineteenth century." It was in
reading this work in a Warsaw library that summer that
I learned of the old-time pilgrimages of wayside inns,
peasant marchers, and beddings of hay in country barns.
And, by dreamy calculation, I transferred the same
to now.

I had read other reports, written mostly by students
and published in Catholic bulletins, of more modern
pilgrimages, and indeed I had met people who had recently participated. It was interesting that while the
younger generation was marked by unadulterated enthusiasm, older Poles to whom I told my plans often said
to me sadly, as they say of so much else in nostalgic Poland, "It's not what it once was." So, I thought, if the
nightlife and the theater, and the kielbasa and the trains,
and the education system and the chocolate, and apartment houses and bookstores, and manners and men's
dress, and the Grand Hotel in Sopot and the intellectual
life in Krakow and on and on and on were not now as
they once had been, why should the pilgrimage be? Yet
what was curious was that while the items and institutions most often cited as suffering from decline did so as
a result of neglect and apathy, the pilgrimage was, to
these people, in the unique position of declining while
in the throes of universal attention and growth. The
numbers of pilgrims increased markedly from year to
year. When, at the end of the school year, I asked my
students their summer plans, I found that there would
be at least one student from every class going on the pilgrimage. That evening going to meet the French we had
found several busloads. And it was this popularization
of the pilgrimage that, these older people feared, had
caused it to lose, if not only its charm, its meaning as well.

The object of the pilgrimage — the Byzantine painting called the Black Madonna — is a national icon of immeasurable importance. Once venerated for her miraculous powers, the Black Madonna is now more strictly regarded as a source of faith, hope, and protection, as well as something of a symbol of the nation itself.

The painting is believed to have arrived in Poland in 1382, a fact that made this year's pilgrimage dually significant; for it marked the six hundredth anniversary of the Black Madonna, as well as the first time the August pilgrimage had been held during a period of self-imposed martial law.

Almost from the time of her arrival, the Black Madonna was revered by Poles. Her image as protectress was indelibly established in the middle of the seventeenth century when invading Swedish armies captured all of Poland, only to be repelled in their siege of Jasna Góra. Henryk Sienkiewicz popularized this historic event in his novel *The Deluge*, and the pilgrimage flourished after its publication in 1886. Though the first walking pilgrimage from Warsaw took place well before this, in 1711. The Feast of the Assumption, on August 15, became a popular date, for it marked the point in the summer at which peasants were usually finished with the harvest.

Yet the fascination that the Black Madonna exerts on Poles goes beyond her role as protectress and is drawn from the mirror-like features and history of the painting itself. She looks out hurtfully with a heavy-lidded, sloe-eyed regard; disturbing her chocolaty complexion are two, long, vertical scars on her cheek, symbols of the desecration perpetrated by bandit nobles in the fifteenth century.

During the Second World War, hidden beneath the

Paulist monastery at Jasna Góra, the picture, like the nation, suffered more damage. It is this, I think, along with the weary, wounded, universal gaze, that makes the Black Madonna such a vibrant symbol for Poles. For she transcends her symbolism and lives and suffers and endures in the same way that her people do. One sees on city churches, for her feast day, banners proclaiming: "Our Lady who is always with us, who has always helped us throughout the centuries." And one is staggered by the fantastic statement of centuries' help from a people so uniformly forgotten. Yet it is her constant succor and embodiment of hope — during plagues, partitions, occupations, martial law — that this thanks refers to. And it is a succor born of its own suffering, for she has come down from above her altar to be made one, in experience and pain, with the people of Poland.

Her power has touched a diversity of men. Hilaire Belloc composed a ballade to her, calling her the "help of the half-defeated," and traveled from England to pin it on the wall of her chapel. The ruling governor-general in Poland, Hans Franck, understood the influence of the Black Madonna well enough to outlaw pilgrimages to her shrine during the German occupation. Franck, who at war's end was tried at Nuremberg and executed, wrote in his journal: "The Church is for the Polish people the focal point around which they rally and which shines out forever in silence; this is the reason it fulfills for them the function of perpetual light. When all the lights went out for Poland, there were always present the Holy Virgin of Częstochowa and the Church. You must never forget it." During the Gdansk shipyard strikes in 1980, Lech Wałęsa took on as one of his duties the passing around of votive cards of the Black Madonna. Regarding the pin of her which became inseparable from his lapel, he told Western news reporters unabashedly: "She protects me." After the signing of the strike agreements in the port city of Szczecin, the strike chairman there, Marian Jurczyk, took the microphone and told the workers' guard: "Take that picture of Our Lady off the gate, but give her all the credit. She kept us going." During martial law young Poles replaced the outlawed Solidarity pins on their own lapels with pins of the Black Madonna set against a backdrop of the Polish flag.

That August afternoon Hania and I found the street in front of the church parked thick on both sides with transport trucks. The doors of the drivers' cabins were printed with the names of the private owners and their firms — an impressive show of the Church's resources. Each group's color combination was indicated on its truck's canvas; in some cases appropriately colored flags blanketed windshields. We found the yellow-and-white truck, a double-hitched affair, near the end of one of the files. Three good-spirited young men were at the back loading the truck; they affixed a number, with a piece of wire, to each bag, then gave the owner a copy of the number. That was all; I would see them next at our first night's camp when they would unload the two full trucks. Then the following morning they would load them up again, for a new unloading, thirty kilometers away, that same night. And so it would go for nine days. Hania asked if the walking was difficult. "Only the first three days," said one of the men. "The first three are the longest. After that you just breeze along." Encouraging as I found that comment then, I was later to see it as nothing more than the facile wisdom of a man who drives to Częstochowa.

A few days earlier I had registered at the church and

had received, with the payment of some złotys, three round, yellow-and-white badges (which were to be sewn, I was instructed, on hat, breast, and hip pockets), a pilgrimage songbook, and a paper containing a schedule of our route and a list of pilgrimage guidelines. Now, with my bags loaded, I had no duties until the evening Mass. Hania left to take the bus back home, and I sat in a nearby park to read over the guidelines of the march:

> The aim of the pilgrimage is an internal transformation and a personal meeting of the pilgrim with God. We want to thank Mary for her care over Poland and to assist Pope John Paul II through our prayers.
>
> Going with the "17" Group are both Christians connected to the church as well as nonbelievers, searching together with us on the path to the center of Christ. The pilgrimage has an uncommon character of wandering retreat with a rich program of various forms of activity, using words and meditations, conferences and discussions, as well as contacts with the Eucharist and sacramental pardon.
>
> The route covers 245 kilometers and calls for about 30 kilometers to be covered each day, in 5 to 6 stages over various roads (often fields) without regard to weather conditions.
>
> You should take on the journey a tent with mattresses, sleeping bags, and blankets. Change of clothes and the rest of your things are to be put in a traveling bag or backpack to be carried by the trucks. You should take on your person a haversack of food for the entire day — fruit, beverage, cooking gear, and an enamel cup.
>
> Shoes are very important — scout shoes, adidas [the general word for sneakers in Polish], or sandals with covered heels (one size too large, stuffed with a filling of

sponge or sea grass — not rubber). Shoes must be comfortable, and it's very helpful if they're already broken in. Socks — doubled; cotton ones underneath and thick woolen ones on top. On your head, a hat with a sun visor.

Personal medicines should also be carried in the haversack, especially salicylic alcohol, talcum or foot powder, vitamins, and lump sugar. En route, bandages, elastic as well as plastic, may be necessary.

The rules of the pilgrimage do not allow smoking, nor the drinking of alcohol either during the march or at night campings, nor the taking off or rolling up of shirts, nor the wearing of shorts. The pilgrimage has a penitential, not carnivalistic, character!

Cooperation for the common good of all is an important part of the pilgrimage. Night quiet will be observed after nine o'clock. On the pilgrimage there are no campfires. During the entire pilgrimage there are as well no coeducational tents or barns.

I got up to go to Mass. The church, on this warm afternoon, was full of pilgrims, mostly young and mostly standing, filling the back aisles, the vestibule, the sidewalk outside. Assisting at the Mass was an East German priest who emphasized the fact that he was the only East German priest who had been allowed by his government to come. Following the Mass came instructions on the next day's start, read by a Polish priest in infused and often whimsical versions of Polish, German, and French. For example, he mentioned in Polish that a group of pilgrims who had left Warsaw that morning had been unable to find water along the first day's route. In French he gave the same distressing news, though amended it, in the throaty admonition of a Parisian market vendor, with, "*Mais . . . il faut pas exagérer.*" Occasionally a particularly persistent French word would work its way into a German sentence or vice versa; this he handled always with good-natured aplomb. We were to meet, he told us, here at the church at seven o'clock the next morning to begin the pilgrimage.

In the evening the leaders of the French group invited Hania and me to dinner at the Victoria Hotel. There, under the chandeliers of the Canaletto Room, we fêted our last night before penitence and sacrifice with unrationed slices of chateaubriand and bottles of Polish Żywiec beer.

"*La bière finale*," said Laurent, with what I took to be a reference to the morning's ban, and not the country's dismal brewing state.

We arrived home late and drank to our health from a bottle of Calvados Bernadette had brought from Normandy. When, at last, I went to bed, it was already the next day, the day of the pilgrimage, and it was with a feeling of satiety and light-headedness that, I knew very well, did not befit a pilgrim.

I

A brilliant blue summer morning. After saying goodbye to Hania, I caught up with the French at the bus stop, where an uncommon commuter circle had formed: half-French and pioneering, half-Polish and staring. One man in particular fed his curiosity. He had on the simplest of Polish summer working dress: a white shirt open at the neck and baggy gray trousers over socks and sandals. He carried the prerequisite worn and tattered briefcase. His face was largely creased and had an air of resigned melancholy. He was old enough to have seen, fought in, the war, and I thought as he watched us: He has lived a harder life than any of us have, and is still living it. I approached him.

"We're walking with the pilgrimage to Częstochowa," I said.

His countenance became transformed.

"Bravo! Bravo!" he said, clasping my arm in his hand. "Excellent. I'm very happy to hear." When he learned that I lived in the neighborhood, he said, "When you return from Częstochowa, come to my place for some coffee. There. You see that balcony straight ahead on the first floor? That's my apartment. Come over some evening when you get back. My wife is no longer living, so I am alone. And I'm always home in the evenings. I'll be interested to hear about the pilgrimage." Our bus came. I thanked him, and he wished us his best.

Reymont's pilgrimage began not at St. Anne's, but at a church in Praga, on the other side of the Vistula. He wrote of the pilgrims gathered there in 1894: "There are here only the real sorts of people . . . their faces frustrated, darkened by the heavy heat, their features are coarse and their clothes gray . . . I feel terribly foreign and alone."

In front of St. Anne's the crowd was predominantly young and had the color and animation of youth. It grew continually as the morning Mass inside proceeded, filling up the street and square so that policemen were brought in to redirect the traffic and to keep an eye on the potentially threatening aggregation. Each bus that pulled to a stop deposited more pilgrims into the Mass. Their dress conjured a pleasant day's outing in the woods; distinguishing it from American clothing was the absence of lettering on T-shirts and the women's preference for skirts (long, unfashionable, floriferous) above boots and socks. There was an impressive array, on many chests, of a sort of religious garden salad: varied pins of the Black Madonna and Maksymilian Kolbe, crucifixes and crosses (some painted in the national colors, red and white), group identification patches, pilgrimage badges. Pilgrims stood or milled about, a bit impatient yet generally buoyant; most seemed aligned to groups of friends or classmates. The only comparison I could make in all this to Reymont's day was the sentiment I felt of alienation. And that was identical.

At last I saw a familiar face, that of a student, Marek, a history major from my four o'clock class. "Have you seen how many people are here?" he asked. "It looks like half of Warsaw is going to Częstochowa."

Finally our group, with its yellow-and-white cross, started out, allowing each of us those gratifying and long-anticipated first steps. (Was it not Belloc who said of such ventures: "Your first step is taken with your soul in the sky"?) The people who had been standing and watching now waved us on, lifting our hearts to where indeed our souls already were.

We marched across Marszałkowska Street, the main thoroughfare of the city, where policemen held up jams of unhurried, Victory-signing lorry drivers and tram conductors beneath the approving gaze of office workers perched on upper-story balconies ("That's the Historical Institute of the Polish Revolutionary Movement," Marek called to me contentedly). Farther down, slicing our way diagonally in a back-street exodus of the city, the crowds persisted, larger always near churches. We passed a government building (the red, convex plaques of crowded script by the door), its ground-floor windows opened wide to the fine summer morning. Through one of them I saw a young clerk standing behind his

desk, reading a file he held in his hands. As the sound
of our march reached his ears, he closed the file and
walked to the window, pausing for a moment before signaling V and turning again to his desk and file. We
passed a factory where the workers sat atop the brick
entrance walls (à la Gdansk) in their baggy, dust gray
coveralls, making this same stub-fingered sign and giving
hard, deep, knowing looks to us, eye to eye.

We crossed over Jerozolimskie Avenue and onto Grójecka. With tram lines bisecting the street, the onlookers
lined only the right side as we reduced the number
of traffic lanes to one. I found the faces of the elderly
women the most moving. They too, many of them, gave
the V sign. When they looked at us it was often with
streaks of tears rolling down their cavernous cheeks and
with such intensity that my own eyes nearly dampened
in reply. "You, you, my son, are going to Częstochowa!
You are going to see the Black Madonna!" I imagined
the feelings behind their gazes were not those of strangers to other strangers, but of mothers to their children.
As the recipient of such an unexpected public outpouring of emotion, I was carried into a sort of ecstasy the
likes of which I had never known before.

We continued in a southwesterly direction down Grójecka, leading into my neighborhood of Ochota. As
we walked, the priest and leader of our group, Father Czuma, spoke, as he'd been doing from the start,
through the microphone: "We would like to thank the
citizens of Warsaw who have so kindly come out today to
bid us farewell and wish us Godspeed. Pray for us in the
days ahead, as we will need your prayers to give us
strength to accomplish our mission. And let us all pray
for Poland, that she may finally be a free and indepen-
dent nation."

Farther along we came to streets dear in their familiarity — Wery Kostrzewy, Opaczewska — there my tram stop, there my newsstand, there my tailor, there my wife, magically incarnated with a plastic cup of nameless juice in her hand (*napój firmowy* — a firm drink) which she broke through the front lines to get to me.

"How do you feel?" she asked, handing me the cup and falling in step by my side.

"Fantastic. I feel like I'm part of an army that has just liberated the city."

"Did you see? . . . No, you couldn't have. . . . There were two girls who stepped out of the march and walked up to two policemen and gave them flowers and a cross. And you know, they just stood there, looking sort of silly, holding onto them . . . and there were a couple of soldiers who were watching the march and giving the V sign back. And there were other soldiers holding flowers. And, Tom, oh, you should have seen the French come out. They're really a lot of them, two full groups, I think, and they marched up chanting, '*Vive la Pologne! Vive la Pologne!*' . . . and in Polish, too, '*Niech żyje Polska! Niech żyje Polska!*' . . . and anybody who wasn't already in tears broke down. And there's an Italian group too, not as numerous as the French, but they sound as if they are. Well, as they came up the boys started running up on the sidewalks and kissing all the Polish girls."

"The liberator's syndrome," I said. "They must have it too."

"Look, Tom," she said, looking around. "I'm not going any farther with you. The rest you do yourself. Take care of yourself, you promise me? And call as soon as you get there. Good luck. Bye-bye."

The crowds diminished as we headed ever farther

out of the city, and into the lilliputian land of stunted streetlamps and wee telephone poles that surrounds the airport. We came to a bridge raised over railway tracks, from the mild rise of which we could look back on the capital from which we had just come, as well as look down upon the open road which bid us on.

"I wonder what happened in Warsaw?" said Marek, looking over the exodus that stretched undiminished to either side. "There seems to be a disconcertingly large number of people leaving."

To either side of us now were simple, flat-roofed houses, often with buckets of water set up at the ends of driveways on small stools or tables. They were unattended (kindness without a human face) or, at some places, surrounded by the entire family. Pilgrims broke off from the march and, with some scuffle, dipped in their enamel cups. Before leaving, they thanked their hosts — *Bóg zapłać* (God repays you) — with the same words that the priests use at offertory. Once back in the march, they either drank the cold and soothing water or tossed it over their shoulders, showering unannounced those treading behind. Few complained. We were walking on open highway through shadeless plains under a cloudless sky; the sun was as fierce this August afternoon as suns ever get in the Polish summer, the temperature probably reaching the low nineties. I readjusted my haversack and noticed that under its strap an identical, inch-thick strip of perspiration darkened my shirt. It was about two o'clock when we pulled off into an orchard lane for lunch, with over half the day's distance already behind us.

I found a seat not far from the highway and leaned my back against the orchard fence. Beside me were

three women seated similarly, each, it seemed, repre-
senting another decade — I guessed one to be in her
thirties, another in her forties, the last in her fifties. The
oldest introduced herself as Maria, the others as Kinga
and Jola. Maria and Kinga were both dressed in loose,
sleeveless white blouses and old slacks rolled up their
thick calves. Jola, the youngest, wore a long, flower-
printed skirt of soft fabric bunched at her small waist,
and a T-shirt. She was fragile and pale and had a distant, preoccupied look that made me think that she was
going to Częstochowa with a definite plea. In her ker-
chief, which she wore against the sun, she looked like a
peasant girl, though she and her companions, I soon
learned, were all from the town of our priest.

None of these women ate before offering to me the
sandwiches they had for themselves. I refused, politely
and with thanks, and extracted from my bag my own
battered products: two crusty, already stale rolls, each
inserted with a sweaty slice of cheese, hardened at the
edges. To wash them down, I drank Ptyś, the Polish carbonated orange drink whose name was a more faithful
representation of the sound of the opening of one of its
bottles than the trade name of any drink I knew: *ptish!*

Maria said, "It seems to me that brother is not Polish.
May I ask where brother is from?"

"I'm from the United States," I said, stopping safely
before a personal address. I had not yet gotten used to
the idea of calling strangers, especially elders, as we were
supposed to on the pilgrimage, brother and sister.

After finishing their sandwiches, the ladies pulled out
plastic, humidifying bags of fruit. These limited rations
of apples and pears were also offered, each to her neighbor, as gifts. "Here, brother from America, you haven't

got nearly enough there. How are you ever going to get to Częstochowa eating like that? Come on, take some of these pears."

Back on the march, this Reymontesque luncheon stuck in my mind. How remote from the voracity of the city food lines! Here food, just as limited, and just as vital, had become a source of charity, rather than contention. The pilgrims seemed to be dissociating themselves, consciously, from the ailments of their society and creating, in this nine-day world, a better, if a bit Utopian, society of their own.

A short time after this rest we turned off the highway and onto the road where our first night's host lived. At about eight o'clock the sun, which all day had seemed motionless, hurried toward setting. The air became chill. We traveled down this new road, passing peasants' houses identified on their gates with the name of the group they were housing, or more appropriately, "fielding," for the night. Ours was at the far left. We found our two trucks, where our bags had already been unloaded and were leaning against each other in groups arranged by numbers. I picked up my three and, walking back toward the courtyard, ran into another student, Michał. He was working as an orderly and promised to find me a place to sleep.

We checked the barn. Girls were already scaling its hay-stacked heights, so that possibility was out. We tried the house, but that too was taken. Finally, we went out through the courtyard and into the field beyond. It was full of pilgrims with their tents, all at various stages of construction. Michał's group had claimed a fine, open spot on the left side near some apple trees. His friends included about six boys and five girls; classmates, I took it, from high school, or the same youth group at church. They had already begun assembling the two tents; one for the boys, one for the girls. Nearby, five nuns had nearly completed theirs. Presently a large woman with arms akimbo came waddling down the field toward us, her mouth sputtering.

"You can't put your tent there! That's right in the middle of the cow path!" This information, meant only for us, rang through the village. We moved to a spot far enough from her censure, yet not her voice.

"Put that hay back! What sort of primitive people do we have here?! And YOU'RE going to Częstochowa? *Jezus Maria*!!"

I walked up to see the object of this abuse: a young woman who was now silently sticking back onto an enormous hay mound the few handfuls she had taken for her night's bedding.

As the tents neared completion, chores were assigned. The girls made sandwiches while two of the boys and I went for coffee, each of us carrying a supposedly clean bucket. The "kitchen" was a good walk away, at the other side of the highway. When we got there we found long queues stretching in front of wheeled carriages, infinitely rusty, and steaming like little train engines. The coffee was brewing inside. Behind them were large, blackened pots and kettles, set over fires of smoky, glowing chunks of wood. A man delicately poured the piping hot coffee into our buckets with a large, long-stemmed, metal ladle. We walked back to our campsite, stopping every few yards to change hands on the bucket, making sure not to spill any of the scalding liquid on ourselves.

When we rejoined the others, it was nearly dark. Michał suggested that we wash. We took his basin to the courtyard, which was animated with the novel enactments of half a dozen causes. There was a general clamor on the back porch as people sought bedding. The barn continued to fill with females. Outside, under the glow of a bare electric bulb, a pilgrim-nurse stood romantically lit in a Florence Nightingale relief against the barn wall; in front of her was a table cluttered with bandages, gauze, and cocoa brown bottles of iodine. A few patients were gathered, exhibiting their blisters and sores.

Near the center of the courtyard was the object of most pilgrims' attention — the well. It was manned by one of Michał's friends, Ryszard, who was obviously enjoying the responsible post. He filled our basin with slightly more than the usual splash. We took it off to the side and, one after the other, removed our shoes and socks and then stuck them into the ice-cold water. We'd forgotten soap. A brother washing nearby shared a bit of his.

It was now dark, and I walked back quickly toward our camp, half jumping over tent lines that threatened to ensnare me in their grasp. Zosia, a woman I had talked to briefly on the march, saw me pass.

"Tom. Hello. Can you join us for supper? You haven't eaten, have you?"

She sat with her legs stretched out, cutting cheese and tomato to put atop stale slices of bread which lay in rows across her blanket. With her was a pimply boy of about sixteen. We ate the sandwiches, and the woman told me that she was a Solidarity journalist, a film critic, unemployed by martial law. I asked her what she did with her free time. She answered that she read a lot, went out with friends, and then her voice faltered, searching for something estimable that she had accomplished in half a year and finding nothing. I did not press her with it. I knew very well the hundreds of accomplishments — finding lemons one day in a neighborhood shop, buying toilet paper on a multirolled spool — that, though significant at the moment, did not particularly stand out in a six-month retrospective.

When I looked at my watch, I saw that it was ten-thirty. In five hours, I thought, we shall be getting up. How nice to sit and talk, but there really was no time. (The thought of not having the strength to make it to Częstochowa was with me from the beginning.) I returned to the tent. A large blanket was spread beside it; I could see, under a small lantern, rows and rows of *kanapki* laid out upon it.

The tent was already full of chattering boys. I found a place next to one of them on the grass under the outer covering. They knew I was Michał's English teacher, and as I rolled out my sleeping bag, they began a discussion on the essential differences between the English and Polish languages. I did not stay awake for their conclusion.

II

A loud, persistent braying of truck horns awakened us, as planned, a few hours later. Inside the tent there was a barely perceptible rustling and awakening of movement. It was still dark, still night. The air was cold and damp with mist. In total darkness I rolled my sleeping bag, deflated my mattress, and then stuffed them both into cases I hoped were mine. We could already see chipper pilgrims headed toward the march. There would be no time for breakfast.

Gradually, light seeped into the world. I thanked my brothers for the lodging and took my bags to the truck. The same men who had loaded in Warsaw worked here, too. Half the group already stood on the highway, waiting patiently for the others. One car passed, its lights still on. Father Czuma called through his microphone: "Let's go, yellow-and-white, come on. We haven't got time to wait." We were the only group on the road, as it was our day to lead the pilgrimage. When it appeared that most of the pilgrims were present, we said the Lord's Prayer. And that otherwise deserted highway at dawn, wrapped through fields of mist, and quiet and still in the mystery of morning, seemed the best place imaginable for doing so. I noticed, too, that I said for the first time in my life with any conviction: "Give us this day our daily bread."

We started off according to schedule at four-thirty, and it was, in my case, with a noctambulist's alertness, for I remember nothing of the march. I first came to at about six, when we made a portentous turn off the open highway and dipped down onto a shaded, blacktop road. This turnoff marked our departure from contemporary Poland, and our entrance into the sheltered and immemorial.

Our first stop was in the town of Tarczyn at about half past six; a good few hours after beginning the day and, I couldn't help but think, a good few hours before I normally begin the day. We came into the center of town and invaded the churchyard. I took my place next to an elderly woman who sat leaning against a tree. She was of solid build and wore a light blue patterned summer dress, white socks, and heavy walking shoes. A stick was by her side.

"Surely not your first pilgrimage," I said to her.

"Twentieth," she answered, looking straight ahead through her spectacles. She paused for a long while, then added, "The first one I went on was the year Piłsudski died. I was still a young girl then." Another pause. "I'm sixty-nine years old now. I start to think I'm too old for it, but every year it comes around and it just pulls me to it. And I can't resist it. I wait all year for it."

I took out my last sandwich from the day before and offered the woman half. With expert eyes, she refused.

After twenty minutes we were on the road again. Now as we walked I varied my pace — sometimes bringing myself to the lead, sometimes dropping back — to get an overall picture of our group. At the very front was the crucifer, carrying the yellow-and-white cross that was actually connected below to a similarly formed M, for Mary. The gaps in the design were filled with bunches of flowers. To either side of the crucifer was a strong front line of marchers. A few feet in front of them, leading the group, was a young crippled man. He rolled along in an antediluvian, three-wheeled chair, with one large wheel in the front which he could revolve using the hand pedal at his chest. He was pale and thin, with a shy, smiling countenance framed by black horn-rimmed glasses. Behind the chair walked a duo or trio of pilgrims, often young girls, alternately pushing and restraining the lugubrious black vehicle.

Also in that tight pack just behind the crucifer were the nuns, about seven or eight of them, each in her long gray habit and blistering black veil. A few wore wide, plantation-style straw hats, which seemed oddly fitting. They walked with bags strung across their shoulders, and crosses and rosaries flapping, keeping lead-position pace in high-laced black work shoes or, in one engaging case, an elegant pair of genuine black Adidas.

Then came the first of the loudspeakers, connected by a wire to a microphone. The pilgrims who walked behind were spread out over a great distance, sometimes, because we were such a large group, falling out of sight, and sound. Here one retreated from the claustrophobia of the pack, or escaped from the persistent patter of sermons and prayers. Here one could converse comfortably, for talking was forbidden during the daily broadcasts. One or two of the young priests, who dotted our group like exclamation marks in their long, black, bead-buttoned cassocks, usually walked here, hearing confessions in a close, rapt, arm-linked tread.

Here also one found the lamed and the bandaged, unable to keep up with the others. Many, on this second day, limped painfully on blistered feet or hobbled in pinching shoes. Others shuffled swollen, gauze-wrapped ankles and calves.

There were a few pilgrims who, by dress or comportment, stood out from the pack. For me the most visible was a short, dark, goateed man with a middle-age paunch, who carried the Polish flag. We carried with us three flags — the red-and-white Polish flag, the yellow-and-white papal flag, and the blue-and-white flag of Mary. Most of the flag bearers took turns, yet this man was rarely without his flagpole, his crutch pointed toward heaven. He spoke to anyone who was near enough to listen; once or twice he had commandeered the microphone and, in a deep and fiery voice trained in dramatics, had recited stirring, nationalistic verses from memory.

There was a batch of girls from a church group, like

church group girls anywhere, unimpeachable, and with a guitar.

There was a richly tanned middle-aged woman who marched in a green tent dress and fashionable sandals.

There was a girl with shoulder-length blond hair, shapely and pretty, who always walked at the front and to the side of the group, setting herself apart from the others not only in distance. She walked barefoot, with the poise of an African. One time I got close to her and saw that the dust had blackened her feet completely, save for the toenails, which shined through with a silvery pink polish, like softly lit windows on a dark night.

There was another, older man in a wheelchair, an amputee deranged of mind as well as body. He was pushed in a more modern convenience than that of the fellow up front, and had no particular place. One was warned of his Apache-like approach by unintelligible cries in a Silesian dialect. Sprays of saliva dampened the picture of the Black Madonna which he wore, pasted on a large piece of cardboard, about his neck.

There was a Dutchman in his mid-thirties, sober and slightly muddled, who walked in casual sport clothes, inevitably holding hands with at least one female Polish companion. He was the only pilgrim, I believe, outfitted in a pair of brown wingtips.

Father Czuma took to the road in hearty strides with enormous black boots, worn by the mileage of countless pilgrimages, poking out from under the hem of his cassock. He talked this day, as we walked, about "Solidarity and Society." These afternoon talks were called conferences; each day a speaker, often a priest, would address an assigned topic, and a discussion would follow.

I was astonished at how strong the statements were.

There was much insistence on the fact, disputed by none, that "the system was sick." "We have a health service," someone quipped, "but it doesn't heal us." Some advocated the "destruction" of the system; others argued that, considering "our situation," that wasn't realistic. "We must work to change the system, as Solidarity had done." There was a debate, all as we were plodding, some five hundred of us, along the road, on the effectiveness of force. One man took the microphone: "I'm not a pacifist. Not in the sense of pacifism at all costs. What is important now is that we stop being afraid. People have this great fear now. But of what? I wonder. There is no reason . . . there is nothing to be afraid of when you have truth on your side. That is why I support demonstrations. Demonstrations are important now. So are strikes. I will tell you that an 'explosion,' if it comes down to that, is necessary." Father Czuma, when the man had finished, thanked him for his opinion and promptly disagreed with it, stressing his allegiance to, and the people's need for, pacifism.

And so it went, as we marched onward. For the first time since leaving Warsaw we had no long views of the countryside. Our road had become hilly, and twisting, and was bordered on both sides by apple orchards. Now in front of the occasional houses, or, rather, at the entrances of lanes, we found, instead of buckets of water, baskets of apples — small, green Polish summer apples — set out for our consumption. Marek, whom I seemed always to find just over my shoulder, had joined me at an apple stop. Then, out of nowhere, appeared a girl with a cane. She smiled at both of us, with wide-open eyes, and asked our names.

Her attire was striking: a sort of peasant, or pilgrim,

chic. She wore a long and rather billowing black skirt with a decorative black hemline, a pale green blouse with a small collar, and a frayed silk shawl — a touch of agrestic cachet — draped across her shoulders. She had flaxen hair and pretty green eyes shaded beneath the wide brim of her straw hat. Her name was Alicja; if she'd been American, it would have been Daisy.

"How are you doing?" I asked her, my eyes drifting toward the cane.

"Terrible. Really. I can't go on."

"Yes you can. Come on. Walk with us."

We started along, now close to the back of the group. She was, for all her country garb, from Warsaw, an artist. Lately she had been commissioned to do a painting for a Krakow church, though generally, work was slow. It was her first pilgrimage.

"I'm not that religious," she said in a carrying voice. "I never used to go to Mass on Sundays. And my mother used to get so discouraged about me. And I got divorced, too. That didn't help. The guy steals letters out of my mailbox." She laughed. "But anyway, this year, when I told my mother that I was going on the pilgrimage, she was shocked." Now a giggle. "She said, 'Oh, Alicja, bless you.' It's like I'm absolved now from all my sins because I'm going on the pilgrimage to Częstochowa. Now, after this, I can sin for the rest of my life." Her giggle had been building, and now it reached loudly up to those ahead of us, who looked back curiously toward the source.

The town of Belsk, which we entered at about two, appeared to consist of only a church, and of that, I confess, I saw only the yard. Alicja and I went out onto the street in front of the church, and there found a

Frenchman, not from our group but from one I had seen in Warsaw before the start. He wore baggy shorts, a shapeless rugby shirt, and a camera that hung to his belly — a sort of short M. Hulot *en vacances*.

We introduced ourselves; he told us his name was Philippe and he was headed toward the restaurant. Would we care to join him? The restaurant — the other visible building in the village — was a short way down the street. It was crowded, though not excessively, and we shortly found a table against the far wall. The room exuded that unappetizing and unhygienic air of Polish village dining — here, as in most places, the bare tile floor was layered with dirt, the tablecloth soiled, the decrepit freezer empty. But here, in contrast to other establishments of the sort, most people were eating rather than drinking. There was the usual, smoky atmosphere, though no one seemed to be smoking.

The waitress — for there was only one — showed no interest in us. She had undoubtedly not seen such a crowd since last year's pilgrimage, and the annual rite did not warm her.

Philippe attempted to address Alicja in Polish, but for complicated phrases turned to me.

"Tell her that we, as Frenchmen, know that the Poles also are great 'partisans' and lovers."

She accepted the compliment modestly, and asked if he were a linguist.

"I work for the Banque Nationale de Paris."

"And did you come here for the religious aspect, or out of curiosity about Poland?"

"Oh, out of curiosity about Poland."

Soon after, a dish of highly curious meat arrived from the kitchen. It was a thin, brown strip of something indistinguishable under a watery gray sauce on a cool white plate. Not having ordered, I excused myself to try the lavatory and, entering the hallway, saw clearly coming through the door — surely it was still too early for a miracle — my wife.

"Hania! Hello!"

"Oh, at last. We've been looking all over for you. Andy and Mercedes brought me in the embassy car. We've got a nice surprise for you. How do you feel?"

We walked out into the brightness again, and back to the church, where Andy had parked his car. The walls in front of the church were whitewashed and nearly blinding. The whole prospect, save for the human traffic, was that of a Spanish town at midday.

"Hey, Tom. Look. We've got Mazowszanka. With ice."

Soon I noticed our group starting to assemble. I thanked our friends and bid them good-bye, then asked Hania:

"Will you come see me tomorrow?"

"There's a chance. We're going with Aneke to Lodz to see the dentist. It depends on the time. Don't count on it, so you won't be disappointed. O.K.? See you."

I strolled down the road toward the restaurant, wondering what Alicja and Philippe had made of my disappearance, and met the goateed actor holding the Polish flag.

"Wait," he called. "Are you from Moscow? Is that a Muscovite accent I recognize there? No, but listen seriously." He had me now.

"Let me tell you honestly, from my heart, that I love the Russian language. I love Russian music, Russian literature. The great Russian artists! The great Russian geniuses! I take nothing away from them. Only I hate, with an equally ferocious passion, the Soviet system!

That monstrous system of slavery, treachery, deceit, poverty, injustice, godlessness — it is that which I loathe! And I loathe it all the more because it has been inflicted on us — on Poland!"

"I'm not Russian," I said. "I'm American."

"I was kidding you, brother."

Without explanation, he altered his abuse.

"My director was a terrible man. A terrible man. He knew nothing about the theater. He held the position because he held the party card." (To each word, he gave the most vivifying emphasis.) "I hated that man as I hate the Soviet leaders. Those were awful years, miserable years with him. Then when Solidarity came along he was kicked out, the bum. And you know what, brother? He couldn't find a job anywhere. He couldn't even find a job in a movie theater. Not even in a movie theater in the countryside. Not even in a movie theater . . . in the countryside . . . that shows Soviet films." His guffaw punctuated the joke.

"I'm an actor," he continued. "I was in the Twenty-seventh Division of the Home Army. Here, I have something to show you. A historical document." He dug into his trousers for his wallet, and pulled from it a laminated identity card. He opened it and handed it to me. It bore the acronym of the Polish Artists Society, and Zbigniew, his name, written underneath his picture. He was handsome and clear-eyed in uniform. "You see how young I look there? Still in my English military uniform. Now," he said, discouraged, stroking his goatee, "I look like Fidel Castro. I told my friend, 'I'm not going to shave my beard until socialism becomes human.' He told me, 'You won't be able to walk down the street for tripping over it.'"

"You know we're all Catholics here," he continued,

looking around the ranks. "Yes, we're all Catholics. But we're all Protestants, too. You know why, brother? Because we're all protesting."

"Let's go, Zbyszek," a small woman by his side said to him. "They're moving." She had stood silently next to us during his communion with me, smiling at stories that, I took it, she was not hearing for the first time. When Zbyszek started to move it was in short, choppy steps, his feet pointed painfully outward.

It was nearing dark when we arrived at Wodziczna, the village of our night's camp. It had more trees than the previous night's; also the peasant's house was larger and newer. It took me a while to find my bags; when I did, Marek, with whom I'd planned to share a tent, had vanished.

"Tom." I heard someone calling me. "Come over here." It was Piotr, the teenage boy from the night before, cheerfully washing his feet. "Don't you have anyplace to sleep? Don't worry, we'll fix you up something. We can make room in one of our tents.

"This is the way it ought to be, huh? Everybody brother and sister. No Poles, no Russians, no Americans. Everyone a human being. That's the way it should always be. Not just on the pilgrimage, but in life."

He finished with his washing and took the basin to the well to refill it for me. He brought it back and set it in the mud by my feet, saying, "Conditions here are not the best. But we make the best of what we have. Besides, that's not important. Material things are not important. What's important is man's soul."

Marek appeared when I had finished. I thanked Piotr and followed Marek to his spot across the road. We assembled his two-man tent in the darkness. As we were about to retire, Piotr's friend Zosia came to ask us if we could squeeze someone else in with us. He had no place to sleep, she explained, and had already been the victim of misfortune: much of his baggage had been lost, his shoes had proven too tight, migraines had tortured him in the backseats of automobiles most of the day, and his remaining suitcase had snapped.

"He has a suitcase?" Marek asked.

"Yes. And another thing. He doesn't speak Polish."

"What does he speak?" we asked in unison.

"French and German and English. At least he speaks to me in French and to Gosia in German and to Iwona in English. Can you help him please? Thanks a lot."

She went off and returned shortly with a man slightly wobbly on her arm. It was, of course, the Dutchman, with a clouded look and an unperceiving gaze. He received us indifferently, preferring to beg a good-night kiss from Zosia, whose arm he was reluctant to let go. Marek and I pushed our sleeping bags to the side to make room for his. We were too tired, and it was too late, to bother with supper.

We heard Peter outside opening his suitcase and throwing a sleeping bag onto the ground. Then he fell on it and lay still on his back in the darkness.

"Peter. Come on inside. You're not in the tent yet," Marek called.

"I'm going to die here," moaned Peter. "I . . . want . . . to . . . die," he repeated, in singsong.

Reymont, too, entertained thoughts of dying on the road to Częstochowa. He imagined how they would place him in a roadside cemetery before continuing on their way. And he imagined how in later years, when new pilgrims passed, they would toss on his grave "a branch of blackthorn" or "a cluster of anemone" and how "I would sleep peacefully, I would dream softly for eternity, I would live in their hearts and in their memories longer than there, in the fair on the grand square of the world."

III

"*Wstawaj! Wstawaj! Wstawaj!*" barked Peter in his freshly acquired Polish. The time was four o'clock Sunday morning.

There was a Mass in the village field at five-thirty. I took advantage of the time to scribble in my notebook; as a non-Catholic, I felt no obligation to attend. By seven-forty-five we were marching, and singing our farewell song, "Żegnamy Was Alleluja" ("We Bid You Farewell, Alleluja") to the villagers, almost none of whom were present at that hour of the morning to hear it.

We followed it with another song, "Oto Jest Dzień" ("O This Is the Day"), an abridged rosary, announcements, and a sermon. Entering the village of Mogielnica, already five kilometers advanced, we passed a small blacksmith shop set back from the road. The simple lettering above it — KOWALSTWO — reminded me that the most common surname in Polish, Kowalski, as in English, Smith, derives from the same, muscular trade.

The town looked little changed from Reymont's day, when he described it as "a hamlet that hardly differs from a hundred others . . . the houses, low and dirty, shock by their ugliness and their state of abandon. The people are thin, one reads the misery on their faces." We came to a spacious square with two-story buildings of light, bleached colors; a shop called Monopoly; a movie theater called Victory; a few wooden houses close to the street, with low roofs of undulating tar paper; and an odd administrative building, heavy, of gray concrete. Some people waved from top-floor windows, white lace curtains flapping behind them. In front of the red brick church, women stood behind stands and tables of gaily colored pinwheels, cheap wheeled toys, plastic dolls, and *obwarzanki*, deceptively fine-looking cracknels, seven or eight looped on a string, like midget bagels, and consisting of nothing but dry, degradable crust and tasteless air, a breadlike cotton candy. There were also pilgrimage postcards that showed a map of the pilgrimage route.

The day was getting gradually hotter, though for the first time since we left Warsaw there were clouds in the sky. I saw Peter walking with two young women in hand, one a tall, Hansel-and-Gretel blonde with waist-length braids running down her blouse like suspenders. The unadulterated heat made the walk particularly difficult for the Poles; I found it less debilitating. It was a pure, dry, dusty daytime heat, and each evening brought relief. Poles are not accustomed to such waves, for which they have the perfect word, *upał* (*ooh*-pow!), with its finely scored plosion at the end.

There were no houses along the road, so no water; we had learned now to fill up our thermoses in the towns to save for these long stretches. We looked forward to an hour's rest and dinner in the next town, where, it was rumored by experienced pilgrims, there was also a river that became on this one day of the year as swelled with bodies as the Ganges.

Nowe Miasto (New Town), we found to be old, and, as Reymont described it, "a small town, dirty and dilapidated." Our presence prompted a good number of male citizens out of the dismal restaurant at the foot of the town — perhaps for the only time all day — who were confronted now, in the glaring sun, with this procession of crosses and hymns.

Hot and sweaty, we mounted the hill of the town, where we were greeted by a jubilant sight: hose-happy gardeners creating a sort of community-sponsored Śmigus Dyngus. Residents appeared behind fences, asking each group if it wanted a squirt; then they would shower us with a fine spray. Neighbors without hoses treated us to buckets of water placed along the street. Everyone turned out, laughing and waving at us as, with plastered-down hair and clinging clothes, we marched past in squishing sneakers.

Once down the hill and out of the town, we tramped across an open field to the sandy banks of the Pilica River. It was not especially clean when we arrived, and we polluted it considerably ourselves. Many pilgrims had dressed for the occasion, with swimsuits under their other clothes, and, slipping off shirts and pants and skirts, now jumped in. Alicja was off somewhere, changing in the grass. She had attracted a leathery, misanthropic man of about forty who now stood next to me in a drooping red swimsuit. He looked at my note-taking with disfavor.

"You a journalist?" he asked, an unusual occupational query from a Pole.

"No. Just keeping notes for myself."

"Just as well. Journalists are bastards who do nothing but lie for a living. I can't stand them."

I asked what he did. He refused to tell. I imagined that, judging from his tan, he was an outdoor physical laborer.

"What physical labor? I sunbathe every day," he said in a husky, defensive voice. "Can't you see how dark and even this tan is?"

I decided on a less personal line of questioning. "Are you from Warsaw?"

"What is this with Warsaw? You think that everybody lives in Warsaw? I don't live anywhere near Warsaw, and I wouldn't if they paid me."

This rather ended our talk. (Reymont, as well, endured a taunt from a non-Varsovian, who noticed that he was traveling without a wife: "But then, sir," asked the man, "you are from Warsaw?" "Exactly." "There all men are like dogs. They stay as long as possible without wives.")

Across the river we came to the entrance of the woods. This next leg of the march was to be the toughest. Our path was sand, softer than usual because of the weeks-long drought, and more powdery. Because cars couldn't make it through the sand, those pilgrims with delicate conditions, who might conceivably falter inside, were advised to forsake this stretch and go around by car to that night's camp. On our schedules the route was measured at seven kilometers, up to a hamlet with the far from encouraging name of Pustelnia (Hermitage).

We sat in the dry grass in preparation, almost as if for battle. Father Czuma spoke in a soft, soothing voice, at one point reading a letter he had received just before coming on the pilgrimage. It was from an interned pilgrim who expressed his regret that this year he would be unable to participate in the walk. We listened quietly. Some had already tied kerchiefs over noses and mouths, looking inevitably like thieves; others, mostly women, had tailored elaborate coverings of cloth and veil, with an equally appropriate desert chic. Eventually the call came to rise and march.

It was all that the worst elaborations had claimed. Immediately into the woods we were immersed in pockets of dust, kicked up most recently by those just in front, though the whole nimbus had been raised noiselessly by groups now far ahead. I carried a tissue across my nose and mouth, and soon noticed a black stain forming where I breathed. The trees were neither tall nor thick, a combination of birch and pine, both parched, the most distant lost in the herd-induced haze. After about twenty minutes we began to see occasional clusters of pilgrims grouped about another one, passed-out and supine, as well as pairs of pilgrims supporting a limping, dehydrated third. I felt a gruff dryness in my throat and took out my thermos, but no sooner had I poured some water into the cup than it appeared tainted and dry. A great admiration grew in me for the older pilgrims. I saw an elderly man walking a good bit ahead of the cross, and Maria, carrying bags in both her hands (low to the ground, for she had short legs), striding without flush. I approached and offered her my water.

"Thank you, thank you very much, brother. But you have it. Kinga's son has some he supplies us with. Thank you. How are you doing?"

I continually looked ahead in hopes of seeing an opening, and each time I found the same infuriating, unbroken line of timber. Then I'd look back on the covered faces and the straining bodies that all seemed to be tilted, harmoniously, the same way, as if to cut more efficiently through the dust. I learned a new word — *kurzyć*, to raise clouds of dust — as many were making this same observation.

And as we stomped and panted, the words from the microphone did not abate. Father Czuma spoke the while of Cyprian Norwid, now read and revered though unsung in his own lifetime, who died penniless in a Parisian old-age home administered by Polish nuns. The poem Father Czuma cited was "Pilgrim."

We came upon an elderly, white-haired man, sitting as though blind on a wooden bench along the side of the route. He wore a shiny, green-brown suit, and held on his lap a hat turned beseechingly upside down. Except for a wooden dwelling espied through the trees, there was no other sign of civilization, and I thought it a curious spot to find our first beggar. In Reymont's time, beggars had congregated in large numbers for the passing of the pilgrimage, usually in front of churches, "holding out their hands while showing their infirmities . . . old professionals . . . each one crying that he is the most unfortunate of all." This lone almsman, surrounded by nothing but dust and pine, enjoyed, by comparison, a quiet and dignified petition. Few stopped, however, to fill his hat.

I had hoped his presence would be a symbol or marker of distance; if not Pustelnia already, a halfway point. Yet when he seemed dust-ages behind, there was still no break in the trees, no opening ahead. We passed more of the fallen, with their feet up on tree stumps, and damp cloths over their foreheads. Others lay with heads back to stop bloody noses. (In September the newspaper *Przegląd Tygodniowy* published an account of the pilgrimage with the news that a nineteen-year-old girl had died here from a heart attack.)

The wood eventually opened up, but the sandy route continued. There, just at the end, at that point where we at last emerged into a less confining wilderness, stood a five-man orchestra. Three men clutched saxophones, one cymbals, another a trumpet. On the ground in front of them was spread a large blanket dotted with the paper bills and silver coins of half a day's donations. They were a dazzling sight — to my mind came Charles Ives's "Two Bands Coming Around a Mountain" — even though they were not playing. (Our own church group girls had already begun a tune, and this woodsmen's five restrained themselves out of sacred, or professional, respect.) Their faces were expressionless; they obviously saw nothing funny in what they were doing. They left one either to delight in or despair at this evidence that even here, in the primeval forest, had penetrated the Polish ardor for *interesy* (doing business, making a buck).

"They're here every year," a pilgrim told me farther along. "Always at the same spot."

We passed through tiny, four-hut hamlets in a world that was becoming, with the dwindling of sunlight and capacity for reason, more and more fey. At a Second World War battle site we said a prayer for the Polish soldiers who had fought and died. As is the custom at this spot, we sang songs of the Polish partisans. We must have made a stirring scene, tramping across the sand and singing these unforgotten songs with a military fervor. A young man crossed my path and, at one heroic strain, threw his clenched fist into the sky. That music, which carried far into the trees, picked up our feet despite dozens of complaints of soreness, as only the music of a march can do.

Yet we were still not home. We came to a pass where there was confusion and a gathering of pilgrims on a hillside. At the top was a shrine to which people climbed on their knees, especially those on their first pilgrimage to Częstochowa and young women about to marry. As we drew closer we could see a low, wobbly file of kneeling pilgrims, some with their hands clasped at their chests in prayer, slowly, rockingly, scaling the hill.

Darkness fell as we were traversing another wood. We began to see lit windows not far off the route and imagined these to be the dwellings of Brudzewice. Then we reached a main street, still sandy and unlit. Occasionally a car passed, showing in the rays of its headlights ever-rising clouds of dust. In this swirling thoroughfare we found our night's farm, and I heard my name called, and saw emerge from the darkness and into my arms, my wife.

"What a time we had finding you tonight!" she said. "Nobody knew when you'd get here. And it's so dark. And this dust all about."

She had driven with our friend Aneke from the Dutch embassy. I introduced them to Marek. Once revived with cups of iced orange juice and Mazowszanka, we described a pleasant day's stroll in the woods. Before they left to drive back to Warsaw, they emptied a hamper of cucumbers, tomatoes, hard-boiled eggs, and two bottles of a Polish cola called, helpfully, Brown. "Food for Poland's Pilgrims." Then they bid us good-bye. "This will be the last time," Hania said to me. "I won't have an embassy car anymore. You know how it is with gasoline these days. And you keep getting farther away. Take care of yourself. Bye-bye."

IV

The horns woke us at five. After Mass at six in an open field, we started out for Studzianna. I found the woman who had been accompanying Zbyszek, the flag bearer. She was alone.

"Oh, he had to drop out. He was in too much pain. But he promised he'd join us yet."

When she learned that I was not Catholic, she said, "So, you're with us from more of a sociological point of view." And after some consideration added with a smile, "You must enjoy yourself observing all of us Poles."

My student Michał, after half a day's rest from traffic, again took to policing, lavishly signaling to motorists.

"You have an obvious bent for the *milicja*," I told him.

"Hey," he called to me, coaxing yet another driver to step on it. "Do you know why our *milicja* always travel in threes?"

"No. Why?"

"So as to have one who can read, one who can write, and one to keep an eye on the two intellectuals."

The sky had clouded over by the time we left Studzianna. Coming to an orchard for rest, we felt some small, sweet drops of rain. We sang "O Idzie Deszcz" ("O the Rain Is Coming"), an old mountaineer's song, and the rain went away. Marek said, "Let us see what the Lord in His unending wisdom still has in mind for us." We spread out before us a Lucullan lunch: two cucumbers, two tomatoes, one hard-boiled egg, kielbasa, wafers with cheese, cola, and water. "*Déjeuner,*" said Marek, "*sur l'herbe.*"

We were in good spirits. It was a calendarless day in a storybook week: we had covered good ground, had eaten our fill, and now rested our bodies — there seemed no other requisites for contentment.

"Hello Tom!" It was my student Maggie with her boyfriend, Dariusz.

She wore a plain skirt down to her calves and high

walking boots that tightly outlined her long legs. Her button nose was burnt red; the rest of her face was as pale as it had been in a February evening English class.

We shared impressions; they were especially interested in mine. I told them my astonishment that all the people here — even the priests — were speaking so boldly against the regime.

"It's always been like that on the pilgrimage," said Dariusz. "As long as I can remember. That's not something new that came about recently through Solidarity. It's always been a good place to learn one's history.

"The pilgrimage has had some hard times," he continued. "It hasn't always been as easy to walk as we are walking now. At one time there were special pilgrims assigned to protect the others as they marched — because rocks and things would be thrown by provocateurs planted along the way. During the Stalin years it was especially hard. They tried to keep bread and other food supplies from the pilgrims. Everything was planned to discourage the pilgrims, to discredit the rite, and, as you see, it had an opposite effect."

Our walk this afternoon took us through an area of delicate beauty. We traveled through fields running up hills and down into dales, the rolling land giving us welcome vistas not only of the countryside, yellow and green, but of the pilgrimage's prodigious, serpentine growth. The sky had darkened in the west, and the birch trees shivered against the fumy backdrop. We passed a peasant woman scurrying home up a dirt field and carrying a wooden basket of potatoes on her arm — one lone figure in a countercurrent against a thousand marching bodies. An elegant line of birch trees sometimes rimmed the horizon; other times they stood clus-

tered in neat, carpeted woods by the side of our path. In
Pan Tadeusz, Mickiewicz paid homage to the birch:

> *Is not our honest birch a fairer one,*
> *That's like a peasant woman weeping for her son,*
> *Or widow for her husband, as she stands,*
> *Hair streaming to the ground, and wrings her hands,*
> *Her silent form than sobs more eloquent?*

It was still overcast when we entered Kunice. Maggie
and Dariusz had told me that the pilgrims are always
well received here, and approaching the church we began to pass small clusters of families gathered to greet
us, the girls and their mothers often in folk costume,
waving shyly. It was the precise opposite of a parade,
with crowds like ours watching in street clothes, as
smaller numbers of costumed people pass. The women
wore white cotton blouses with billowy sleeves and
furled lace cuffs and collars; over these, black vests embroidered with floral designs of dark red and green and
studded with silvery bangles and beads. They had on
two visible layers of skirts — one a sort of apron with
bright vertical stripes and a white lace trim over a skirt
of even sharper stripes of gold, green, and black. In the
front yard of the presbytery, flags flew as welcome —
Polish, papal, Italian, French, American — and at the
doorway the bishop waved. We responded with a song
in his honor. Then we took our rest in the churchyard.

Marek and I found a place with Ryszard, who had
manned the pump that first night, and Bogdan, another
orderly. With nothing to eat, we talked about food: the
soups — *żurek* in winter, *chłodnik* in summer; *pierogi*
("Yes! yes! But which? Meat *pierogi*? Or *pierogi* stuffed

with sauerkraut and mushrooms? Or cream cheese and potatoes?"); *bigos*; mushrooms, fried in butter, breaded, or with cream. . . . "I'll tell you what I can't stand, how's that?" I suggested. "Groats, pig's feet, compote . . . I'm a bit tired of boiled potatoes . . . sandwiches spread with lard, and black pudding."

"What about duck's blood soup?" Ryszard asked.

"Never had it."

"You're lucky."

"Why?"

"In the villages it was the soup traditionally given to the suitor by the girl's parents as a sign that they didn't approve of him."

The white-haired man next to us had listened attentively to this, with an acknowledging smile on his up-turned face, as he lay on his back with his head resting comfortably in his wife's lap.

"Your talking just now about food," he broke in, "reminded me of during the occupation. My brother lived in Warsaw then and used to have a supper every Sunday evening for whomever of us could make it, and with whatever any of us could bring. You know the sort of rations you got back then. Well, the supper never lasted very long," he said, chuckling. "There wasn't that much to eat. When we finished, the general rule was that each person would describe the food he most missed having there in front of him. You had to prolong the supper, you see. And you couldn't repeat anyone else's food; you all had to think of something different. If we had a good group, they would think up foods that covered every course, from soup to dessert, so that we had an entire second meal in narrative, so to speak. And some people went into lengthy descriptions, full of detail and told very passionately. Well, it became the most popular part of the suppers. Everybody came forgetting about what they were going to have to eat, and anxious to hear the descriptions. I look back on those evenings with fondness now."

After a silence, Ryszard said, "We may start them again soon."

"You never know. You never know." The man chuckled again.

More unpaved road ran through more fields. At each lane, a peasant woman stood, having walked to the edge of her land from an unseen house to watch us pass. She would stand motionless, her arms folded and her shoulders covered in her pastoral cape, dark stripes of green, red, yellow, pink, and black. Farther along, in the small villages, we were famously received. At one crossroads a little wooden roadside bench was crammed with grannies and urchins. Outside the village, a peasant's whole brood had gathered in recumbent spectator postures on a haystack; other families had spread blankets on the grass. One peasant man stood in a field and waved at us, cupping his hand in the way of a little child.

Tonight, as on each evening, various pilgrims took turns at the microphone, requesting prayers.

For my mother, who is sick
For the dockworkers in Gdansk
For my father, that he may overcome his alcoholism
For the people who are interned
For doctors who kill children
For the Pope, a unique pilgrim, that he may come to his
     fatherland in an atmosphere of peace

For the actors and artists and writers with us, that they may
   glorify God in their works
For all who are going with us because they have been
   "assigned" to
For the miners who were killed at Wujek
For my parents, that God will give them the faith to believe
   in Him
For the Polish family, that it may learn love and solidarity

In the last village of the day we came upon an unusual greeting. A *milicja* van — the first we had seen in
days — was parked along the road, and an officer stood in
front of it. Another policeman popped through an opening in the roof — like a constabulary jack-in-the-box —
stretched in enthusiasm and signaling V.

"Is he being ironic?" I asked Marek, well aware that
that is not a trait by which Polish policemen are generally known.

"No. No. He's quite sincere."

"But how?"

"Here in the villages everybody thinks the same and
they all know it. The fact that he's a policeman doesn't
change anything — it's just a job, maybe one of the few
he can get. But he's still a Pole. In the countryside, that's
the way things are generally. The people all think the
same, so they don't worry about showing how they
think. They're together. It's not like in Warsaw."

V

On the way to church this morning, I found a sprightly
Zbyszek, clutching the Polish flag. His quiet companion
walked beside him.

"I'm very happy you've rejoined us," I said to him.

"As Mickiewicz writes in 'Ode to Youth,'" he readied to recite, "'Happy is he who falls in the fray.'"

We came to the village pond, there in the geographical heart of the settlement. A flotilla of ducks paddled about.

"I wanted to go in there for my morning bath," said Zbyszek. "But they" — he pointed to the ducks — "wouldn't let me. No. They are envious of their place. But they were smart. Do you know why? Because I'm an old fox," and he laughed.

The street leading back to the church was a courtly route, shaded on both sides by trees. Zbyszek orated to all around him: "Poland is a rich, blessed country. We have four beautiful seasons of the year. We have splendid and varied scenery. We have mountains, we have the sea, we have lakes, we have plains. We have this beautiful countryside and these lovely villages. We are wealthy in minerals and natural resources. We have so much good farmland that our cities should be full of plenty, we have so much milk that it should flow in rivers to the markets . . ."

Mass was said outside the church, a graceful, aged structure like those in the Tatras: all roof, its wooden tiles sloped sharply down to the ground, like a child wearing a grown-up's hat.

The nun in the Adidas sang *Godzinki*, beatific refrains that lasted an hour or more. The tune was something like a Gregorian chant; the words, I was assured, of a very old and elegant Polish.

In late morning we took a rest in a field already cut for harvest. From this site we could see the church spire of Paradyż, where a Mass was to be said for us in French. Marek and I found an insignificant spot and lay down to rest. Two girls solicited us with underground Solidarity booklets. As we hesitantly answered the call to move out, we saw a group, including the priest, gathered in the middle of the field. They were receiving with hugs and kisses an Amish-looking young man in beard and glasses. As we came closer we heard that this was the man who had written the letter from prison. He had been released, it seemed, only the day before. Friends had driven him out this morning to meet the pilgrimage en route. I saw Jola standing off to the side and gazing at him as he greeted more old friends. Father Czuma turned to us as we walked by, a great smile breaking across his face, and said, "Uncanny." We got started late. I found Maria, looking pleased.

"Did you see that Jola's husband has come?"

"Aha. That's Jola's husband."

"Yes. He's been interned. I knew she was hoping he'd make it. She didn't want to talk about it, of course. But I knew she was waiting for him."

Then we passed Jola, standing alone by the side of the road.

"Come on with us, Jola," Maria said.

"*Idę blisko mojego*" (I'm going next to mine), Jola replied, in her soft, firm Polish.

A little later I looked for them behind us, and found them; their faces forward, their eyes straight ahead, walking hand in hand toward Paradyż.

What Nowe Miasto is to the modern city, Paradyż is to Eden. These small Polish towns have nothing of the "picturesque poverty" of some equally small towns in Mediterranean Europe, and they are antipodal to the manicured, front-porch respectability of American small towns. In America we still talk of someone, favorably, as possessing small-town virtues; in Poland, rather, drunkenness and fatuity are traits of the municipality.

The Polish writer Marek Hłasko captured the quid-

dity of the Polish small town in a short story entitled
"The Duck's Ass Cut, or Everything Changes." A Warsaw journalist, returning home after an assignment,
stops in a small town for a haircut. He tells the stationmaster, "Nothing changes in these small, shitty towns.
I myself was born in such a hole."

He finds the barber, who asks if he wants his hair cut
in the "duck's ass" style, but the journalist prefers a
"normal cut." The barber tells him how, years ago,
everybody wanted the duck's ass cut, and leads into a
lengthy discourse on how things have changed in the
small town. By the end of the sitting the journalist's
mood has improved, as he's convinced that progress
does reach even to these hinterlands. He thanks the barber generously. When back at the station he sees his re-
flection in a window, he discovers that the barber has
given him the duck's ass cut.

After a quick look inside the church — curiously baroque in this austere town — I walked the main street,
continually passing fellow pilgrims. We had taken over
the town completely, just as in war, divisions engulf entire cities. The buildings set off from the street were low,
dusty, run-down, in hues of mustard yellow and bruised
peach. The air was muggy under a gray and darkening
sky. I found the bake shop at the far side of the square,
with a sign in the window — on this one landmark sales
day of the year — reading: CLOSED DUE TO LACK OF MA-
TERIALS. I ambled over to the town restaurant, set back
from the main street by a trampled plot of dirt and
sparse, dehydrated blades of grass. A girl sat on the
front steps tending a nose bleed, the trail of blood leading up through the doorway and across the unwashed

tile inside. This restaurant looked like a hundred others: the great, clouded front window; the nicotine-stained curtain hanging to the floor and lapping against tumbleweeds of dust and the accumulated ash of countless cigarettes; the small, red-and-tan-checked tiles, some missing, none clean; the square, naked linoleum tables with their metal legs scraped thin at the bottoms; the refrigerated case, vintage fifties, displaying a plate of ham *kanapki*, the dove gray slices of dessicated ham brittlely curled atop each slice of bread; the wilted flower in its vase; the rotting apple core in its ashtray; the plump blonde grumpily dispensing medicinal brown bottles of crude fruit drinks, the bottles seldom labeled, and if so, crookedly.

There was a custom in such establishments to place alluring bottles of wine or beer on shelves behind the service bar. When the customer asked for one of these, he was told, in abusive terms, that the restaurant was all out of wine and beer, that the bottles exhibited were only "for display, can't you read?" And looking again, the humbled customer saw that, indeed, posted next to the bottles was the word DEKORACJA. In this restaurant, however, the shelves on the wall were bare, save for a sign that read: OUT OF DECORATION. Meaning, of course, that the bar didn't have the bottles to show what bottles it didn't have — an admission of a want within a want that went beyond commerce.

We came into Przyłęk, a make-believe hamlet of thatch huts and birch groves that seemed, in its compactness, merely a larger example of the educational models one finds in natural history museums, depicting settlements of the Middle Ages.

Half a dozen humble dwellings clustered about the

dirt road in a tribal, clannish hunch. Each house, turned sideways to the street, was low and wigged with a woolly, tenebrous thatch. Hearth and home of the northern Slav. A few were painted a soft, cerulean blue, as if from pigments dripped from the summer skies. They nestled in gardens of sunflowers and bean stalks, surrounded by brown picket fences. In the dirt courtyard between house and barn drilled a troop of ducks, or sometimes geese, but never with the accompanying goosegirl:

> *Once in Poland, far away,*
> *I was in the little sip*
> *That fell betwixt the cup and lip.*
> *Down I spattered on a rock*
> *Between a goosegirl and her flock.*

We had only six more kilometers to call it a day. Yet how long those short stretches so often seemed. This one no less so, as Ryszard had been relieved of his loudspeaker harness and had hunted me down. He was an unequivocal Americanophile, and I suffered at his side a relentless catechism: "Who is your favorite American actor? What Polish actor do you like? Who is your favorite Polish football player? Who is your favorite American president?" In this landscape so exotic to me, I was the most exotic thing to him. "Where did you learn French? Why do the French like to eat frogs? Do Americans eat frogs? Do you like hamburgers? Do you ever eat frogs with hamburgers?" As he asked these questions, he would pull out of his pockets handfuls of wheat, blow away the feathery husks, and pop the grains into his mouth. He asked me, as I knew he would, to repeat: "*W Szczebrzeszynie chrząszcz brzmi w trzcinie.*" It is the Polish version, in laborious phonetics, of "How much wood would a woodchuck chuck . . ." In English it is: "In Szczebrzeszyn the cockchafer sounds in the reeds," which is not all that easy, either. "All right," I said. "Veshechebyreshinya hhshonsh," and then I lost it. "No, no, no!" he said. "*W Szczebrzeszynie chrząszcz brzmi w trzcinie.* Repeat." I repeated. It was a long way to Skorkowice.

We arrived well before sundown and were able, for the first time, to set up our tents leisurely and in light.

I joined a queue for canned goods at the back of a truck. Soon the "porters" handed me one tin of sardines in tomato sauce from Thailand and one tin of West German corned beef. Everyone got the same allotment. Marek borrowed some bread ("Can brothers and sisters spare us a portion of your bread? God repays you"), and we ate our first unhurried supper, garnished by near-rotted tomatoes I had forgotten in a tin.

A little before nine we left to join others who were walking in the darkness toward the village chapel for the "Apel Jasnogórski." I thought people would be too slack after a day's marching with hymns and prayers to gather in any number for evensong. But the church was filled when we got there, and we crowded into the back. There was a violin solo; then the "Apel Jasnogórski" was sung three times, as is done at nine o'clock of every evening of every year inside the chapel at Jasna Góra: "Mary, Queen of Poland, we are with you, we remember, we are vigilant."

I had been at many services in Poland, both for the church's feast days and the nation's remembrance days, and I found this simple refrain, sung in the village chapel, as moving as anything that had preceded it.

Around me were mostly young people, standing tall and singing these familiar words with a look of serenity and intense conviction. Walking with them on the road, I had thought them not unlike myself and my American friends, but watching them this night I saw in their faces, so openly and devotedly turned toward Mary, a hint of how different we really were.

VI

The horns blared as usual, though a humane tinkling sounded, too, as an unfortunate soul with a bell walked amidst our tents, like a plague victim. It was not yet five, and we had another, though our last, thirty-plus-kilometer day before us.

The nun in sneakers carried us through the mellifluous sounds of *Godzinki* — those plaintive cadences of the matinal cloister, here scattered to the trees. Fewer were limping and hobbling than in the first few days; the assumption was that those who couldn't make it by about the third day had dropped out, and those who did make it, would walk the distance. But still enormous energy was spent, just as painful efforts were made. Occasionally Father Czuma would speak soothing words of encouragement over the loudspeaker, especially toward the end of the day: "I know how you're feeling, but try not to give up now. When you feel you have nothing left inside you, reach deep down and you'll find you do still have the energy and strength you need." Though my feet and legs were free from pains and sores, I was, each day, growing a bit more weary of the monotonous task of putting one leg out in front of the other, ad infinitum, it seemed. (Who has counted the steps from Warsaw to Częstochowa?)

On the road I came upon Alicja, in sun hat, shawl, and billowy skirt, advancing with a large wooden staff in her hand.

"You look like a shepherdess," I said.

"I am," she replied.

"Where are your sheep?"

"Here," she said, and held out her arms in a wide, encompassing gesture to the flocks of pilgrims in front of us.

We hung toward the back with the confessors. Every day we saw priests dropped back and coupled with pilgrims in hushed, attentive tones as they walked. Only the Swedes, it is said, went to Częstochowa without confession. Farther along we came to a parked peasant wagon. The owner wore an old cloth cap and tilted a tall wooden barrel of pickles toward us as an offering. Pilgrims rushed over with rolled sleeves, submerged their arms to the elbows, and pulled out, with the delight of Little Jack Horners, bright, briny handfuls of tumescent green pickles, sprigs of dill still clinging to their fingers.

"God repays you," echoed in exuberance.

"But sir, you must be an angel," Alicja said, and the peasant turned his eyes downward, with modesty.

Watching Alicja eat her pickle, I was reminded of the peasant girl in Andrzej Wajda's film *Wedding*. With infinite dexterity, she holds between her fat forefinger and middle finger a stump of kielbasa, between her middle finger and ring finger a portly pickle, and with her thumb and pinky a shot glass of vodka. Then with one quick, delirious flick she downs the vodka, chomps the pickle, chomps the sausage — a pert, five-finger administration of the national cuisine.

We entered the village of Trzebce before sundown.

A few hours later we went to sleep to the tune, played on a nearby pilgrim's guitar, of "Let's Twist Again (Like We Did Last Summer)."

VII

After the initial morning crawl, our pace picked up, as did my spirits with *Godzinki*. Maria said to me, as I came up beside her, "*Mamy pagodę*" (We have weather), meaning, of course, that it was good.

We passed a dark, ploughed field and a peasant sowing. His cloth sack hung waist-high and slightly to the side. He reached in the bag, and every two steps — with a rhythmic flick of his wrist (the frame that painters' canvases always freeze) — he scattered his seeds. I watched him a long while as we walked, with that almost disbelieving reverence that one has when coming upon living subjects of ancient labors. His movement was one of venerable beauty and mechanical exactitude. Neither his step nor his toss faltered, and watching him solitary in that morning calm, I recalled Sebastian Klonowic's sixteenth-century verse:

> *Fair Poland nestles on a fertile sod,*
> *Content as though within the lap of God.*

These lines never occurred to me while standing in the city's queues.

Marek and I ate with Laurent, who had left the French group and joined us for the day. His hat was covered with jangling pins and badges he had collected along the way, so that he resembled the pilgrim in *Piers Plowman* who had "An hundreth of ampulles on his hatt seten." There were, indeed, many marks among us of those medieval pilgrims and their treks: the collection of

badges, the carving of wood crosses to present as offerings, the barefoot path, and the staff, which a few carried, once an integral part of the pilgrim's dress, symbol
of faith, and a helpful tool for the beating off of wild
dogs. We had yet to encounter real bandits.

The sun grew hotter in the afternoon. Marek and I
were joined by a tall, brightly dressed *Flamande*, journey-
ing in the Belgian group. We asked of her impressions.

"Well, as far as the pilgrimage itself, I think it's mar-
velous. You have a feeling of walking in unity with the
entire nation. We have nothing to compare to this at
home. It's quite extraordinary, really, *all* these people,
engaged in something like out of Old Europe.

"In our group there are these Jesuit priests. I must
confess I'm quite attracted to Jesuit thought. Well, they
walk about with Polish girls on their arms. That's rather
shocking to me, but I like it. It seems to me very Polish.

"And I'm surprised to see how fit and healthy everyone looks. After reading about all the hardships here, I
expected people to look grim and undernourished. But
they don't — they look good. Especially the young.

"It's interesting to see the people who come to meet us
along the route — some simply giving, some selling,
what they have."

"It's like the nation," explained Marek. "There are
those who act out of charity and those who are more interested in making money."

The afternoon walk was hot and grueling, but I began
to sense that, when the pilgrimage was over, I would
miss these marches: the biblical entries into new lands;
the consistent, snail-like, barely discernible progress
through the country; and the sheeplike joy of unmapped
following.

There was a sense of solidarity in walking with a

group. How many of us, I sometimes wondered, could have walked this far alone? Walking en masse, one enters a curious trance that comes from the day-to-day wearing down of one's resistance and the numbing of one's senses — all the better to receive the end epiphany. And with a group, there is that added cinematic effect that one observes in films, to heighten a scene, and says, "Yes, but there's never the background music in real life." Here there was. As we marched, a cast of thousands, we sang our own score.

Of all the songs we sang, there were two that especially moved me. They were both patriotic. The first, the well-known "Rota"; the second, the lesser-known "Hymn of the Bar Confederates," with its many verses, each begun defiantly and ending somewhat hauntingly:

> We don't ask for blood, to conquer is not our plea,
> We don't want killing, for pillage we have no gift,
> We want only to regain our Fatherland,
> Only to be free.

Soborzyce, into which we filed for the night, was a larger version of Przyłęk — more extended, though just as hunched. Some of the thatch houses here seemed smaller and more withdrawn, set back deep in gardens as if trammeled in the vines. One cowered behind soaring bean stalks; another edged out into the road, and walking by it I found that the roof thatch touched my shoulder. I was reminded of a Polish friend who had said to me once, after I'd returned from the mountains: "I like the mountaineers. They're proud and forthright and they stand up to you in greeting. Not like the peasant who is always so humble and shrinking next to strangers." Here that aspect was unmistakable in the architecture.

Marek went off to the evening Mass, while I set out to explore the village. I passed a peasant woman bringing her cows home from pasture, four of them following her, all tied to one central chain she held in her hand. Behind them a stooped, shirtless peasant shuffled, a hay rake balanced on his shoulder. They walked with their elongated shadows well out in front of them, the orange globe of the setting sun behind.

If, as Mickiewicz writes, "No frogs sing as beautifully as Polish frogs," then, I will add, no cows look as pitiful as Polish cows. They seem among the sorriest of God's creatures. The Polish cow is uniformly black and white, with the inevitable matting of caked mud on her hind side. Her skeletal structure, if not protruding, is sharply defined. She enjoys none of the healthy sheen of her Dutch sisters (not to mention the floral plumage of the Swiss), yet her worst disgrace is that she is so often alone and tethered. Frequently her only company is a peasant, stretched and dreamy, while the oppressive chain deprives her of even her ruminative grace and makes her out a grazing convict. *La vache punie.*

At a dirt crossroads I decided to knock at one of the tumbledown cottages and ask for a look inside. There was another one that appropriated part of the street for its living space and, walking around to the front, I sought entrance. The front door was open, and I walked into a low, windowless hallway of stone. I entered the doorway to the left and came in full view of the lady of the house.

"Now if you want milk," she rattled off to me, "you won't find any here. So there's no use trying. We milked our cows a good two hours ago and already there's been pilgrims in here asking. If I had some I'd give it to you, but the fact is I haven't got any."

She stood, a not very large woman, in the center of the room, her arms akimbo. She wore a blue apron over a flower print dress, and her expression to me was neither threatening nor withdrawing — simply indifferent. A little girl came out of the back room and sat down on the couch. I explained that I simply wished to see the house.

"Well, if that's all you want, help yourself," she said.

The room had a wooden floor; a low, wood-beam ceiling; and a small window on two opposite walls. There were three principal pieces of furniture — a couch, a table, a stove — giving it, no doubt, its three principal functions — bedroom, dining room, and kitchen. The couch and table were both shoved against the walls, allowing space in the center, and giving the impression — aided by the jutting angle into the street — that the house had recently been lifted up and twirled by a tornado before being set down here. The ancient stove, with faded tiles, squatted not far from the center of the room. Over the table hung a yellow strip of gluey paper dotted with flies. Oddly, there were no religious paintings. A man came in and sat down next to the little girl on the couch.

"It's a house like any other house," said the woman. "It's two hundred years old. We came to it only about thirty-five years ago. I wasn't always a village woman. No . . . no. I was a nurse. I worked as a nurse in Wroclaw during the war. Yes . . . yes. That was in Germany then. I saw plenty of things those years. Terrible, terrible things. So many people killed. Oh, it was a horrible time. My uncle and cousins were killed. Yes. My uncle got hit with a bomb that blew everything to pieces.

Things flew all over the place. When I got over to him, all that was left of him was his belt. Terrible, terrible times. Well, after the war I should have stayed there in Wroclaw. I could have got an education. I could have seen many things. Met many people. But I couldn't. I had to have something to live on. We came here, and we have been here ever since."

I left and walked to the other end of the village where our kitchen was set up. (These presumably were established at every campsite, though far enough from our group that, except for the first night, I never saw one.) A roped-off area was set with wood fires and enormous pots and kettles, the bubbly, open-air broth reinforcing the medieval aspect of the village. The kettles were charred black to the rims, licked by orange flames. To transport them, two men caught long wooden poles under the handles and then carried the kettles, like pashas, to another spot.

A few pilgrims stood behind a sagging rope, enamel cups in hand, waiting for soup. A man stood only a head above the kettle and stirred the broth with the exertion of someone rowing against a tide. The warm evening, plus the fire's heat, doused him in sweat. Soon the supervisor walked over. He was covered with filth, a little, simian man in a sleeveless T-shirt. He dipped a ladle in and, with the appropriate culinary ponderousness of a man of his position, tasted the soup. The pilgrims waiting made critical noises.

"You don't think it's good?" he called to them defensively. "One of you come here and try. Come on."

A girl eagerly jumped the rope. The man artfully stirred the contents, then dredged out a ladleful. She sipped.

"Now tell me if that's not good soup," said the chef.

"It is!" she said, turning to her doubtful brothers.

The men dipped in large buckets, and then brought them over to the waiting queue. It was, again, tomato and noodle, from some undisclosed Western country's mix. With my filled cup, I went to join Alicja, who was sitting on the grass with a man dressed like a hippie.

"Shame on you for not going to Mass," said Alicja.

"Aren't you having any soup?" I asked her friend.

"No, he eats only natural foods," said Alicja. "Remember I told you there was a vegetarian with us?"

"Poland's always seemed to me a good country in which to be a vegetarian," I said.

"That's not true," said Alicja. "O.K. There's not that much meat, but there are not that many of the protein substitutes, either, such as you have in America. I was just trying to figure out what Rafał *does* eat."

"Oh, Alicja, there are many things." He spoke in a soft, childlike voice. "Especially now in summer, all the different berries, wonderful berries, there are to eat. And then all the various pastes of the rich Polish cuisine . . . *kluski* [balls of boiled paste, which he pronounced lovingly], noodles, delicious dumplings, flour dumplings, potato dumplings, potato pancakes . . . and *kasza* [groats], oh, Alicja, such *kasza*, and cereals and grains, gruels and rices."

VIII

A great rosy pig greeted us this morning as we marched out of the village. He stood to the side, unattended, and gazed fixedly at us as we passed. A few of the girls broke over to pet him; one of the boys called out: "Somebody take a picture! The last pig in Poland! Quick! Get a picture. This can't go unrecorded."

A black mourning ribbon had been tied atop the Polish flag, for today was the thirteenth, commencing the ninth straight month of martial law. Father Czuma informed us: "We've heard that they are saying on the news that those going to Częstochowa are going in an 'anti-State' spirit. We don't accept that. We are serving our nation well." Another priest replied: "If the nation continues, it's because it gathers its pilgrims. When you get home, you tell your friends that there was nothing 'anti-State' here. Only the truth."

We had another short day — only twenty-two kilometers — ahead of us, and the morning passed quickly. We began to see, placed in the windows of some of the houses we passed, pictures of the Black Madonna, often bordered by heavy gold frames. At one bend in the road we passed a barn, freshly whitewashed and with the movements of a chessboard painted as curious decoration on one of its sides. Underneath was written: "White is leading and winning."

We were instructed, in orders from the pilgrimage head, that no superfluous signs would be permitted for the arrival into Częstochowa. The black ribbon of mourning had already been removed from our Polish flag. The only flags we were allowed were our present three. There were to be no additional banners or slogans — written or chanted. Our comportment on arrival was to be in the spirit of the pilgrimage itself, penitential, with nothing that bespoke of demonstration.

It was a still, muggy afternoon, with ever-darkening skies ahead of us. I broke out of the march at one point with a powerful thirst and went behind a house to seek the well. It was surrounded by dark-haired pilgrims speaking Italian. I took some water from the bucket and, turning, came face-to-face with a pretty girl, her large brown eyes peering over the rim of her cup. Drawing it from her mouth, she unveiled a lovely, liquidy smile, and said: *Acqua.*

Woda, I replied, with an equally soggy grin.

We came upon a road sign farther along — the first we'd spotted — for Częstochowa. It reminded me of car trips that my family used to take to Philadelphia and how, outside Doylestown, we would always pass a certain exotic place-name, the only one in the sixty-mile route that none of us could pronounce.

A helicopter arrived and hovered above us, then followed along our length, before returning again. Outside one small town we passed a plain upright granite staff, like a girder, stuck on a gray rectangular plaque at the base. "That's a monument to Soviet soldiers who fought in the Second World War," Marek told me. "It's often repeated in other towns. It's known familiarly as 'the Eternal Banana.'"

Later that afternoon a storm came upon us. For a long time we could see the lightning up ahead and the gradual darkening of the world into which we were walking. The thunder bellowed. Everyone reached into his haversack for the folded plastic raincoat he kept there — like a pilot his parachute. I wondered if it would not be advisable to pull off the road until the storm passed, but then I remembered the pilgrimage dictum of walking "without regard to weather conditions." The air, which had been still for a week, now gusted, and literally knocked pilgrims off their strides. I looked up with consternation at the electric wires swaying above our heads, as the first, fat, refreshing drops of rain plopped down. The lightning crackled. Visions came to me of a single bolt, shot into our midst and bowling us down like so many defenseless pins along that black macadam alley. In minutes, we were soaked. The march continued fearlessly on to the assured rhythms of the rosary, toward which my attitude had changed throughout the march. At the beginning I thought it uniquely laborious; soon after, aided by an ignorance of its words, I discovered that its monotonous cadences were highly conducive to marching. Now, however, I found the chant personally inopportune. It occurred to me that I was the only one not praying.

It was still raining when we came into the village of what was to be our last encampment, Zawada (which in America would be the municipality of Obstacle). The lightning had passed and the roadway was littered with blown leaves and felled branches. The sun hinted at appearance. I was walking down the hill when Father Czuma approached and asked if I would mind doing duty that night as an orderly.

Presently Laurent joined me, and he and I continued down the hill to the house that was serving as the headquarters. A blond boy with an armband stood on a roofless cement porch and blocked our entrance. I explained that I was the volunteer from the yellow-and-white group, and his expression softened. He said my first duty was to find the French group and tell them to appoint two pilgrims to stand guard overnight.

On our way, we were met by a Renault jeep driven by a Pole traveling with the French as interpreter. His sister sat next to him.

"Urszula," Laurent said to the girl, "you have somebody to speak English with."

"Really?" the girl exclaimed in soft, unaccented tones, and turned around. "Are you English?"

"No, American."

"Really? It's nice to see you. I study English. My brother studies French. But we're going to stop so we can sell cakes."

"Cakes?" I asked.

"Yes, our father has a cake shop in Warsaw," the boy explained in English. "I have one more year until I get the equivalent of my master's in French literature. When I get out next summer there will be no jobs, so I'll go into baking cakes with my father. My sister will be there too, because she couldn't even get into university," he said with mock criticism, and they exchanged knowing smiles.

We arrived at the French camp. Laurent found me a priest, and I relayed to him my orders. He exhibited no misgivings, nor, even more baffling to me, any doubts as to my integrity. He assured me he would comply. Laurent and his friend Wojtek went back to the car to search for Krakovians; Urszula asked me: "Can I walk with you back to the base? I'd like the chance to speak English."

Urszula's English, similar to that of some of my more gifted students, was untouched by native accent or inflection. It was an English in which the only giveaway as to her identity as a foreign speaker might have been the unaccustomed care with which she uttered each phrase.

"Did you learn English at school?" I asked.

"Well, at the beginning. But then last summer I went to England, where I worked as an au pair. It was so easy to get a passport and go abroad. I'm glad I took advantage of the chance when I had it. Now I don't know when I'll be able to get back to England — or anywhere."

"What's this your brother said about your not getting into the university?"

"That's true. I failed the entrance exam."

"For what department?"

"English."

"Impossible."

"No, listen. I took the exam at Warsaw University. It was an oral exam. And do you know what they asked me? They asked me which member of the British royal family fought in the Falklands war? I didn't know," she said, strangely apologetically.

"But was that all?"

"They asked me to speak at some length on Polish-Australian relations."

"Oh God. What did you do?"

"I just got up and said, 'I'm sorry but I can't answer your questions,' and walked out."

"So what will you do now?" I asked.

"*Cakes!*" she said triumphantly.

We reached the base.

"Well, thank you for putting up with my poor English," she said. "Maybe when you get back to Warsaw you can stop by our cake shop." She wrote down the address for me. "It's quite in the center of the city. They're really good cakes, too. Private, you know. We used to have much more variety, but now it's so hard to get sugar and the right flour. Still, I think they're the best cakes in Warsaw. But then I'm prejudiced. Thanks again."

"Did you get the message through to the French?" Jacek, the blond orderly, asked me as I came up toward the porch.

He was about seventeen. We sat down on the stoop with another orderly and the kindly, clubfooted man who ran the lost and found, and chatted among ourselves. And so we prepared for the long watch. My only apprehension was that I might not get the rest I needed to make the last day's walk to Częstochowa. (The prospect of failing was still with me.) Jacek suggested that the three of us alternate at two-hour sleeping shifts, to begin soon after ten o'clock. "You know," he said to me at one point. "I have many acquaintances in America. Yes, many. Father Doroszewski in New York, Father Świtkiewicz in Atlanta, Fathers Borowicz and Jastrzębski in Los Angeles, Father Skarzyński in Chicago. I could do all right once I got there. They'd help me out, for sure. It's not like I'd be going there without knowing anybody. What about" — now he lowered his voice and moved closer to me — "sending me an invitation when you get back to the States? It wouldn't be any trouble, would it? That's all I'd need. Just an invitation. You wouldn't have to worry about me after that. As I told you, I have lots of acquaintances there. Father Doroszewski and Father Świtkiewicz. . . . But I can't go . . . I can't do anything without the invitation. Listen," he whispered now, even more confidentially, standing nose to nose with me, "you know what the situation is like now in this country. True? So, you understand. Let me give you my address." He wrote it into my notebook, exasperatingly legible. "O.K. You won't forget?"

We resumed normal tones on more neutral grounds, as if the plea had never been made. A little past nine o'clock a tall, middle-aged man in sport clothes appeared and identified himself, in correct Polish, as a Swedish journalist.

"You can see Father as soon as he's free," Jacek told him. "He's in conference at the moment. Too bad you didn't come a little earlier, you could have seen some action here."

The Swede took a seat with us on the stoop. "Really? What happened?"

"They caught some provocateurs on the march this afternoon. It seems a car drove up full of men, stopped, and one of them got out and started walking with the pilgrimage. A priest saw it and thought it looked suspicious. He went up to the man and asked to see his identity card. The man refused to show it. They brought him down here for questions. Too bad we didn't have a tape recorder. The priest made him look like a fool."

"What did he say?"

"He said he just wanted to have a look at the pilgrimage."

"So what did they do with him?"

"Nothing," said Jacek. "They just let him go. What could they do? Turn him over to the police?" And the irony of the question hit us all at the same moment, namely, that this man *was* the police.

"The thing I find most astounding," said the Swede, "is how incredibly well it all seems to be organized."

"You know," I said, "an elderly Pole told me in Warsaw before I came, 'You will see on that pilgrimage something miraculous. You will see thousands of people, young and old, with and without supplies, travel for nine days, during which not one soul will go hungry nor will one soul be left without a place to sleep. And that in a country short on food and with fifteen years' wait for an apartment.'"

"How many people are there on the pilgrimage?" he asked.

"I heard about forty thousand," I said. "The group I'm in has about seven hundred. We started out at five hundred, but people joined us from the villages and towns we passed through. Now that group — my group — is only part of a main unit that comprises about twelve other groups. The unit is number seventeen. There are sixteen other units ahead of us. The figures go into the tens of thousands. And this is only from Warsaw. It doesn't include the thousands coming from other cities and towns."

A "secretary" came and said that Father was free to see the visitor, and the Swede entered the house. One by one, sometimes two by two, somber young men appeared and stood in expectant circles in the backyard. Many carried flashlights.

"Who are they?" I asked Jacek.

"They're the night patrol. Father's going to come out soon and talk to them."

When the priest did emerge, after the conclusion of his interview with the Swede, it was near eleven o'clock, and the patrol gathered in two regimental lines of about ten men each. They looked like a sheriff's midnight posse. The priest expressed his appreciation to the volunteers for their service and gave them their instructions. They were to go about the encampment in pairs. If they saw anything suspicious, one of them was to come and report it immediately to headquarters. Any people sneaking about were first to be given a warning. If the same person was caught a second time, he said, "then I leave it up to you to use your own good judgment."

As they dispersed to make their rounds, the priest started back toward his office. Jacek halted him a moment and said, "Father, we have an extra guard tonight. An American."

"Well," he said, and turned to me with a smile. "So we are in good hands."

IX

As I awoke I found myself, strangely, in a bed, and, even more strangely, bathed in light. Jacek stood in front of me.

"What time is it?" I asked him.

"Five o'clock."

"What happened? Why didn't anybody wake me? I was only supposed to sleep two hours."

"Don't worry. We decided to let you sleep. After all, you're not Polish, you shouldn't have to work. Besides, it was very quiet."

I gathered my things and said my farewell to Jacek, who walked me out to the porch. As I was about to go, he said: "You'll remember about the invitation?"

I walked up that lifeless village street intensely happy. I passed courtyards yet still and inactive in the nascence of morning, and thought, Today we go to Częstochowa. And I will make it!

In the garden of a thatch hut, I saw a pilgrim girl gathering flowers for a Częstochowa bouquet.

"What are they called?" I asked, for they were the daisy-like flowers that sprout before every peasant house in Poland. She didn't know (nor did anyone of the dozens I asked later), but she came forward and bestowed on me a fine yellow one to keep and carry.

An hour later our group assembled. According to our schedule, we had eighteen kilometers to Jasna Góra.

Late in the morning we turned off the road and continued on a dirt path between sun-beaten fields. Now a considerable space grew between each group, and when, after a long haul, we reached the farthest end of that plain, we (as we'd seen the previous sections doing) fell to our knees. The tower of Jasna Góra was before us. It was only after our prayer of thanks to Mary that I discerned it. It did not appear, as Reymont described it, "like a hurricane." Maria, who had seen it countless times before, picked it out of the mist for me: over-topping the hill in front of us, a slender spear of high-lighted gray in a gray horizon. I was struck by how far away it appeared. It was the first time on the pilgrimage that I had actually glimpsed ahead of me our destina-tion. And just as well, for looking into those shrouded depths it seemed to me startling that I was going to walk that distance, and even more startling that that distance, when translated into figures, we had all considered pid-dling. I remembered that earlier pilgrims used to crawl on their knees from this point, or carry heavy rocks, and took courage from the thought. And I found solace in recalling the ancient adage that "the powers of the devils can do nothing in a circle where the tower of Jasna Góra is visible."

We lifted ourselves up and careened down a rocky path into a small valley between two hills. Here, we were told, we would have a rest of undetermined time to await our placement in the congested procession into Częstochowa. Pilgrims scurried up the hill to stake out places, I thought to eat or sleep, and when next I looked at that mound I saw everyone turned to each other, in couples, and kissing — a sudden, mass outbreak of affection on a hillside. Pilgrims stood at all levels, young with old, brothers with sisters, sisters with sisters, broth-ers with brothers, pecking one another the customary three times on the cheek. ("Oh yes, three," an American friend said once, greeting my wife, "everything in Po-land is odd.")

"What is going on?" I asked Marek.

"It's a tradition here, before arriving to Częstochowa, to make apologies to your fellow pilgrims for your sins, and misdeeds, and for them to forgive you, so that you will have a clear conscience when you come before Mary. The name of the place is *Przeprośna Górka* [Hill of Forgiveness]."

All about us an equal number of people were begging forgiveness and being forgiven — a redoubtable ratio. Tears dampened hundreds of eyes, with both joy and sadness: joy, for we had nearly made it; sadness, for it was nearly over. An hour after we'd landed on that hill, a couple of straggling hugs were still being offered, a few remaining *przepraszams* could still be heard. A long and lovely moment that had been.

We rose to march. Some pilgrims carried bouquets of flowers; others bore wooden crosses they had carved during the long days of the walk. Our pace was quick with expectation. We came down a built-up street and saw the smokestacks of factories and the tops of apartment towers. Below us lay a city, the first since Warsaw, and we were back, from wherever it was that we had been.

We rumbled onto a black iron bridge and then, very shortly, we were on the Avenue of the Most Blessed Virgin Mary. It is a tree-lined street with a walkway in the middle, which runs laterally through the center of town, up to the foot of Jasna Góra. Its whole length this day was lined with citizens to greet our arrival. They stood close together on both sides, now in the late afternoon hours under a leaden sky. We met them, not as in earlier years, with songs and hymns, but with a rosary: a constant, solemn chanting of the mysteries. The stage was

altered from that in Warsaw. Here, in place of the sunlight and levity, was grayness and zeal. The lowered sky
and the closeness of the crowd lent a dramatic imme-
diacy to the scene, and the effect, as the tear-strained
voices chanted with us, was, if possible, more moving
than in the capital.

> *Święta Mario, Matko Boża*
> *Módl się za nami grzesznymi*
> *Teraz i w godzinę śmierci naszej. Amen.*

> Holy Mary, Mother of God
> Pray for us sinners
> Now and at the hour of our death. Amen.

Maria saw me and motioned to me to step ahead of
her, leaving a place that she somehow knew I'd desire,
on the end with a view to all the people who passed.
They looked, collectively, older, sicklier, more indigent,
than in Warsaw, their faces paler and more sunken. I
tried to look into each one of the faces, but we walked
too quickly — no sooner would I register one than another would take its place. I grew numb from the chanting, and the stillness, and the sweetness of the *fait ac-
compli.*

> *Święta Mario, Matko Boża*
> *Módl się za nami grzesznymi*
> *Teraz i w godzinę śmierci naszej. Amen.*

I had learned to say this much. We halted several times.
At the briefest of pauses a man in the crowd reached
out and clasped my wrist, tightly pressing it in wordless
communion until we moved. A small boy stepped forth

and handed me a warm bottle of carbonated soda, looking up at me as if to a Sunday's hero. Farther along
a rubicund worker, no less delirious than I, sprinted
out into the street to give me a stem of gladiola, crying hoarsely: *"Żeby Polska była Polską"* (Let Poland be
Poland).

I had never before in my life been, nor do I expect
ever again to be, the recipient of such a complete and
passionate demonstration of public approbation. I realized that as a foreigner I could not appreciate the full
significance of this display; yet I understood enough,
and, more importantly, felt enough, to be lifted immeasurably by it. If, when we at last reached the foot of
Jasna Góra, I found it tricky to walk, it was not because
of fatigue.

> *Święta Mario, Matko Boża*
> *Módl się za nami grzesznymi*
> *Teraz i w godzinę śmierci naszej. Amen.*

We inched our way up that royal pass and rose gradually on its incline, first between the tall trees of the
park — the crowds forming a triumphant alley — and
then into the great, open grounds amassed with bodies.
We viewed, ever and ever clearer before us, the monastery: the high, fortress walls of brick and ivy; atop them
the cluttered lines of balcony, roof, and statuary; and,
rising high above it all, slightly to the left, the beacon
tower.

By the church wall, now clearly visible, a great sheet
rose for several stories. It showed an enormous, feathery white eagle, the national symbol, crowned, as before
the last war. In the center, or heart, of the eagle was

painted the Black Madonna with child. At the bottom, by the eagle's outstretched claws, were sprigs of thorn, or, depending on one's viewpoint, snips of barbed wire. Running the whole length of the fortification wall, at its top, was a banner reading: THE QUEEN OF JASNA GÓRA — BE ALWAYS WITH US.

We moved up for the official announcement and greeting of our group. Every one of us fell to his knees. High above the walls one could espy a tribunal, canopied and niched insubstantially into that stone edifice as if afloat. I could vaguely discern faraway priests within. Lay bodies perched on every available inch of balcony and ledge. I felt like part of a Roman legion, ceremoniously bowed before the emperor.

After the introduction, it took us a long time to work our way around the southeastern bastion to the monastery entrance. After perhaps half an hour we reached the main entranceway and pushed on through the Lubomirski Gate. "Here," Pope John Paul II had said, "the Poles always were free." Both ledges of the high, semicircular walls were deep with flowers, and I placed my gladiola among them.

We pushed through a series of arched gateways and found ourselves in a bustling courtyard, as if having passed over medieval causeways into a magnificent walled city. Father Czuma asked all the young men to step to the sides and link arms, forming a protective wall for the rest as they moved toward the chapel. I found the push extreme, though the boy whose arm I linked said, "This is nothing. In fact, it's pretty good this year. Last year it was bedlam." We were dragged closer, and then, at last, inside. The chapel was somber and, with so much traffic, strangely still. The ceiling was high and vaulted; the side walls dripped darkly with the collective spoils of pilgrims' devotions over six centuries — chains, trinkets, badges, medals, bibelots. Ahead of us the massive rood screen was studded with a high, semicircle of old wooden crutches. Behind it, the picture: uncovered, yet so dark the features were indistinguishable. I centered my eyes on a brown space the shape of an acorn, a tall golden crown atop it, bejeweled robes below; the entire image embedded, above the altar, in an ornate burst of silver, gilt, and crystal. Each of us knelt momentarily in individual prayer, then was whisked away.

I slept for a few hours in our campground behind the monastery, and then awoke at two A.M. A special service was to be said in the chapel for the Warsaw group. There were no other pilgrims on the path, and alone I passed tents heaving with mortal snoring. Uncertain as to which way to go, I turned and saw in the distance a bright cross, lighting the sky above the tower like a lodestar. ("When all the lights went out for Poland . . .") Not until reaching the outer walls of the monastery did I find movement, that nightlong drift of sleepless souls, like travelers at a station. Gaining the courtyard, I found even more pilgrims gathered, and once in the chapel I was immersed in a fanfare of humanity.

Immediately inside the doors there were pilgrims sleeping at my feet. They were parked three- and four-deep against the walls, mostly women, some next to their children, all unmistakably from the provinces. They offered a profusion of colorful head scarves, lumpy travel bags, thick stockings, blunt shoes. A few wore their majestically striped capes draped across their shoulders. They had traveled from their homes and villages and, with nowhere to sleep in the city of Częstochowa, had made humble bedding here in the shrine of their Lady. At first they seemed to me, with their bodily sprawl and human stench, an affront on her holy chapel, yet eventually I was to see them as a tribute, and living example of her protection and care. As the great Polish painter, playwright, and poet Stanisław Wyspiański wrote in *The Queen of the Polish Crown,*

> *Before you — O Mother of God.*
> *Before you the poor people kneel in misery and despair,*
> *The people of God of this Polish land.*

I worked my way into the nave. The pews at either side were full of the elderly and middle-aged who had conquered them the day before; some kneeling, their hands folded in prayer, fast asleep. A tremendous flourish of music crashed — a brittle chorus of brass and string which sounded more Gaelic than Slavic — and pounded uproariously between the walls. Halfway into the nave I met the groping swarm of penitents and was washed into its incontinent wave. Anything that I had, in the pilgrimage or in life, beheld as a crush, was here dispelled. I could not walk, I could barely breathe.

I squirmed my way through. The jacket that I had put on against the chill was tugged half off me, and my face burst out in sweat. I strained ever closer inside, not knowing how I would get out safely. For there was no exit other than the one we had come in. We were hundreds strong, all pushing into an even smaller space. Each person was making his own individual indentions, though we expanded, and contracted, as one body. Sometimes I was flipped sideways, nose to nose with a stranger; once I looked and saw Alicja impaled against a man's chest. I reached the rood screen, which seemed itself almost to bend from the pressure. I tried to stop there, but it was not the crowd's will, and I was popped in deeper. People who had never felt a fear of claustrophobia did so now, while others hosted thoughts of death by suffocation. It was strange to think that in this same chamber, a few yards away, people lulled in untroubled sleep. Odd, also, to think it two o'clock in the morning.

I found it more and more difficult to catch my breath, and turned to fight my way out. It was, obviously, with much more effort than I had used coming in. When, at the back of the chapel, I broke free, I saw the peasants still bunched on the floor, their sleep undisturbed.

Outside I breathed in the cool air and took a seat against a wall to hear the service through the loudspeakers. Pilgrims were parceled all about the courtyard in similar positions, many sleeping with their families bundled under blankets. Near me a young nun dozed, her habited legs stretched out in front of her. An elderly, white-haired man approached me in his good black suit, asked if the paint rubbed off, then took a seat beside me. He told me he had come from Poznan; I said I'd come from America. Soon he was fast asleep.

At the end of the service all but the sleeping stood, inside and out, their arms raised purposefully in V's, and sang the occupation version of "Boże Coś Polskę," which ends, "God, return our free country to us."

The next morning I wandered around the monastery grounds alone. "I have weather," I said to myself, though it didn't sound the same in the singular. Outside the entrance walls, I found the inevitable religious commerce — rosaries, statues, pins, plates, baubles — assembled on portable tables along the walk. Men had set up primitive games of chance: a rickety wheel spun with five numbers on it; cutout paper horses galloped to the deciding roll of a pair of dice. It was such a feeble assembly that it seemed almost quaint, and had none of the garish effrontery of such commercialism at Western shrines. Here, at least, the church could thank the Communists for a certain purity.

Then I walked through to the interior streets again, still busy, as they would be for days, with pilgrims. In great happiness, I found Laurent.

"You've made it!" I said.

"And you too!" We embraced.

"How is everybody?"

"Fine. Everybody's here and in good shape."

We climbed a flight of open steps that took us to the top of the ramparts, from which we had a commanding view of the city. At such a point Sienkiewicz's hero Kmicic could have stood, shelling the Swedes.

I asked Laurent what he had thought of the previous day's entrance. "It was very different from last year's," he said. "Much more solemn. And the people greeting us showed that too. Their faces were harder and more intense. There was little display of joy."

A young man and woman approached and presented Laurent with two pins of their group.

"I heard him speaking French," the man told me. "We are very grateful to the French for all the medicine and food their country's sending us. And we're very grateful that they came to participate in the pilgrimage with us."

"Laurent was here last year," I explained. "And he was just telling me how much more solemn the procession was this year."

"Yes, because of the tragic situation in the country," he said, and I translated. "When our group came up this hill yesterday, our leaders placed a branch there by the Virgin Mary as a symbol of our hurt." He pointed to the statue, with its back to us far below. "Many people in our group wouldn't accept flowers or gifts from the people, also as a sign of the penitential aspect of the march. But there was a tremendous following this year, a tremendous number of people who walked, and that is a very important thing. And many of them were young.

"You see, nothing can happen now, for the time being. We must wait a few years. In the meantime, we will come here again, as we did this week. And we'll try to live our lives according to what we learned here, and on the way here. And then something is going to happen in this country. You see all the young people. We have a whole generation on our side. In previous times there may have been a majority, but not such a majority as now. The government could always buy some young people off, with promises of apartments, cars, etc. Now that's no longer possible. The government has no money with which to offer any of these things to anybody. It's bankrupt. It's lost face as well. While here, every year, more people gather. Now we wait. We must wait until this new generation grows up a bit. And then we'll see."

VI
Waiting for the
Stefan Batory

AS EARLY AS MARCH I had booked passage on the *Stefan Batory*, which, sadly, is no longer in service. I enjoyed the languor of ships, which gives a person time to contemplate the uprooting from one home to another. Fourteen days at sea on a Polish ship would do nicely, I thought.

My farewells began in June, when I gave my last classes at the Methodist School. In the final week I ran into Magdalena, who had been mysteriously absent for weeks, missing the final exam and thus forfeiting the semester. "I have been in a terrible state," she told me. Several weeks earlier, just before she was to defend her thesis on Mallarmé, she had received a telegram from her fiancé in Paris. "We were to be married this summer. He said in the telegram that he was going on to his family in Chicago. I had no idea of any of this." He told her that perhaps some day, if things got better in Poland, she would be able to get out and join him. "Join such a man!" she said. "And this after five years of going together!" I asked her how he had acted the last time they had been together. "Perfectly normal." She already had a wedding dress. They had an apartment ready, which, as a single woman, she would lose all rights to, and have to go on living with her parents. She related all of this with remarkable candor and control, concluding philosophically, "One must live" (the Polish variant of "Life goes on"). At the break I went out onto the stone balcony and told Eliza, one of the teachers, this tale. She looked down at the colorful Fiats jockeying around the square, which was bedded with tulips, then said quietly: "Do you know how many stories there are like that now? It's our complete moral decay." I had momentarily forgotten that her husband had left her in the sixth month of pregnancy to move in with her best friend.

On the last day of classes I arrived as nervous as I had on the first, nearly four years before. Walking into a sunlit Room 26 at four o'clock I found a message written on the board by my intermediate students: "Dear Tomasz, Best Wishes on/at (Choose One) the Last Lesson." They presented me ceremoniously with flowers and stood to sing a rousing chorus of "Sto Lat" ("May You Live a Hundred Years"). I was terribly moved and told them so, in terrible Polish: "*Jestem wru . . . zwru . . . wzruszony.*" Jacek struggled equally to get a picture out of his camera, which, the others loudly advertised, was Russian-made. I received a book, an album of Warsaw photographs bearing the front-page inscription in Polish, signed by all: "To fine Tomasz — In thanks for the excellent method of conducting lessons, the great pedagogical talent, and the sweet smile — Faithful listeners."

My five o'clock students gave me a single, long-stemmed yellow rose and the newly reprinted antiquarian book entitled *Sketches and Pictures from Warsaw Life.* Inside, on a separate sheet, they had signed their names below a Stanisław Lec aphorism, "Everything passes, even the longest snake." Beside this were the words, in equally unsentimental Polish, "To the nicest American we know. (We know only one.)"

At each break I returned burdened with more flowers, and the ladies in the smokers' room scurried around to dig up vases. At tea Miss Wiaderny gave me a matchbox-sized collection of poems by Julian Tuwim, a gesture that touched me greatly. On the way home, I passed the flower vendors on Narutowicz Square, and noted with satisfaction that my supply exceeded theirs.

I spent my last September in Warsaw as I had my first: endlessly traveling the city. It seemed, after the dilapidation I'd seen in the provinces, a true metropolis, wondrously grand and elegant. Sitting on buses I wrote down the simple names of the shops we passed: OBUWIE, KSIĘGARNIA, ZABAWKI, APTEKA, FRYZJER, SŁODYCZE, MIĘSO. I studied the city's features — shop windows, cars, cafés, doors, trams, apartments, kiosks, queues — for who knew when I would see them again? As much as Warsaw had become a second home to me, it was still a prohibitively long distance from my first.

I went to the Malaysian embassy to see Stefan and accompanied him to a smoky neighborhood café for lunch. He apologized for being so long out of touch, explaining that illness had run through his entire family, ending up in jaundice for his wife. He himself looked pale and tired. His work was going all right, he said, but I knew that it held neither challenge nor advancement for him. He promised to write, wished me and Hania well, and shook my hand firmly. (Unlike most Polish men, he was not inclined to kissing.)

Soon I was down to a week. I paid my last visit to Dr. Zięba. She greeted me warmly and led me into the living room, where various gifts were laid upon the table: a hand-carved wooden letter opener from the Tatras, a bottle of a Polish brandy long unobtainable, and another matchbox-sized volume, this one complete with illustrations, of *Pan Tadeusz*.

I played one last game of tennis with Andy at the Warszawianka courts. The old, bare-chested groundsman raked the clay as always, and when he came up behind me, commented, barely lifting his head: "So, sir, you are leaving the country." They were the first words he had ever spoken to me. The verb he chose, *opuszczać*, is actually much stronger than "leave," rather like "abandon" or "desert," and is sometimes used, with patriotic insinuations, for young Poles who decide to emigrate. No one in that last week made me feel more at home, or sad for leaving.

The night before my departure, the mood in the apartment was high-pitched, not only over my leaving. (Hania was staying for another few months, to allow me to get settled, preferably with a job, in the States.) Leszek had just been offered a year-long contract with a French engineering firm in Iraq. It meant that he would earn Western money, which would serve him and Gosia well when, on his return, they would finally marry.

The following day broke dull and wet. I sat anxiously at the kitchen table, looking out onto the gray, windowless wall of the tenement opposite. Jadzia cooked me a special, spicy casserole that I was too excited to enjoy. At last the hour came for the train, and Hania and I gathered my traveling bags in the hall. (Leszek was driving the boxes up in his Syrena after us.) I hugged Bocia awkwardly, finding the retrieval of appropriate salutations in Polish difficult. Jadzia got up from comforting the dog and embraced me. Tears watered her eyes as she made the sign of the cross upon my forehead with her thumb. Then Gosia kissed me. Once downstairs, I looked up to our fourth-floor kitchen and found Jadzia newly seated at the open window, making the sign of the cross in the drizzly sky.

At Warsaw's Central Station, Hania and I boarded the train to Sopot. As we started to move, I sat glued to the rain-streaked window. "I think it's probably best that your last view of Warsaw is like this," said Hania. Jadzia had explained the weather: "The angels over Warsaw are crying at your departure."

We arrived in the seaside resort town of Sopot that evening and took a taxi to the Grand Hotel. I remembered it from a trip to Gdansk four years before: the graceful shingled building among the pines, the once elegant gardens, the sweeping beachfront prospect. Leszek, and Hania's girlhood friend Ewa, who had accompanied him, were waiting in the lobby as we came in.

The next morning we drove the boxes to the port in Gdynia. The *Batory*, with its handsome, black and white lines, sat regally at the dock. A porter loaded the collection onto a freight elevator and took us upstairs to an enormous, airy terminal for customs inspection.

Sunday, we awoke to a fine day of sunlight and soft, blue skies. The road to Gdynia was colored by trees turned yellow, and the already fallen leaves skittered about in a dance of Polish golden autumn.

We said our farewells in front of the terminal. Leszek kissed me in a manly fashion three times on the cheek, then presented me with a small cross, embedded with the Polish eagle, which I could attach to a chain. To remember. Hania and I embraced, and then reluctantly I walked away. High up on the gangway I stood a moment and waved down to them, before ducking quickly into the ship.

After a few hours the *Batory* eased out of its dock, while a small orchestra played the haunting polonaise of Ogiński, "Adieu to the Fatherland." Two stocky tugs turned us around and then set us on our course across the Gulf of Gdansk. I stood at the railing of the stern and watched as the crowd on the quay contracted and the terminal receded. Once out beyond the Hel Peninsula, and into the Baltic, I continued watching as the features of the land grew indistinguishable and Poland became a faint, anonymous bar stretching along the watery horizon.

Epilogue ═══════

ONE OF THE FIRST THINGS the air traveler sees upon landing in Warsaw is a modest band of people gathered on a raised walkway outside the terminal to welcome the flight. Okęcie is a small airport, arrivals are rarely simultaneous, and if friends or family are waiting for you, chances are they are in that crowd. It is always reassuring to find the gathering unchanged, intimate in size and purpose and with a poignancy that comes of long separations. You look up from the airport bus at the expectant faces — the young father standing patiently with a child in one hand, roses in the other — and feel immediately rewarded for coming in a way you seldom do at larger airports in happier countries.

When Hania and I first returned together, in the fall of 1985, Bocia, Jadzia, and Gosia greeted us here enthusiastically, with flowers, while Leszek snapped pictures. He and Gosia had been married earlier that year. For our arrival three years later, only Leszek and Gosia showed; Bocia had died and Jadzia was unwell after a massive heart attack. Leszek drove us to their new house in Otrębusy, a small suburb southwest of Warsaw. Despite the accumulated savings of his two years in Iraq, followed by two in Kuwait, they had been unable to afford a decent apartment within the city. The following spring we received a telegram of Jadzia's passing.

On a Friday morning in the fall of 1990, Leszek met

me at Okęcie. Hania was in Washington, working temporarily as a consultant to the World Bank. She now frequently came to Poland with a mission devoted to the country's housing crisis.

It was, of course, my first trip ever to the Republic of Poland, as it now called itself. During my previous visits, I had had to look for themes, in the overall stagnation, to write about. In 1985 I focused on the drift of many Poles, in light of the mandatory retreat from politics, toward private enterprise. In 1988 I concentrated on the phenomenon of emigration, which seemed, along with the economy and pollution, to be among the most serious and insoluble problems facing Poland. Not only were people leaving at an astounding rate — an estimated 600,000, though not all for good, between 1980 and 1988 — but a large percentage of them were young and talented. Just as the Soviet army, at Katyń, had destroyed the promise of the new generation, so, years later, was the Soviet system driving it out.

In the fall of 1990, however, there was no need to search for a story. There was only one — the return of freedom and independence (in the words of our pilgrimage priest just eight years before) — and its reach extended far beyond Poland. But as always in Poland, there were countless interpretations.

Leszek and I went to the hospital to pick up Gosia and from there we drove to the Wilanów Café on Ujazdowskie Avenue. They both looked well, little changed from two years before. Leszek's time in the desert had aged him only slightly, most notably with a becoming tinge of gray in his boyish blond hair.

We ordered tea and cakes, for thousands of złotys, and caught up on news. Because of the scarcity of capital, little new building was going on, and Leszek's engineering firm, not for the first time, was short of work. He was greatly concerned about the advent of foreign investment.

"Western firms will come in," he explained, "bringing their own materials and their own managers, their own people who understand the technology. The only thing they will need us for is the simpleminded physical work. And they will exploit us. They will take away the profits while we are left to do the dirty work. Poland will become renowned as a source of cheap labor." He knew the process well from Iraq and Kuwait.

"These are very uncertain times," he continued. "Very uncertain. Germany is strengthening itself. It is conceivable that we will become even poorer. And that could be a catastrophe. Because when you are a poor, weak nation, you are not important to anyone. If you have no valuable resources, no powerful trading partners, who cares whether you survive or perish? And it is precisely then that larger nations look to take you over." The decline of Communism, which many in the West had viewed as giving birth to a new, united European order, Leszek and other Poles saw as opening the door to ancient, historic aggression. At first I was tempted to laugh at this bleak and characteristic perspective — Poles again obsessing on their national fate — until I remembered how often throughout history such dour analyses have proven true for Poland.

"And it will take years to get rid of this system," he continued. "Not on paper, perhaps, but in people's minds. Gosia and I, no matter how much we detested it and protested against it, are infected by it. It is still here," he said pointing, "in our heads." I was startled to hear Leszek admit this, having for years heard from him nothing but the most personal condemnations of the system. "The next generation," he said, "will be the first to grow up uncontaminated."

In the following days, I did as I always do on returning to Warsaw: I walked. The weather was cold and wet, and finding it exactly as I rememberd it did not lessen my discomfort. I entered familiar cafés for glasses of tea. Unlike my new home, Florida, where it rains for fifteen minutes and then the sun comes out again, here the sun peeped through for fifteen minutes between the rains. Pedestrians grimaced, poking their way with umbrellas. Leszek had complained of the increase in potholes, and I thought he had meant in the streets until I stepped on several loose pavement stones in the sidewalk, which tipped up their opposite ends to send small bodies of water washing across my shoes.

Rain dripped incessantly from vendors' stands, and those without tops covered their merchandise with plastic tarp. These sidewalk entrepreneurs clustering around the downtown streets provided the most striking physical change in Warsaw. In front of the Palace of Culture and the department stores on Marszałkowska Street, they ran tiny booths that they folded up and locked at night; along Nowy Świat and other streets, they generally spent the day sitting passively behind card tables. (The national passion for bridge had finally proved useful.) The most elementary business operation I saw was along Jerozolimskie Avenue, where a couple had simply parked their car and placed a few possessions atop the hood. The old grizzled women still sat with their timeless gifts of flowers and pumice stones and now looked almost historic.

The result of all this was that Warsaw seemed less a city than a teeming bazaar. People still filled the streets at all hours of the day — you cannot walk in Warsaw without wondering who is left in the offices — and now were slowed in their progress by the endless number of things to see, items to inspect. The popularity of this trade was most evident along Marszałkowska Street, where shoppers unanimously turned their backs on the display windows of the department stores to examine the counters of the private booths.

You could do a decent shopping without ever entering a shop: these vendors sold food, clothes, jewelry, health and beauty products, music tapes and books. Except for the last two, many of these products bore German labels, explaining why one of the daily trains to Germany carried the nickname "Vendors' Express." Just as 1980 had been the year of the worker — with its own documentary film, *Workers 1980*, about the August strikes — so, it seemed to me, 1990 was the year of the vendor. (I wondered why no Polish director had made *Vendors 1990*.) Walking the streets of Warsaw, I could not help but feel that Poland had become, in less than a year, a nation of small shopkeepers — without shops, of course — just as for years it had been, and still was, a nation of apartment dwellers without apartments.

A number of my Polish friends bemoaned this commerce from an aesthetic viewpoint; and indeed, the clutter of booths along Marszałkowska Street successfully made the downtown of a European capital resemble the honky-tonk midway of a county fair. However, a foreigner I met who had spent some time in Poland in the early eighties was surprisingly encouraged. "At least there's something going on," he said. "You have all the hustle and bustle of a real free market.

I'd rather see that than long queues waiting for meat." I agreed with him, but still found the phenomenon disturbing. It was an artificial, evanescent busyness; the only thing being made was money. And to have so many people, many of them young, spending their days idly selling another country's merchandise struck me as an untimely waste.

Elsewhere, I found subtler changes, familiar sights with unfamiliar twists. The great signboards still stood in Constitution Square and in front of the Palace of Culture, but their socialist slogans had been replaced by Western advertising. The same groaning trams ran, but now of three types: those identical to previous ones, with their pale red cars; those with small advertising signs painted on the sides; and those wholly given over to the colors of their sponsors, the most startling example being the new Milka chocolate tram that made its way in purple passages through the city. It looked even more farfetched as the same drab commuters climbed through its now fancifully painted doors.

The *woda sodowa* vendors still clung to their parasoled carts, but now in addition to seltzer water, they carried elegantly labeled bottles of kiwi and mango juice. The prevalence of exotic fruits in a country that had recently been starved of oranges amazed me. One day on the train to Otrębusy, I noticed an odor I never associated with Polish public transport: seated in front of me was a young girl nonchalantly eating a banana. In the late seventies, the term "banana children" had been used to describe the offspring of the privileged few.

Long lines for visas still formed in the courtyard of the American embassy, though just across the street one enterprising man had parked a small trailer and offered photos in three minutes. The eagles decorating the plaques of government buildings had all been given back their crowns. And on the steps of the deserted party headquarters teenagers fearlessly rode their skate-boards.

There were, as well, new features that had already taken on inveterate characteristics. The Marriott Hotel had set up a reception booth at the airport which, when I came through shortly before noon on a Friday, was un-occupied. The telephone rang and rang, unanswered, suggesting at least one fundamentally unchanged at-titude.

Western newspapers and magazines were now avail-able in hotel lobbies and bookstores. In the latter they were usually layered with the local press, and instead of standing out with their high-quality color, they seemed somehow to take on the dull sheen of their neighbors. I noticed that the tabloid *Kurier Polski* had embraced the idea of a sensational press and enthusiastically applied it to national obsessions. A headline one evening, suggest-ing a kind of thinking man's *National Enquirer*, read: "Did Stalin Poison Lenin?"

The lights of a sex shop blazed on Marszałkowska Street, and a few international firms — Benetton, Puma, Salamander — had added their names to the cityscape. Benetton added as well a whole new class of manne-quins that were, in their outfits costing several months' salary, as far removed from the reality of most Warsaw women's wardrobes as the Raggedy Ann mannequins in the state clothing shops.

Inside the classical gates of the University of Warsaw, the underground booksellers had been replaced by a trailer dispensing hamburgers and hot dogs. What they had once handled exclusively was now easily obtained in the Prus bookstore across the street, or, at slightly lower prices, from the card tables set up along the sidewalks. Émigré Polish writers and statesmen — Miłosz, Kołakowski, Mrożek, Brzeziński — were well represented, as were still local talents like Kapuściński and Konwicki. A translated edition of Timothy Garton Ash's book on the Polish revolution had taken its place between the sunbleached postcards and shampoos in kiosks. The national passion for lavishly illustrated books seemed to have reached its apotheosis with one elegantly produced volume entitled: *Wieliczka: Seven Centuries of Polish Salt.*

A few new stores had opened with large front windows proclaiming the name and year of founding, as some families had been given back the shops taken from them after the war. One address downtown now served authentic pizza, and almost as important, its aroma traveled several blocks. A Greek restaurant had opened recently near the university, allowing moneyed students a taste of souvlaki.

Also new this time were graffiti. The underground passage in front of the university carried them in profusion — it was here, I was told, where the practice had begun — while other instances were sprouting all over the city. Scribbled across the foundation of a soulless apartment house, graffiti didn't seem all that regrettable, especially when, as happened frequently, they offered amusing messages in a foreign language. One day, from a tram in Żoliborz, I read on an otherwise undistinguished wall: "E.T. go home." But seeing the defacement of the King Zygmunt Column on Castle Square made me bristle.

One day walking down Nowy Świat I ran into a cousin

of Hania's who was in town on business. We ducked — it was still raining — into a café. Czesław had left Poland in 1981, shortly before martial law was declared, and settled in the States. He had found work with an investment company and was now coming to Warsaw regularly to look into possible business ventures.

He was nearly as glum as Leszek, not because of the nature of foreign investment, but the lack of it. "There is not as much investment going on here now as people think," he said, "nor in the rest of Eastern Europe." I asked him why. "Here, it's twofold," he said. "On the one hand, Western firms are being cautious — they are waiting to see what happens next. On the other hand, they are not being given all that much encouragement. The present government, which says it wants the business, has not dismantled enough of the barriers that are holding it back. In this sense it is still very socialistic in its approach.

"There are other problems, too," he continued. "The telephone system, for instance." Indeed, getting a telephone — a difficult enough achievement in Poland — was no guarantee of access. Frequently I would try to call someone only to be connected to someone else, often in another city. "It makes the whole concept of fast deals and transactions rather hopeless. And what Western companies will want to put up with the bother?

"Another thing," he said, now for the first time grinning slightly. "The white socks. I understand — I'm from here. But you go into a minister's office and he's in his suit and then he sits down and crosses his legs and there you see his socks." He shook his head understandingly. "They don't realize it makes a bad impression. Some of them haven't been abroad. Sometimes I will tell an assistant — it would not be good etiquette if I did it — to suggest to them that they should wear more subdued shades."

One evening I took a tram to see Stefan. He still didn't have a telephone, but he had written that if I dropped by most any evening after eight I should find him at home. In the same letter he told me that, after nine years at the Malaysian embassy, he had "left the Muslim brotherhood." His new job, he said, was as a translator and proofreader for *Gazeta International*, the new English-language weekly that was a sister to *Gazeta Wyborcza*, Poland's largest national daily paper.

The lot in front of Stefan's building was still (as on my last two visits) being excavated for a future subway station. I had to ask my way, from three bored teenagers on bicycles, through the piles of dirt. Then I took the aging elevator to the anonymous door.

Stefan greeted me with his delightful, mischievous smile and led me into the living room. It looked exactly as I remembered it, except that now a computer sat atop the dining room table. His teenage daughter was playing a game on it.

"Any trouble finding us?" Stefan asked, going to the kitchen to get some beers.

"Not once I got used to the purple tram."

"Milka chocolate," he said instantly. "That's the one I often take. It's a bit disappointing that they don't give free samples."

Stefan was using public transportation, I soon learned, because his car had recently been stolen. "Appropriately enough, the morning I'm to start my new job, I go out and find the car missing." That had been in

June; since then the police had had no further word on it. Friends had told me about the hopelessness of the police force, now woefully understaffed and ineffectual. It was one of the many factors contributing to the increase in crime.

I was eager to hear about his new job. "To tell you the truth," he said thoughtfully, "I'm already thinking of quitting." The work, he admitted, was more interesting than at the embassy. "We get stories from *Gazeta Wyborcza* primarily. A few other people and I translate them into English. Then before they're sent, a native English speaker — the editor is American and we have some help from American embassy spouses — reads over our translations." The hours were much to his liking (except for the day the paper went to press, he came and went pretty much as he pleased), and his coworkers were pleasant. But he just didn't seem to have found his niche. The money wasn't all that good either, and, with rampant inflation, money had suddenly become an important consideration.

"I'm thinking of going back to teaching," he said. "You know, I view life as cyclical — and I think I am coming back around to where I started, as a teacher. Someone's contacted me about getting involved in a new British school for business English. And it sounds interesting. I've started going over some of my old papers on body language as a teaching tool. You know, some woman actually applied my theories in her classroom," he said in a tone of astonishment, "and found they worked."

We turned to talk of the general situation. "In my opinion," Stefan said, "Poland has become a boring country. The fascinating place right now is the Soviet

Union." I asked if he'd seen the article in one of the papers that day of name changes being considered there. One suggestion was Union of European and Asian Republics.

"Yes, but that would include *all* of the republics," he said, grinning, "even Japan.

"But really," he continued, "this idea of capitalism in the Soviet Union intrigues me. I can see the slogans now: 'Go east, young man.' 'The Vladivostok Trail.'"

I asked him why he found Poland boring. "There's no great enemy anymore," he said sadly. "No one to fight against. Life has lost its edge. You know, I have been reading this book." He got up from his chair and went into the bedroom to get it. "*Happiness* by Tartarkiewicz. He quotes in here a psychologist who says that Poles are among those people who can only be happy in those situations when they have no reason to be."

The assessment gave me pause. I thought of the scene — ten years before, almost to the day, in this very living room — of Stefan proudly, purposefully addressing the teachers on the school's new Solidarity union. I thought of Stefan, again in this room, rejoicing at the "end of the myth of socialism" in the first hostile week of martial law. And I thought of him now, kvetching about a fresh start in the free press of a suddenly sovereign homeland.

I left at about ten-thirty, as I was worried about catching the last bus (at eleven) back to the apartment where I was staying. Changing at Świętokrzyska Street, I took my place at a lonely bus stop. It was a few minutes before eleven on a Saturday night in the center of the city, and the sidewalks were bare. A few cars moved down the street, even fewer buses. Had it been any other year,

I would not have thought twice about walking. But the familiarly dark, empty streets, which before had evoked only a feeling of tedium, now suggested menace. I had heard reports about the increase in robberies and muggings, often from American travel writers who had fallen victim. Their stories always caused me pain, not for their lost travelers' checks, but for the resulting image of Poland. Now that other people were finally coming to write about the country, I thought sorrowfully, the lasting picture they would give the world would be one of greed and lawlessness. And I grew even more depressed wondering how people unfamiliar with Poland would react when I now found myself watchful and untrusting. But it wasn't only from Americans that I had heard these stories; Poles themselves talked of the gangs who worked the central train station, converging on foreigners once they had boarded and deftly relieving them of their wallets. Hania told me of her World Bank colleagues who had fallen prey to these bandits, creating, it seemed to me, one of the most direct, hands-on channels ever devised for financial assistance to an underprivileged people. Shortly before leaving the States, I received a postcard from a friend: "Looking forward to seeing you, as are, I'm sure, the pickpockets."

Over the course of my stay, it was not only the idea of crime that grated. No one could expect instant efficiency in government, but many of my friends complained about the inordinate amount of time spent in debate, often on the most peripheral issues. I watched a few of the afternoon telecasts from Parliament and was quick to see their point. Of course, you could interpret such debate as the blessed fruit of the revolution — that, after years of unanimous voting, lawmakers could be ex-

cused for reveling in argument, which was a proof of
their new democratic status if not also the time-honored
cliché of Polish fractiousness. But pursuit of debate for
debate's sake seemed dangerously tempting, especially
while the country, and its economy, floundered.

The Church, which I had seen at its best — the brave
defender of the nation against the occupying power, the
guardian of national identity and culture, the speaker of
truth (historical as well as spiritual) — was not adjusting
well. In trying to enlarge its own realm, it had succeeded
in procuring the introduction of religion classes into
public school curricula. My wife's friend Ewa said to me:
"Now students who may not even believe, whose parents
may not even believe, will get more religion than I did at
my Catholic boarding school." Which was, I suppose,
the Church's point. But what of the pluralism that had
been as important an idea in the struggle against Communism as religious freedom? Other issues were heating up; the first non-antigovernment demonstration I
ever saw in Warsaw marched down Nowy Świat one Saturday afternoon with antiabortion signs held high.

One day I saw a note on the wall in front of Holy
Cross Church calling for a demonstration at the Soviet
embassy to protest the lack of forthcoming facts about
Katyń. Someone with rather infantile penmanship had
scrawled across it: "Denounce the Soviets? For Jewish
crimes?!?" Having read so much in the States about
the rise of anti-Semitism in Poland, I came upon this
graffito almost with a feeling of fulfillment. "There is
more written about it in the West than there actually is,"
some of my friends had told me, somewhat irritably,
when I brought up the subject.

Nevertheless, a dislike of Jews was compatible with

the creeping, general mood of intolerance. It seemed to me that before there had been one Poland, united, even if artificially, by the common struggle against the foreign occupier. Now, in the absence of that unifying force, there was a proliferation of special interests, each one set against the other. This was as evident in the growth of pickpockets as it was in the divisiveness of the politics. I sensed it, too, when a woman on the bus one day berated me for not giving her enough room. Of course, rudeness existed before the fall of Communism. But in earlier days, I think, this woman would have been more inclined to see the person squeezed next to her on a bus as a fellow sufferer in the cause, a compatriot, a brother, and kept her mouth shut. Now she probably wondered, because I was wearing a nice trench, why I didn't drive.

Feeling rather depressed, I went with Ewa one night to a cabaret. I rarely go to the theater when I am at home; I almost always go when I am in Warsaw. In Warsaw it has a make-believe quality that goes beyond the action on the stage. The lobby is invariably filled with attractive, smartly dressed young women whose hair shines under lighting that is not fluorescent. They smoke cigarettes with an unconcerned grace and seem magically removed from the realities of the street where you, and somehow they, recently were. Just as the poorer classes in Poland drink to forget, the educated ones go to the theater.

This theater, one of Ewa's favorites, was Rampa, situated at the far end of Praga on the other side of the Vistula. The lobby did not disappoint. The troupe, both men and women, came on stage dressed in tuxedos. There were no costume changes. The songs were witty, or sung with humorous exaggeration. They seemed to be blissfully, desperately, striking out against the encroaching bleakness of, in the words of director and emcee Andrzej Strzelecki, "the capital of a major European country whose citizens are all in their homes by eight o'clock." But toward the end of the evening the players gathered around Strzelecki and sang a melancholy song, which caused him to lay his head face down on his desk in despair. The refrain: "We are growing smaller. And we don't know what to do about it."

A few days later I visited the English Language College. I arrived at about four and found the usual crowd of students pressing against the windows of the downstairs office. Mrs. Kuczma stood behind one of them, answering questions, just as I had left her. Jolanta, recently named director in the wake of her father's retirement, came out to welcome me. We sat in the tiny office, catching up on news; the charwoman greeted me warmly and rushed off to get us tea. The janitor brought in some cakes. As if to complete the ceremony, a woman tried to enter with a box of Wedel chocolates as an aid in getting her daughter registered after the cutoff date.

The school was still thriving, Jolanta told me, despite a blossoming of private English schools in Warsaw. English was more popular than ever; now anyone with a good knowledge of it could, it seemed, find a job of some sort. A friend of Jolanta's, who had studied American literature, was now captain of the bartenders at the Marriott casino.

Jolanta seemed cheerful, despite misgivings. "Nobody knows what to do now," she said in her pensive way. "Before, our life was very rigid. There were certain ways you acted, certain rules you followed, certain people you depended on. Now that's gone and people are slightly paralyzed."

At six o'clock, of course, I went up to the teachers' room for tea. "Mr. . . . Mr. . . . Mr. Swick," Miss Wiaderny said thoughtfully, after only a few seconds of deep concentration. "Are you going to be teaching this year?" Except for a bandage on her left hand, she looked the same as I remembered her, an ageless grammarian untouched by the tide of history. Mr. Romanowicz greeted me. "We have *Newsweek* now. We can buy it right downstairs in the bookstore. It's expensive, of course, but it's available. And BBC — we get broadcasts of the BBC. It's wonderful."

Someone found a seat for me at the head of the table in the smokers' room, which still contained, I was happy to see, most of the same ladies. They too were just as I remembered them: sharp, discursive, animated, and welcoming. I thought with regret of all the fascinating teatimes I had missed. I was thirsty for a month of teas. "What do you think of Poland, Tom?" they asked. I told them it was one of the most fashionable countries in America now. They howled with laughter.

In my final days I experienced similar, though less personal moments which seemed to cancel out my deeper disappointments. I had somehow forgotten that much of the beauty of Poland for me was always in these small, graceful notes that survived, unexpectedly, in an atmosphere of decay. It was the appeal of the diamond in the rough: the cheerful Catholic aunts in an officially atheistic state, the lavish spread in a season of shortages, the cozy apartment in the dilapidated tenement, the beautiful girl in the leathery-faced crowd, the witty remark in the drunken café.

By the last day I was almost ready to stay — rejoin the school, or even set up a card table with English books on Marszałkowska Street. Visiting Jolanta at her apartment in Praga, I gave her a copy of the quarterly in which I had recently published an article on Poland. She turned to the piece and immediately began counting. "Twenty pages?" she asked disappointedly. "So short?"

On the way back, I watched a tough-looking teenager with a surly expression board the bus. He seemed typical of Praga, a delinquent in denim. Standing toward the rear, he pulled a tattered paperback out of his pocket and started to read. I moved closer until I could make out the title: *Cannery Row*, in English.

A few hours later, going with Ewa to the theater again — she refusing to let me pay, refusing even to tell me how much these expensive tickets were setting her back on her meager savings — we passed a drunk. He and Ewa did a little dance before Ewa swerved widely out of his path.

"Madame, why are you afraid?" the drunk addressed her, rousing himself to a brief moment of not only sobriety but clairvoyance. "You are going to the theater!"